THE TRANSFORMATIVE MAGIC
of Power Query M Code
in Excel and Power BI

A Beginner's Guide to Mastering the Art of Data Metamorphosis to Get Just the Data Structure Needed to Create Insightful Data Analysis Solutions

by
Mike "excelisfun" Girvin

T0293320

Holy Macro! Books
PO Box 541731
Merritt Island, FL 32953

The Transformative Magic of Power Query M Code in Excel and Power BI

Author: Mike Girvin

Tech Editor: Geert Delmulle

Layout: Bronkella Publishing LLC

Copyediting: Kitty Wilson

Cover Design: Shannon Travise

Indexing: Cheryl Lenser

Published by: Holy Macro! Books, PO Box 541731, Merritt Island FL 32953, USA

Distributed by: Independent Publishers Group, Chicago, IL

First Printing: September 2024

ISBN: 978-1-61547-083-9 Print, 978-1-61547-169-0 e-Book

Dedication

Dedicated to our amazing online Excel team at YouTube, LinkedIn, and the MrExcel Message Board!

About the Author

Mike "excelisfun" Girvin has been a Microsoft Excel MVP since 2013 and a Highline College business instructor since 2002. He is the creator of the excelisfun YouTube channel and has been the internet leader in bringing free Excel and Power BI education to the world since 2008. The channel has 1 million subscribers, 3600 videos, 10,000 downloadable files, 100 playlists, and 20 different free classes focusing on Excel basics, advanced Excel, Power BI, data analysis, analytics, statistics, math, and much more. Mike Girvin has also authored several Excel books and DVDs and has won numerous awards for teaching Excel.

Before joining academia, Mike "Gel" Girvin ran the boomerang manufacturing company Gel Boomerangs in Oakland, California, from 1984 to 2002, where he won numerous boomerang design and competition awards. It was while Mike was running Gel Boomerangs in the 1990s that Steve Kavanaugh showed him Excel for the first time. From that point forward, Mike couldn't resist the power and fun of Excel, and he went on to be an Excel teacher for the world. Currently, when Mike "Magic" Girvin is not creating Excel and Power BI solutions, you can find him each weekend out racing and parking BMX bikes with fellow rad old guys and his kid Isaac "Iceman" Girvin.

Acknowledgments

My number-one Excel guy in the world is Bill "MrExcel" Jelen, who was the first person to make Excel videos. He inspired me and many other Excel people to make and share videos. MrExcel also started the MrExcel Message Board, where I learned many of my advanced Excel skills. Plus, MrExcel has written more than 60 Excel books!

I also want to thank the more than 1 million subscribers at YouTube; in the comments below every one of the videos I post, I get to learn new things about making efficient Excel and Power BI solutions—and having fun doing it! I must also thank Geert Delmulle, who diligently did the technical edit for this book. Saving the biggest acknowledgement for last: I want to thank the world's greatest editor: Kitty "Magician" Wilson!

Contents at a Glance

Introduction xiv

Chapter 1: Power Query and M Code 1

Chapter 2: M Code Values 10

Chapter 3: Custom Functions 44

Chapter 4: M Code Lookup Formulas 56

Chapter 5: Unpivot, Append, Join, and Group By 78

Chapter 6: Data Connectors 121

Chapter 7: Data Modeling 161

Conclusion 209

Table of Contents

Introduction vii
  Who This Book Is For vii
  The Microsoft Power Query M Language Specification vii
  Files to Download So You Can Follow Along vii

Chapter 1: Power Query and M Code 1
  History of Power Query 1
  Power Query and M Code 1
  Comparing the Four Function-Based Languages 1
  The User Interface and M Code 2
  Three Locations to Edit M Code 3
  The let Expression, Keywords, Identifiers, and Expressions 6
  Three Different Load Data Buttons 8
  Summary 9

Chapter 2: M Code Values 10
  Type Values and Data Types 11
  The if Expression 18
  The Table.AddColumn Function 19
  Date, Time, Datetime, Datetimezone, and Duration 20
  Working with Date- and Time-Related Values 27
  Using let Expressions to Define Variables in Formulas 32
  Calculating Hours Elapsed from Datetime Values 34
  Tables, Records, and Lists 35
  Binary Values 42
  Summary 43

Chapter 3: Custom Functions 44
  Creating Two Reusable Function Queries 45
  Creating a Custom Function in a Function Argument 48
  Using each and an Underscore to Create a Custom Function 49
  Creating a Custom Function Query Step in a let Expression 50
  Recursion with Custom Functions 51
  Using List.Accumulate to Simulate Recursion 54
  Summary 55

Chapter 4: M Code Lookup Formulas 56
  Exact Match Lookups 56
  Approximate Match Lookups 69
  Summary 77

Chapter 5: Unpivot, Append, Join, and Group By 78
  Unpivot and the Table.UnpivotOtherColumns Function 78
  Appending: Table.Combine vs. Table.ExpandTableColumn 81
  Join Operations Used by the Merge Feature 85

The Table.Group Function and the Group By Feature...93

Other List Functions and Table.Sort, Too 113

Three Table.Group Tricks 118

Summary...120

Chapter 6: Data Connectors 121

CSV Files vs. Text Files 121

On-Premises File and Folder Paths 125

Using the Locale Feature to Import Data from Different Locales..149

ISO Dates..152

Online Data Sources...152

Summary...160

Chapter 7: Data Modeling..161

Project 1: Using From Folder and Combine Files to Combine Multiple Excel Files, Each with a
    Single Object...161

Project 2: Using a Custom Column to Combine Multiple Excel Files, Each with a Single Object 166

Project 3: Appending Multiple Text Files with Table Structure Problems 167

Project 4: Appending Tables with Inconsistent Column Names...172

Project 5: Appending JSON Tables with Filename Attributes...175

Project 6: Importing Multiple Excel Files, Each with Multiple Objects 177

Project 7: Combining Two Fact Tables into One Fact Table...182

Project 8: Converting a Single Column of Badly Structured Records into a Proper Table 189

Bonus Topic: Privacy Levels and Data Security..193

Bonus Example: Dynamically Connecting to SharePoint Server Files from Within an Excel File 200

Conclusion...209

Introduction

This book will teach you the fundamentals of how to use and write Power Query M code in Excel, Power BI Desktop, and Dataflow in the online Power BI service. The M code can be slightly different in each tool, but all the fundamentals of M code are the same in each tool.

Power Query's M code is a case-sensitive, function-based data-shaping computer language. There are more than 800 M code functions in Excel and more than 1000 of them in Power BI Desktop and Dataflow. You will learn about many of the amazing functions that accomplish data tasks that no other language can do quite as easily. However, you cannot easily understand most of the functions until you learn about M code fundamentals such as the let expression, M code values, data types, custom functions, and M code lookups.

To prepare you to use M code, this book covers the following topics:

- The user interface
- Where you can edit M code
- Identifiers, keywords, and expressions
- The let expression
- M code values
- Data types
- Custom functions
- M code lookups
- Drill-down and primary keys
- How to unpivot, append, join/merge, and group by
- Data connectors
- Data modeling

When you have assimilated the content of this book, you will be able to understand some of the wild M code that the user interface generates, build custom functions to make the many unique data transformations that are not possible with the user interface, and author custom let expression queries to accomplish any data scenario, including the seemingly impossible.

Who This Book Is For

This book is for you if you have learned to use Power Query through the user interface, are familiar with navigating through Power Query, and want to take your Power Query abilities to the next level by learning the function-based language behind every query: M. It is also for you if you are an analyst using Excel or Power BI who wants to learn and understand the syntax and structure of the M language so that you have full access to the power of Power Query to get, clean, and transform data. This book will give you a solid understanding of the M language so you can edit and create efficient queries for all your projects that involve data. Some say that you don't really know Power Query until you know M—and I agree. So, if you want to learn M to gain data-shaping skills in Excel and Power BI, this is the book for you!

The Microsoft Power Query M Language Specification

The Microsoft Power Query M Language Specification is a guide worth checking out because it speaks to every minute detail about M code. You can find it at https://learn.microsoft.com/en-us/powerquery-m/power-query-m-language-specification.

Files to Download So You Can Follow Along

Following along and trying examples as you read about them is a great way to learn. I've therefore provided all the Excel and Power BI files that you see in this book as a zipped file that you can download from https://excelisfun.net/files/MCodeExcelisfunBook.zip.

Here are a few points to keep in mind about the files for this book:

- Almost all of the queries in the Excel files use Excel tables from the current workbook file as the source data to avoid on-premises file path errors. In addition, almost all of the queries in the Power BI Desktop files use data that was pasted in using the Enter Data feature, which uses a combination of the M code functions Table.FromRows, Json.Document, Binary.Decompress, and Binary.FromText. Pasting the data avoids on-premises file path errors.

- In some cases, in both Excel and Power BI, this book also uses intrinsic tables as the source data to avoid data source errors.

- Almost every query in the files is loaded as a connection only and is not loaded to a final location in order to make the file size much smaller and more manageable.

- Many query names end with the letter Q to differentiate them from the data source Excel table names.

If you are using Dataflow (in the Power BI online service), you will have to import the tables and queries from the Excel files.

Chapter 1: Power Query and M Code

History of Power Query

For quite some time, using a PivotTable was the preferred method of converting a table of data into useful summary reports and chart visuals. It was easy to use a PivotTable if it was based on a correctly structured table with column names and records. But often the data came from many different sources and did not have the correct table structure to create the reports and chart visuals. To get the correct structure for the PivotTable tool, it was necessary to use VBA code or manually convert the data to the correct structure.

Power Query was first introduced in Excel in 2013, two decades after the PivotTable was invented. Power Query made it dramatically easier to take data from different data sources and then clean, transform, and load the data to the best location in an Excel workbook file. Then, in 2015, Power BI Desktop was invented to help us easily report and visualize data. Microsoft embedded Power Query in Power BI Desktop to make connecting to and structuring data easy. Finally, in 2023, Microsoft gave us the full Power Query tool in the online Power BI service; many call it Dataflow. Now, with whatever tool you may be using, Power Query allows you to connect to almost any data source and transform the data into exactly the structure you need to create your data analysis and analytic solutions.

> **Note:** Throughout the book, I talk about the Dataflow tool. "Dataflow" isn't the official name for the tool, and you won't see this name in any title bars; what you will see is "Power Query." Dataflow is the name many use for online Power Query, which is available in the online Power BI service.

Power Query and M Code

Power Query is a Microsoft tool that allows you to create queries that can connect to, import, clean, transform, and load data. The amazing Power Query tool is embedded in Excel, Power BI Desktop, and the online Power BI service (where we refer to it as Dataflow). All Power Query queries are created with the M programming language (so named because the language is used to "mash up data"). **M** is officially defined as a case-sensitive, function-based language that can deliver **M code values**, such as tables, lists, numbers, and 12 other data-related values. (M code values are covered extensively in Chapter 2.)

When you create a query in Power Query, you can use the user interface to write the M code, you can type your own M code, or you can do a combination of both. The function-based M language is a complement to and works closely with the other three Microsoft function-based languages in Excel and Power BI: worksheet formulas, standard PivotTables, and Data Model DAX formulas. All four function-based languages help you perform calculations, analytics, and data analysis. To place Power Query M into the correct context, it's helpful to look at the main characteristics of each of these four function-based languages.

Comparing the Four Function-Based Languages

The beauty of a worksheet formula is that you can point it to any cell, range, column, or table in an Excel worksheet. The other three languages cannot do that: They are all confined to structured data, such as tables and columns. With worksheet formulas, you are free to incorporate any part of a worksheet, such as tables, columns, ranges, or cells. You are not limited to a strict column-and-table data structure, as you are with standard PivotTables, DAX formulas, and M code. There are also many convenient worksheet functions, such as XLOOKUP, NETWORKDAYS.INTL, and BINOM.DIST.RANGE, that are not available in the other function-based languages. Finally, worksheet formulas allow a solution to instantly update when the source data changes. Although the other three languages do not allow instant updates when the source data changes, each of them has its own power and magic to help you make calculations and perform data analysis:

- When it comes to summing, counting, and calculating percentages, no other calculation tool is as fast and easy to use as a standard PivotTable.
- With DAX, you can work with big data more quickly than you can with any of the other languages, and you can create tables at various levels of granularity inside DAX formulas to help reduce the complexity of the calculation process. The DAX language has powerful functions that the other languages do not have, such as CALCULATE, AVERAGEX, and RELATEDTABLE.
- The M language allows you to work with data, tables, and data sources such as SQL Server databases, columns of tables, columns of files, and other structures that contain data in ways that none of the

other languages can. M is specifically programmed to work with data, and it allows you to shape and form data into efficient structures that can be loaded to worksheets, the PivotTable cache, or the Data Model in either Power Pivot or Power BI. In addition, M is the only language that allows you to write most of your formulas using the user interface.

In this book, we focus on Power Query M, which gives you unique abilities to work with and shape data.

The User Interface and M Code

Even when you become proficient with M, you will often use the user interface to write M code. Sometimes the M code the user interface generates is perfect, and other times you need to edit the generated M code to better meet your needs. I usually use the user interface to create M code, and then I edit and hack the code to get just what I want. Throughout this book, I show you hacks to get the user interface to write as much of your M code as possible.

Figures 1-1 through 1-3 show the user interfaces in Excel, Power BI Desktop, and Dataflow.

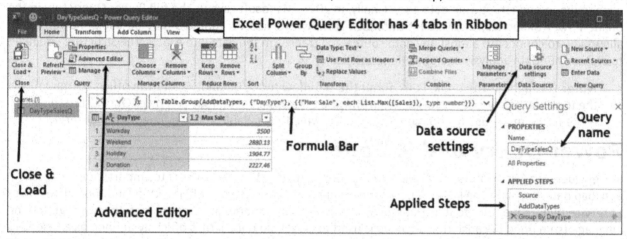

Figure 1-1 *Power Query Editor in Excel.*

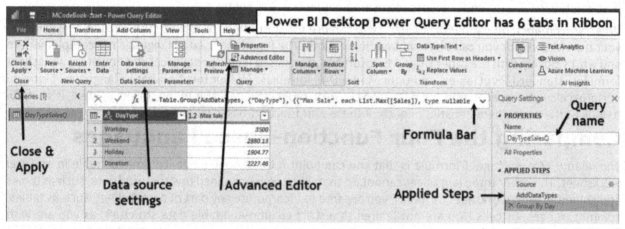

Figure 1-2 *Power Query Editor in Power BI Desktop.*

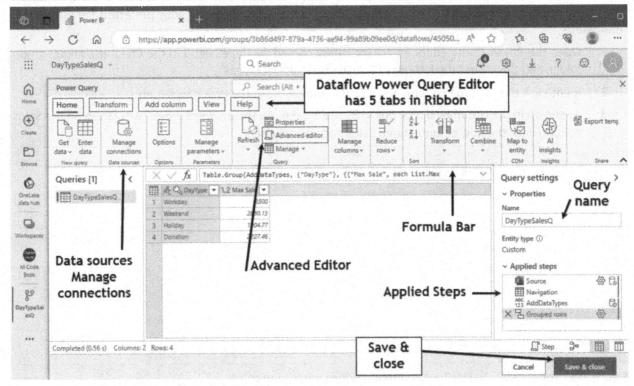

Figure 1-3 *Power Query Editor in Dataflow.*

> **Note:** For this book, I've created the figures almost exclusively in the Power Query Editor in Excel. When there are differences in the user interfaces, I indicate the differences.

Now that you have seen the user interfaces, you're ready to see how to create a query using the user interface and then dive into M code.

Three Locations to Edit M Code

You can follow along with the examples in this book by opening the Excel file named MCodeBook-Start.xlsx or the Power BI Desktop file named MCodeBook-Start.pbix, or you can load the source Excel tables from inside the Excel file to Dataflow in your preferred Microsoft online service and work there.

> **Note:** The files MCodeBook-Start.xlsx and MCodeBook-Start.pbix include many queries that have been loaded into the Power Query Editor but that are not loaded to a destination such as the Data Model or worksheet. Throughout this book, we will almost always be working in the Power Query Editor without loading to any final location.

To get started learning M code, you are going to build a query using the user interface, and then you will edit the M code. To do this, you will use the DayTypeSales table, which has three columns: Date, DayType, and Sales (see Figure 1-4). Your initial goal for this query is to group by the DayType column and add the sales for each unique day type. Then you can use the query to learn about the three different locations where you can edit M code.

The **Group By command** is a common command in all data analysis tools that allows you to select one or more columns, generate a unique list of conditions from the column(s), and makes aggregate calculations based on the items in the unique list.

	Date	AᴮC DayType	1.2 Sales
1	8/3/2018	Workday	3500
2	8/4/2018	Workday	1048.36
3	8/5/2018	Weekend	106.75

Figure 1-4 *DayTypeSales table.*

To learn about the three places that you can edit and create M code, open your preferred file and follow these steps:

1. Open the Power Query Editor, select the query named DayTypeSalesQ in the Chapter01and02 group folder, and then select the last query step, named AddDataTypes.

2. Right-click the DayType column and select Group By from the dropdown menu.

3. As shown in the Group By dialog box in Figure 1-5, create the aggregate sum calculation on the Sales column with the new column name Sales and then click OK.

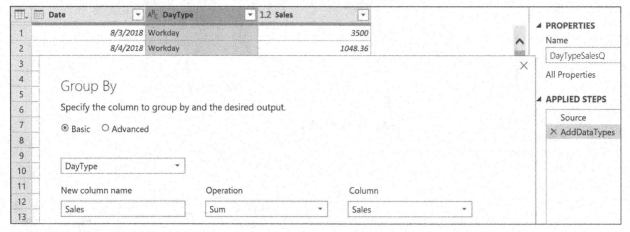

Figure 1-5 *Grouping by the DayType column to aggregate a sum total.*

As shown in Figure 1-6 a new step named Grouped Rows is added to the Applied Steps list. The resulting table displays a unique list of day types and the sum of sales for each. There are three locations where you can now edit the M code:

- Applied Steps list
- Formula Bar
- Advanced Editor

Note: In Power BI Desktop and Dataflow, Advanced Editor is in a different location, as shown back in Figures 1-1 and 1-2.

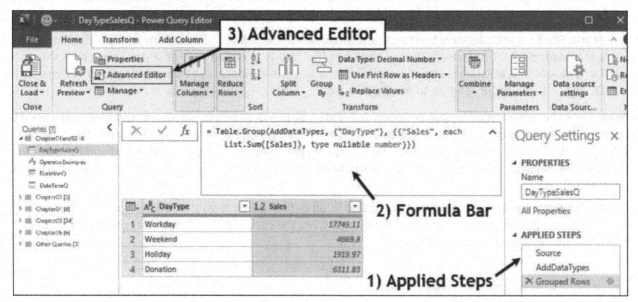

Figure 1-6 *The three locations to edit M code.*

4. To view the complete M code for this query, open the Advanced Editor in your preferred app.

You now see the user interface–generated M code, which should look as shown in Figure 1-7. (The specific M code formula used in the Source step is different in each app.) The let expression shows three query steps followed by the in keyword and the name of the last step. We will come back and cover the let expression and the components of the let expression later in this chapter. All you need to notice for now is that the step named Grouped Rows in Applied Steps and the formula in the Formula Bar are listed together on the third line of the let expression. This illustrates that the three locations where you can edit M code work together so that if you change the code in any one place, it changes in the other places as well. To see this in action, continue following these steps.

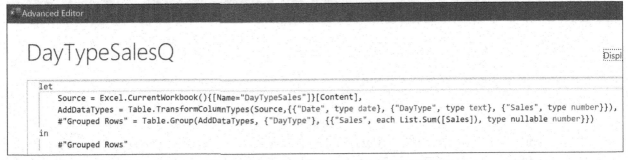

```
× Advanced Editor

DayTypeSalesQ                                                                              Displ

let
    Source = Excel.CurrentWorkbook(){[Name="DayTypeSales"]}[Content],
    AddDataTypes = Table.TransformColumnTypes(Source,{{"Date", type date}, {"DayType", type text}, {"Sales", type number}}),
    #"Grouped Rows" = Table.Group(AddDataTypes, {"DayType"}, {{"Sales", each List.Sum([Sales]), type nullable number}})
in
    #"Grouped Rows"
```

Figure 1-7 *The Advanced Editor showing the user interface–generated M code.*

5. In the Advanced Editor, in the third line of the let statement, change the aggregate sum column name from Sales to Total Sales and then click Done. Figure 1-8 shows that the formula in the Formula Bar and the column name in the table now reflect your change.

		fx	= Table.Group(AddDataTypes, {"DayType"}, {{"Total Sales", each List.Sum([Sales]), type nullable number}})

	A^BC DayType	1.2 Total Sales
1	Workday	17749.11
2	Weekend	4669.8
3	Holiday	1919.97
4	Donation	6311.83

Figure 1-8 *The formula and column name reflect the changes made in the Advanced Editor.*

6. In the Applied Steps list, click the Grouped Rows step (making sure it turns dark green to indicate that it is correctly selected), press the F2 key to put the query step name into edit mode, type the new step name Group By DayType, and press Enter.

7. To change the aggregate function used by the Group By feature, click in the Formula Bar and then, in the third row of the query, after the each keyword (which causes the formula to make a calculation in each row of the table), change the function name from List.Sum to List.Max and change the column name from Total Sales to Max Sale. To enter the formula, either click at the end of the formula and then press Enter or click the check mark on the far right side of the Formula Bar.

8. Open the Advanced Editor. As shown in Figure 1-9, the changes that you made in the Applied Steps list and Formula Bar are reflected in the Advanced Editor.

```
× Advanced Editor

DayTypeSalesQ                                                                              Display O

let
    Source = Excel.CurrentWorkbook(){[Name="DayTypeSales"]}[Content],
    AddDataTypes = Table.TransformColumnTypes(Source,{{"Date", type date}, {"DayType", type text}, {"Sales", type number}}),
    #"Group By DayType" = Table.Group(AddDataTypes, {"DayType"}, {{"Max Sale" , each List.Max([Sales]), type nullable number}})
in
    #"Group By DayType"
```

Figure 1-9 *Applied Steps list and Formula Bar changes are reflected in the Advanced Editor.*

So where is the best place to edit your M code? It depends. Each of the locations has efficient uses. For changing the names of steps in the Applied Steps list and making small edits to formulas, it is usually fastest and easiest to use the Applied Steps list and then the Formula Bar. For more complex edits or when you want to completely hack your code, the Advanced Editor is the best location.

The let Expression, Keywords, Identifiers, and Expressions

Figure 1-10 shows the DayTypeSalesQ query let expression (with some hard returns and tabs added to make the query easy to see). Notice the keywords let, in, each, and type. They're easy to spot because in M code, keywords appear in blue.

```
DayTypeSalesQ

let
    Source = Excel.CurrentWorkbook(){[Name="DayTypeSales"]}[Content],
    AddDataTypes = Table.TransformColumnTypes(Source,{{"Date", type date},
        {"DayType", type text}, {"Sales", type number}}),
    #"Group By DayType" = Table.Group(AddDataTypes, {"DayType"},
        {{"Max Sale",  each List.Max([Sales]), type nullable number}})
in
    #"Group By DayType"
```

Figure 1-10 *DayTypeSalesQ query let expression.*

A **keyword** is a reserved word that has a predefined use. For example:

- **let** is a keyword that indicates the start of a let expression.
- **in** ends the query steps and precedes the query output.
- **each** allows a formula to calculate in each row of a table or list.
- **type** assigns the data type.

Figure 1-11 shows a list of some of the possible keywords in M code. You will learn about these keywords as you progress through the book.

and, as, each, else, error, FALSE, if, in, is, let, meta, not, otherwise, or, section, shared, then, TRUE, try, type

#binary, #date, #datetime, #datetimezone, #duration, #infinity, #nan, #sections, #shared, #table, #time

Figure 1-11 *A list of reserved keywords in M code.*

Notice in Figure 1-10 that M code uses operators. For example, in Figure 1-10, the #"Group By DayType" step uses the {} list operator to group together the three elements for the aggregate max calculation. Figure 1-12 shows the operators used in M code. (You will learn all about operators in Chapter 2.)

, ; = < <= > >= <> + - * / & () [] {} @ ! ? => ..

Figure 1-12 *Operators in M code.*

The next thing to notice in Figure 1-10 is the identifiers, such as DayTypeSalesQ, Source, AddDataTypes, and #"Group By DayType". An **identifier** is a name used to refer to an expression that delivers an M code value (such as a number, a list, or a table).

Note: If an identifier includes one or more spaces, you must enclose the identifier in quotation marks and place a # sign at the beginning (for example, #"Group By DayType"). This is how you distinguish an identifier from text, which requires quotation marks but not a # sign. To make your M code easier to read, avoid spaces when creating identifiers. For example, use the identifier GroupByDayType rather than #"Group By DayType". I used spaces in the identifier in this case for illustration purposes. Throughout the rest of the book, I do not use spaces in identifiers.

A **generalized identifier** is an identifier that may have spaces without needing the # sign and quotation marks. Generalized identifiers are allowed in two situations:

- In the name of a column in a record literal, such as [Boom Product = "Quad", Sales = 43]
- In the name of a column in a field access operator, such as [Boom Product]

You'll see examples of generalized identifiers throughout the book, such as in Chapter 2 when you create record literals and in Chapter 4 when you learn how to do lookups.

An **expression** is any M code that delivers an M code value. (Chapter 2 covers all 15 M code values.) To see an example of an identifier and an expression, look again at Figure 1-10. In that example, the #"Group By DayType" step uses the identifier #"Group By DayType" to refer to and name the query step expression:

```
Table.Group(AddDataTypes, {"DayType"},{{"Max Sale", each List.Max([Sales]),
type nullable number}})
```

That expression then delivers a table with the group by results. A query step identifier can be used throughout the let expression, but it cannot be used outside the let expression.

As another example of an identifier and an expression, the query identifier DayTypeSalesQ refers to the let expression and delivers a table as the query output. The identifier can be used throughout the Power Query Editor, and the output result is the table.

Looking once again at Figure 1-10, notice the built-in M code functions Table.TransformColumnTypes and Table. Group. Built-in **M code functions** are case-sensitive functions with specified arguments that are programmed to achieve specific tasks, such as transforming column types or performing the group by operation on a table. **Power Query functions** are premade built-in functions, whereas **custom functions** are user-defined functions. (You will learn about custom functions in Chapter 3.) The built-in Power Query functions come from the standard library, which is a list of functions and constants. One thing you can say for sure is that the Microsoft programmers named the built-in functions with self-explanatory and helpful names. For example, there is little doubt what the Table.Group function does. (You'll learn more details about each of the functions shown in Figure 1-10 later in this book.)

A **let expression** allows you to define **variables**, also known as **query steps**, and use them throughout the let expression to deliver a final query value (that is, query output). You can use let expressions in any M code to define variables, but most often you use a let expression to define a new query and deliver query output. Every time you start a new query and select commands from the user interface, Power Query automatically records the commands you select in a let expression.

These are the syntactical rules for a let expression:

- A let expression starts with let (lowercase).
- Each variable, or query step, starts with an identifier, followed by an equals sign and then the expression. The identifier represents the expression throughout the query.
- Variables are usually used in the first argument of a function to modify the previous step, but they can be used anywhere throughout the let expression. A let expression's variables cannot be used outside the let expression.
- Each variable in a let expression is followed by a comma that allows the let statement to deliver an intermediate value, such as a table that can then be acted on further or used in other locations in the query.
- The last variable ends without a comma. When the let expression finds no comma, it expects the in keyword to come next, followed by the query output.
- The let expression ends with the in (lowercase) keyword followed by the identifier for the final value to be delivered by the query. The output of the query is almost always the identifier of the last query

step; however, the output can be any of the variables defined in the let expression, any other query in the file, or any expression.

- You can add non-executable comments to your M code by adding two forward slashes (//) for single-line comments or using multi-line comments that begin with /* and end with */.

Figure 1-13 shows an example of a let expression in a query, and Figure 1-14 provides a cheat sheet that helps you understand the parts of a let expression.

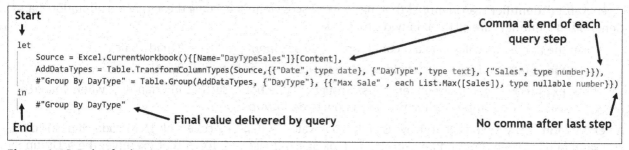

Figure 1-13 *Rules for let expressions.*

```
let
    VariableName1 = Expression,
     #"Variable Name 2" = Expression,
    VariableName3 = Expression
in
    Output
        (Output is usually the last variable name, but can
        be any variable, query name or expression)

// one-line comment
/* multiple line comments */
```

Figure 1-14 *Cheat sheet for the syntax of a let expression.*

Three Different Load Data Buttons

There are three locations where you can load the output of a query let expression. If you take a look back at Figures 1-1 through 1-3, you will notice that Excel, Power BI Desktop, and Dataflow each has a different load button in its respective Power Query Editor: Excel Power Query has the Close & Load button, Power BI Desktop Power Query has the Close & Apply button, and Dataflow Power Query has the Save & Close button.

In Excel, when you click the Close & Load button, Power Query applies the query steps and loads the data to the worksheet. But if you click the dropdown arrow at the bottom of the Close & Load button and select Close & Load To, the Import Data dialog box pops up, giving you five options:

- **Table:** This loads the data to the worksheet as an Excel Table object.
- **PivotTable:** This loads the data to the PivotTable cache.
- **PivotChart:** This loads the data to the PivotChart cache.
- **Only Create Connection:** This does not load the data, but the query and data connections are preserved in the query editors.
- **Only Create Connection with the checkbox Add This Data to the Data Model checked:** This loads the data to the Power Pivot Data Model.

In Power BI Desktop, you can only load data to one location: the Data Model. When you click the Close & Apply button dropdown arrow, you get these three options:

- **Close & Apply:** This applies the query steps, loads the data to the Data Model, and closes the Power Query Editor.
- **Apply:** This applies the query steps, loads the data to the Data Model, and leaves the Power Query Editor open.

- **Close:** This closes the Power Query Editor without applying query steps or loading the data.

In Dataflow, you can only load data to one location: the Dataflow workspace in the online Power BI service. The data is available to people who have access to the workspace and therefore is available in tools such as Excel, Power BI Desktop, and various Microsoft online services. The Save & Close button applies query steps, loads the data to the Dataflow workspace, and closes the Power Query Editor.

For Power BI Desktop and Dataflow, when you want to load a query as a connection only, without loading the data to the Data Model, in the Power Query Editor, you select the query in the Queries pane, right-click the query, and uncheck Enable Load.

Summary

In this chapter, you learned a bit about the history of M, and you learned about the Power Query user interface and places where you can edit M code. You also learned about some of the building blocks of M code, such as keywords, identifiers, expressions, let expressions, queries, and standard library built-in functions. To finish up the chapter, you learned about the different load locations in the three tools that contain the Power Query tool: Excel, Power BI Desktop, and Dataflow. Chapter 2 covers the heart and soul of everything you can create with M code: the 15 different Power Query values.

Chapter 2: M Code Values

In Chapter 1, you learned about some of the building blocks of M code, such as identifiers, expressions, let expressions, queries, and built-in functions. You learned that identifiers refer to expressions; expressions (such as let expressions) deliver M code values; queries use let expressions, so they deliver M code values; and built-in functions deliver M code values. Because everything you do in M delivers M code values, M code values are the heart and soul of M code. Having a good understanding of them is the key to becoming an M code guru. If you understand the M code values, everything else will fall into place.

An **M code value** is what is produced when you evaluate an expression. Figure 2-1 lists all 15 M code values, briefly describes each one, and shows the M code used to hard-code each value.

Value	Description	M Code to Hard-Code a Value
Null	The absence of data.	Example: null
Logical	A Boolean: true or false.	Example: true or false
Text	A string of Unicode characters.	Examples: "Quad", "A430G"
Number	A numeral used in numeric and arithmetic operations.	Examples: -43, 0, 43.46, 9.9e-5
Time	A time for a 24-hour day as a decimal between 0 and 1.	#time(hour, minute, seconds) Example: #time(11,10,57) = 11:10:57
Date	A date as a serial number (Common Era Gregorian calendar). Dates span from 01/01/0001 to 12/31/9999.	#date(year, month, day) Example: #date(1598, 01, 15)= 1/15/1598
Datetime	A value that contains both date and time.	#datetime(year, month, day, hour, minutes, seconds) Example: #datetime(2021,10,01,11,10,57)) = 10/01/21 11:10:57 AM
Datetimezone	A UTC (Universal Coordinated Time) date and time with a timezone offset (in the last two arguments).	#datetimezone(year, month, day, hour, minute, second, offset-hours, offset-minutes) Example: #datetimezone(2021,10,01,11,10,57,09,00) = 10/01/21 11:10:57 AM + 9 hours
Duration	An amount of time in units of days, hours, minutes, and seconds. (This data type is not supported in Dataflow.)	#duration(days, hours, minutes, seconds) Example: #duration(01,01,10,0) = 1 day and 1 hour 10 minutes
Table	A table with field names and records.	Example: #table({"Boom Product", "Sales"}, {{"Quad",43},{"Aspen",35}}) =
Record	An ordered sequence of fields.	Example: [Boom Product = "Quad", Sales = 43] =
List	A sequence of M code values.	Example: {"Quad","Aspen"} =
Binary	A sequence of bytes.	Example: Excel file =
Function	A custom function that defines the variables and the mapping for those variables to deliver a value.	Example: Function calculates the effective rate = (APR, Periods) => Number.Power(1+APR/Periods, Periods)-1
Type	A value that classifies other values with 1 of 16 data types.	Example: "type number" for defining the decimal data type

Figure 2-1 *M code values.*

In this chapter, you will learn about all the M code values except for the function value, which is covered in Chapter 3. This chapter defines each of the other M code values, shows how to hard-code it, defines the operators that work for it, and shows at least several expressions (formulas) for it.

> **Note:** Although hard-coding values in M code is much less common than importing data sets that contain the values, by hard-coding the values, you will become more familiar with the structure of the different M code values.

There are several ways to hard-code M code values:

- **Use literal syntax:** This means just typing a value into your M code, such as typing null for a null value or "Quad" for the text value Quad.
- **Use an intrinsic function:** For many values, such as date and table values, you program an intrinsic function to hard-code values into M code.
- **Use initialization syntax:** For a sequence of elements, like a list or a set of record values, you use initialization syntax to start, populate, and end the value.
- **Use function-expression syntax:** You create function values by using *function-expression syntax.*

You will learn about hard-coding techniques throughout this chapter. The first M code value we will look at is the type value.

Type Values and Data Types

A **type value** is a value that classifies other values by using the data types shown in Figure 2-2. **Data types** are safeguards placed on columns to produce consistent data and accuracy in calculations and can change the underlying value to a new value, if necessary.

Data Type	Icon	Description	M Code
Decimal number	1.2	A number with up to 15 decimal places	type number
Currency (fixed decimal number)	$	A number with up to 4 decimal places	Currency.Type
Whole number	1²₃	A number with no digit to the right of the decimal point, rouded using banker's rouding	Int64.Type
Percentage	%	A number with up to 15 decimal places with % number for	Percentage.Type
Datetime	📅🕒	A serial number date and time together	type datetime
Date	📅	A serial number date	type date
Time	🕐	A serial number time	type time
Datetimezone	🌐🕐	A UTC date and time with a timezone offset	type datetimezone
Duration	🕐	A serial number representing length of date and time (not supported in Dataflow)	type duration
Text	AᴮC	Text	type text
True/false	✗✓	A Boolean	type logical
Binary	📄	A file, such as an Excel file or a text file	type binary
Any	ABC 123	A number such as a date or decimal number, set according to regional settings	type any
Nullable		A keyword added to a data type such as a number so that the column can have the number or a null	type nullable number
Anynonnull		Any non-null value	type anynonnull
None		A keyword that causes no values to be classified	type none

Figure 2-2 *Data types that classify M code values.*

A value that is classified by a data type is said to *conform* to that data type. For example, if you apply the whole number data type to a source column of number values with digits to the right of the decimal point, new number values are created that are rounded to the ones position so that the new numbers conform to the whole number data type definition. In addition, if you load the whole number data to the worksheet or Data Model, all your calculations are based on the new whole numbers, not the original source number values. Further, if you change your mind about applying a data type, you are allowed to revert to the original source values from before the data type was applied. This is possible because the Source data step stores the original values in a query step that occurs before the query step that applies the data type. When you revert to the original source data or change the data type from one type to another, the query, the loaded data, and any analysis based on the loaded data are all updated to match the new data type.

A common example of using data types to change the source data for analysis purposes is with ISO text date values (which are in YYYYMMDD format). These values do not work as true dates in the worksheet or Data Model. But if you apply a date data type to the text date values, the text date values are converted to date values. The date values will then work as true dates for your analysis.

Operators, Values, and Data Types

Operators are applied to **operands** to form expressions. For example, in the expression 43 + 7, the number values 43 and 7 are operands, and the operator is the addition operator (+). Figure 2-3 describes the M code operators and provides at least one example for each one. There are 36 M code expression examples in the figure. These examples are in the query named OperatorExamples that is available with the book's files so that you can view and experiment with all of these examples.

The figure presents the operators in order of **expression evaluation precedence**, from highest to lowest; that is, it shows the **order of operations**. Operators in the same category have equal precedence. Many of the operators in the list are the same operators that you use in an Excel worksheet and in DAX. However, the application of operators works very differently in M code than in a worksheet and in DAX. For example, in a worksheet and in DAX, if you want to add the number value 10 days to the date value 11/01/2023, the formula is 11/01/2023 + 10 = 11/11/2023. This type of formula does not work in M code.

In M code, with most operators, the operands involved must be the same data type. In M code, you can subtract a date from a date because both are date values, but you cannot directly add a number to a date because a number value is not equivalent to a date value. Calculations like adding a number to a date are easy to perform in M code, but the process works differently than in most other systems. If you need to add a number to a date, you use the easy-to-interpret function Date.AddDays or you add a duration value to the date, which is one of the exceptions to our rule that with most operators, the operands involved must be the same data type.

In addition, each M code value has a different defined set of operators. For example, the only math operators defined for time and date values are addition and subtraction, whereas for number values, the operators multiplication, division, addition, subtraction, and unitary plus and minus are defined, but the exponentiation operator (^) is not. As you will see later in this chapter, exponentiation operations require the use of the Number.Power built-in function. Also, as noted earlier, when you need to add a time to a date in a worksheet and in DAX, you use the addition operator. In contrast, in M code, you use the join operator.

> **Note:** As you can see, it is crucial to learn the designated set of operators for each M code value type. To this end, as I cover each value type through the rest of this chapter, I list the defined set of operators for that value.

There are two keys to applying operators to operands:

- Make sure both operands have the same value type. (However, there are a few exceptions, such as duration, null, and datetime join values.)
- Check the list of defined operators for the given M code value.

It's also important not to confuse data types with values when applying operators. For example, if you apply the any data type to a column of number values and to a column of text values, you cannot apply an operator between the two columns because, although the data type is the same for each column of values, the underlying values are different. However, when you apply the data type decimal or currency (which is equivalent to fixed in Power BI) or whole number or percentage to a column of number values, the underlying numbers are all still number values, and you are allowed to mix and match those data types with operators. In M code, a number value is used for numeric and arithmetic operations. So regardless of whether a column of number values has the decimal, currency (fixed), whole number, or percentage data type applied, the number values are all numbers that can be used in arithmetic operations. It is the M code value, not the data type, that determines the type of operation.

M Code Operator Category (in order of precedence)	Operator(s)	Description	Example
	i	Identifier	Source
	@i	Recursive identifier	let Repeat = {0, @Repeat} in Repeat
	( )	Parenthesized expression	2 * (2+3) = 10
	Table[ColumnName]	Column lookup	#table({"A", "B"}, {{2, 4}, {6, 1}})[B] = {4, 1}
	Table{RowNumber}	Row lookup	#table({"A", "B"}, {{2, 4}, {6, 1}}){0} = [A = 2, B = 4]
	Function(...)	Function invocation	List.Sum({4, 1}) = 5
	{x, y,...}	List	{4, 1}
Primary	[i = x, ...]	Record	[A = 2, B = 4]
	+x	Identity	+3 = 3
	-x	Negation	-3 = -3
Unary	not	NOT logical test	not (-3 = -3) = false
Metadata	meta	Record of metadata	3 meta [Sales = "Low"] = 3
	*	Multiplication	2 + 3 / 3 * 1 = 3
Multiplicative	/	Division	2 + 3 * 3 / 1 = 11
	+	Addition	2 + 5 - 1 = 6
Additive	-	Subtraction	2 - 5 + 1 = -2
		Join text values	"You are " & "Rad!" = You are Rad!
		Join list values	{43} & {2, 17} = {43, 2, 17}
		Merge record values	[x = 3] & [y = 2] = [x = 3, y =2]
		Merge time and date values	#date(2024, 6, 1) & #time(8, 0, 0) = 6/1/2024 8 AM
		Append table values	= #table({"B"},{{43}}) & #table({"B"},{{37}}) = #table({"B"},{{43},{37}})
Join/merge/append	&		
	>	Greater than	2 > 3 = false
	>=	Greater than or equal to	2 >= 2 = true
	<	Less than	"a"<"b" = true
Comparison (logical)	<=	Less than or equal to	10 <= 10 = true
	=	Equal	"Quad" = "Quad" = true
Equality (logical)	<>	Not equal	"Quad" <> "Quad" = false
			43 as number = 43
Type assertion	as	Value assertion	43 as text = error
			43 is number = true
Type conformance	is	Check value type	43 is text = false
AND logical test	and	AND logical test	("Quad" = "Quad" and 100>5) = true
OR logical test	or	OR logical test	("Quad" = "Quad" or 100>5) = true
		From left to right,	null ?? 43 = 43
		the coalesce operator	28 ?? 43 = 28
		returns the first	These two formulas deliver same result:
Coalesce	??	non-null value	value ?? 43 = 43 and if value <> null then value else 43

Figure 2-3 *M code operators, in order of precedence.*

Null Values

A **null value** represents the absence of an M code value. The literal syntax for hard-coding a null value into M code is null (all lowercase). When using a null, an operator, and any of the other value types in an expression, the result is a null value. For example, 5 + null = null, "Quad" & null = null, and 43 >= null = null. As mentioned earlier, the null value is an exception to the rule that operators must work on equivalent value types, but the result will always be null.

To examine the null value and other values, follow these steps:

1. In the Power Query Editor, create a new blank query and name it MCodeValues. To move the function query to the Chapter01and02 group folder, right-click the query in the Queries pane, hover your cursor over Move to Group, and click the Chapter01and02 group.

Note: Here's how you create a blank query in each of the three different tools:

- **Excel:** In the Home tab of the Ribbon, go to the New Query group and click the New Source dropdown, hover over Other Sources, and click Blank Query.
- **Power BI Desktop:** In the Home tab of the Ribbon, go to the New Query group, click the New Source dropdown, and click Blank Query.
- **Dataflow:** In the Home tab of the Ribbon, go to the New Query group and click the Get Data dropdown, click Blank Query, and click Next.

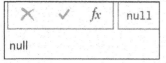

Figure 2-4 *The delivered value is null, and the literal syntax is null.*

2. Click in the Formula Bar, type null (all lowercase), and enter a value by clicking the check mark on the left side of the Formula Bar (or just click on the background outside the Formula Bar). As shown in Figure 2-4, the query result shows as null, which is the same as the literal syntax.

3. In the Applied Steps list, select the query step, put the name in edit mode, press the F2 key, and name the step Null. (The capitalization of the first letter in this identifier distinguishes the identifier from the keyword null. If you really wanted to use the lowercase identifier null, you could use #"null".)

4. To add a new step to the MCodeValues query, click the Fx icon on the left side of the Formula Bar, delete what is in the Formula Bar, and type the following formula:
   ```
   =null + 5
   ```

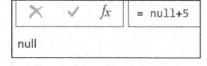

Figure 2-5 *Adding 5 to a null value results in a null.*

5. Click the check mark on the left side of the Formula Bar and name the query step NullPlus5. As shown in Figure 2-5, using an operator on a null value results in a null value.

Logical Values

A **logical value** is one of two possible Boolean values: true or false. The literal syntax for hard-coding logical values is true or false (all lowercase). Figure 2-6 shows the operators defined for logical values.

Operation	Operator
Greater than	>
Greater than or equal	>=
Less than	<
Less than or equal	<=
Equal	=
Not equal	<>
Logical tests	and, or, not
Coalesce	??

Figure 2-6 *Operators that are defined to work between two logical values.*

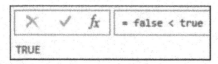

Figure 2-7 *The delivered value is TRUE, and the literal syntax is true.*

To type the literal syntax for a true value and build two formulas using logical values, follow these steps:

1. Add a new step to the MCodeValues query, delete what is in the Formula Bar, type the logical value true (all lowercase), and click the check mark on the left side of the Formula Bar. Name the query step Logical. As shown in Figure 2-7, the query result shows as TRUE, which is different from the literal syntax true.

2. Add a new step to the MCodeValues query, delete what is in the Formula Bar, and type the following formula:
   ```
   = false < true
   ```

3. Click the check mark on the left side of the Formula Bar. Name the query step FalseLessThanTrue. As shown in Figure 2-8, false is less than true.

Figure 2-8 *The less than operator is defined for logical values.*

4. Add a new step to the MCodeValues query, delete what is in the Formula Bar, and type the following formula:

```
= false & true
```

5. Click the check mark on the left side of the Formula Bar and name the query step JoinLogicals. As shown in Figure 2-9, you get an Expression.Error message that warns you that you cannot apply the join operator (&) to logical values. Although a formula like this is allowed in a worksheet or in DAX, in M code, the join operator is not defined for logical values.

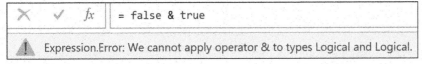

Figure 2-9 *In M code, the join operator is not defined for logical values.*

Text Values

A **text value** is a string of Unicode characters. The literal syntax for hard-coding a text value into M code is to put the characters in quotation marks—such as "Quad" for the word Quad. Figure 2-10 shows the operators defined for text values.

Operation	Operator
Equal	=
Not equal	<>
Greater than or equal	>=
Greater than	>
Less than	<
Less than or equal	<=
Concatenation	&
Coalesce	??

Figure 2-10 *Operators that are defined to work between two text values.*

To type the literal syntax for a text value and build two formulas using text values, follow these steps:

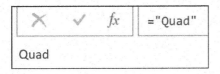

Figure 2-11 *The literal syntax is "Quad", and the delivered value is Quad.*

1. Add a new step to the MCodeValues query by deleting what is in the Formula Bar, typing the text value "Quad", and pressing Enter. Name the query step Text. Notice in Figure 2-11 that the query result appears as Quad, with no quotation marks. As you can see in the figure, the query result is different from the literal syntax.

2. Add a new step to the MCodeValues query by deleting what is in the Formula Bar and typing the following formula:

```
= "Quad" & " is a rad boomerang"
```

3. Click the check mark on the left side of the Formula Bar and name the query step JoinText. As shown in Figure 2-12, the two text values are joined into one text value.

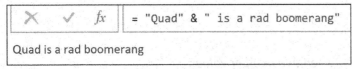

Figure 2-12 *The join operator is defined for text values.*

4. Add a new step to the MCodeValues query by deleting what is in the Formula Bar and typing the following formula:

```
= "43" + "20"
```

5. Click the check mark on the left side of the Formula Bar. Name the query step AddTextNumbers. As shown in Figure 2-13, Expression.Error warns you that you cannot apply the addition operator (+) to text values. Although a formula like this is allowed in the worksheet or in DAX, in M code, the addition operator is not defined for text values.

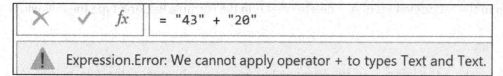

Figure 2-13 *The addition operator is not defined for text values.*

Number Values

Number values are used for numeric and arithmetic operations. The literal syntax for some possible number values is shown here:

- 1210
- -43
- 20.3524
- 12.5874441875555
- 0.025 or 2.5%
- 0.00157 or 1.57E-03
- 2560000 or 2.56E+06
- #infinity (which is the result of the operation 1/0)
- -#infinity (which is the result of the operation -1/0)
- #nan (which is the result of the operation 0/0)

A number is represented with at least the precision of a double (although it may retain more precision). The double representation is congruent with the IEEE 64-bit double precision standard for binary floating-point arithmetic defined in IEEE 754-2008. The double representation can be zero or can range from -1.797693134862315E+308 to -2.225073858507201E-308 or from 2.225073858507201E-308 to 1.797693134862315E+308.

Figures 2-14 and 2-15 show the operators defined for number values.

Operation	Operator
Greater than	>
Greater than or equal	>=
Less than	<
Less than or equal	<=
Equal	=
Not equal	<>
Sum	+
Difference	-
Product	*
Quotient	/
Coalesce	??
Unary plus	+x
Negation	-x

Figure 2-14 *Operators that are defined to work between two number values.*

Operator	Left Operand	Right Operand	Meaning
x * y	duration	number	N times a duration
x * y	number	duration	N times a duration
x / y	duration	number	Fraction of a duration

Figure 2-15 *Number values can perform three operations with duration values.*

Whereas Figure 2-14 shows operators defined for number values, Figure 2-15 shows that for three operations, the duration value can be used with number values. As mentioned earlier in this chapter, in the discussion of operators, the duration value is an exception to the rule that operators must work on equivalent value types.

> **Note:** We have not studied the duration value yet, but I list the duration-related operations in this section so that when you need to look up the operators for numbers, you can find them all in one place. Briefly, a **duration value** is an amount of time, in units of days, hours, minutes, and seconds. So, the fact that you can multiply a number value by a duration or divide a duration by a number makes sense. For example, 2 times the duration 2 days would yield 4 days. You will see how to make this type of duration and number value calculation in the upcoming section on duration values.

To type the literal syntax for a number value and build two formulas using number values, follow these steps:

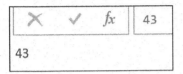

1. Add a new step to the MCodeValues query, delete what is in the Formula Bar, type the number value 43, and press Enter. Name the query step Number. In Figure 2-16, notice that the query result shows as 43, which is the same as the literal syntax.

Figure 2-16 *The literal syntax is 43, and the delivered value is also 43.*

2. Add a new step to the MCodeValues query, delete what is in the Formula Bar, and type the following formula:
   = 23 * 2

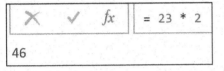

3. Click the check mark on the left side of the Formula Bar and name the query step MultiplyNumbers. As shown in Figure 2-17, the multiplication operator works with two number values.

Figure 2-17 *The multiplication operator is defined for number values.*

4. Add a new step to the MCodeValues query, delete what is in the Formula Bar, and type the following formula:
   = 2 ^ 4

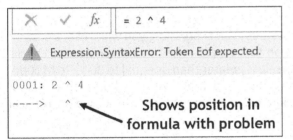

Shows position in formula with problem

5. Click the check mark on the left side of the Formula Bar and name the query step ExponentNumbers. As shown in Figure 2-18, Expression.SyntaxError warns you that there is a syntax error in the formula at the position of the exponentiation operator. As shown in Figure 2-14, the exponentiation operator is not defined for number values. In fact, the exponentiation operator does not exist in M code. In contrast, in a worksheet and in DAX, a formula like 2^4 works without error. In M code, when you need an exponent in a formula, you use the built-in function Number.Power.

Figure 2-18 *The exponent operator is not defined for number values.*

The Number.Power function calculates a result from a base and an exponent. For example, if the base is 2 and the exponent is 4, the math that the function performs is 2^4 = 16. The Number.Power function has two arguments:

=Number.Power(*Base, Exponent*)

6. To see how the Number.Power function works, add a new step to the MCodeValues query by deleting what is in the Formula Bar and typing the following formula:
   = Number.Power(2,4)

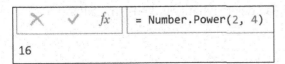

7. Click the check mark on the left side of the Formula Bar and name the query step NumberPowerFunction. As shown in Figure 2-19, the Number.Power function delivers the correct result: 16.

Figure 2-19 *The Number.Power function makes exponential calculations.*

The left side of Figure 2-20 shows the 12 query steps (identifiers and expressions) in the let expression that Power Query has written for you in the Advanced Editor. The right side of the figure shows the query step names in the Applied Steps list.

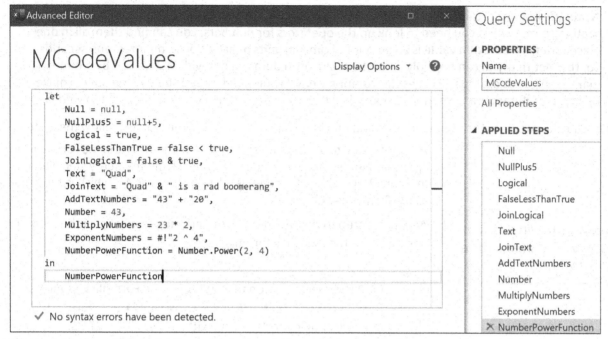

Figure 2-20 *The Advanced Editor and the Applied Steps list, side-by-side.*

The if Expression

Now that we have talked about the five M code values type, null, logical, text, and number, let's look at how to use all five values in a single expression (formula).

To see how you might use the null, logical, text, and number values in an expression, you will create a custom column in the DayTypeSalesQ query and use an if expression to create a conditional formula that checks whether DayType is equal to Workday and whether the max sale is greater than or equal to 3000. In M code, the if expression uses the same logic as the IF function in a worksheet or in a DAX formula, but it uses different syntax. You use an **if expression** when you want the expression to deliver one of two items based on a logical test. The syntax for the if expression is as follows:

```
if  logical_test  then  expression_if_true  else  expression_if_false
```

To create a conditional column, you can start by creating a reference to the first query that you created, named DayTypeSalesQ; this will pull the table result into the current query. Then you can add a column by using the **Custom Column** feature, which allows you to create a new column, name the column, and create a formula (expression) in each row of the table.

> **Note:** If you do not have a Power BI Premium license, you cannot reference another query in Dataflow; in this case, you can add the if expression formula to the query named DayTypeSalesQ rather than create the reference to the query DayTypeSalesQ in the current query named MCodeValues.

Follow these steps to create a conditional column:

1. To add a new step to the MCodeValues query in order to create a reference to the DayTypeSalesQ query, click the Fx icon on the left side of the Formula Bar, delete what is in the Formula Bar, and type the following formula:

   ```
   = DayTypeSalesQ
   ```

2. Press Enter to pull the DayTypeSalesQ query result into the current query. Name the query step GetDayTypeQuery.

3. To create a custom column, in the Add Column tab of the Ribbon, in the General group, click the Custom Column button. The Custom Column dialog box appears.

4. As shown in Figure 2-21, in the New Column Name textbox, type the name IfExpression. Then, in the Custom Column Formula textbox, type this formula:

```
if [DayType] = "Workday" and [Max Sale] >= 3000 then true else null
```

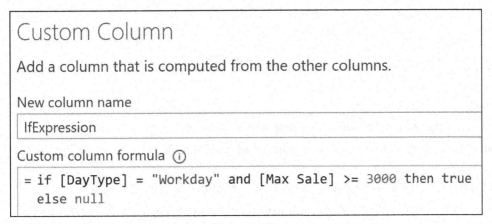

Figure 2-21 *An if expression in the Custom Column dialog box.*

Figure 2-21 shows the formula in the Custom Column dialog box, with the "Workday" text value, the 3000 number value, the true logical value, and the null value. Also in this formula are the if expression keywords if, then, and else. The formula also contains two comparison operators: equal to (=) and greater than or equal to (>=). In addition, the **field access operator**—the square brackets around the column names, [DayType] and [Max Sale]—allows you access to the column it wraps around. (You will learn more about the field access operator in Chapter 4.) Finally, the logical test checks for two conditions and performs an AND logical test (where all tests must be true). In M code, the (lowercase) **and operator** is used to perform an (all uppercase) AND logical test. The two other types of logical operators (not shown in this formula) are the **or operator** to run an OR logical test (where at least one test is true) and the **not operator** to run a NOT logical test (which switches true to false or false to true).

5. Click the Done button and name the query step FormulaWithValues. As shown in Figure 2-22, the formula delivers one of two possible M code values in each row: TRUE or null.

	A^B_C DayType	1.2 Max Sale	ABC 123 IfExpression
1	Workday	3500	TRUE
2	Weekend	2880.13	null
3	Holiday	1904.77	null
4	Donation	2227.46	null

Figure 2-22 *A new custom column with either TRUE or null In each row.*

Next, you will learn about the M code function that allowed the if expression to calculate an answer in each row in this example.

The Table.AddColumn Function

When you create a formula in the Custom Column dialog box, behind the scenes the formula is placed in the **Table.AddColumn** function, which adds a column to a table by running a formula in each row. Figure 2-23 shows the Table.AddColumn function that you used as part of your if expression in the preceding section. The arguments for the function are as follows:

```
Table.AddColumn(
    table as table,
    newColumnName as text,
    columnGenerator as function,
    optional columnType as nullable type) as table
```

When reading the Table.AddColumn argument description above, keep in mind that as table, as text, and as function use the as keyword to communicate what type of M code value you should put into the argument. as table indicates that the function delivers a table value. In Figure 2-23, notice that the Table.AddColumn function does not use the fourth argument.

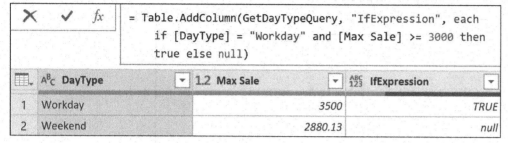

```
= Table.AddColumn(GetDayTypeQuery, "IfExpression", each
        if [DayType] = "Workday" and [Max Sale] >= 3000 then
        true else null)
```

A^B_C DayType	1.2 Max Sale	ABC₁₂₃ IfExpression
1 Workday	3500	TRUE
2 Weekend	2880.13	null

Figure 2-23 *The Table.AddColumn function has four arguments but is using only three of them here.*

To edit your formula and add a data type to the fourth argument of the Table.AddColumn function, follow these steps:

1. Expand the Formula Bar with the expand arrow on the right side of the Formula Bar.

2. As shown in Figure 2-24, in the Table.AddColumn function, add a line break before each of the four arguments by pressing Shift+Enter and adding five spaces to indent each argument. (This formatting makes the formula easier to read.)

3. In the Formula Bar, after the null value but before the closing parenthesis, type a comma to get to the fourth argument and then add a new line break and five spaces. Finally, type the following:
    ```
    type nullable logical
    ```

4. Click at the end of the formula after the closing parenthesis and press Enter.

Figure 2-24 shows the result, with the data type applied to the column. Now your formula contains the five M code values: the text value "Workday", the number value 3000, the logical value true, the null value null, and the type value nullable logical. (nullable logical means that the column has the logical data type but allows null values.) Finally, the Table.AddColumn function delivers a sixth M code value: a table.

```
= Table.AddColumn(
        GetDayTypeQuery,
        "IfExpression",
        each if [DayType] = "Workday" and [Max Sale] >= 3000 then true else null,
        type nullable logical)
```

A^B_C DayType	1.2 Max Sale	IfExpression

Figure 2-24 *The nullable logical data type is added in the fourth argument.*

Date, Time, Datetime, Datetimezone, and Duration

M code has a number of values related to time and date: date, time, datetime, datetimezone, and duration. When you hard-code each of these values, you use an intrinsic function to deliver the value. The following sections describe these values, provide an example of each intrinsic function, and give several expression examples. Because duration values interact with the other date- and time-related values, we will look at them first.

Duration Values

A **duration value** is encoded as a serial number that represents an amount of time in units of days, hours, minutes, and seconds. A duration can be negative or positive. There is no literal syntax for durations, but you can use an intrinsic function to hard-code a duration value, as shown here:

```
=#duration(days, hours, minutes, seconds)
```

Here's an example of this intrinsic function in action:

```
=#duration(1,0,10,0) = 1:00:10:00 = 1 day and 10 minutes
```

Duration values are important in M code because they can interact as operands with the date, time, datetime, datetimezone, and number values. For example, if you want to add 10 days to a date, you cannot use the formula 1/1/2023 + 10 because the value types for the date and number are not equivalent. But you can use the formula 1/1/2023 + #duration(10,0,0,0), and the result will be 1/11/2023. As another example, if you want to add 2 hours to a datetime value, you cannot use the formula 1/1/2023 8 AM + 2:00 because the value types for datetime and time are not equivalent. But you can use the formula 1/1/2023 8 AM + #duration(0,2,0,0), and the result will be 1/1/2023 10 AM. In addition, if you subtract an earlier date from a later date to get the number of days, the result will be a duration. For example, 1/11/2023 - 1/1/2023 = #duration(10,0,0,0), or 10 days. Finally, if you have an amount of time as a duration and you want to double that time, because multiplication is defined between numbers and durations, you can simply multiply the time duration by two.

Microsoft's documentation says that duration values are not supported in Dataflow. I have found that I can use a duration value embedded in a formula if the formula does not deliver a duration value and does define a duration data type. Duration values do not exist in worksheets or in the Data Model. If you load them to a worksheet or the Data Model, they are converted to datetime values. Figure 2-25 shows the operators defined for duration values. The defined operators that work between duration values and other values are shown later in this chapter.

Operation	Operator
Equal	=
Not equal	<>
Greater than or equal	>=
Greater than	>
Less than	<
Less than or equal	<=
Coalesce	??
Sum	+
Difference	-

Figure 2-25 Operators that are defined to work between two duration values.

Next, you will see how to use duration intrinsic functions to create a hard-coded duration value and then create two formulas that use duration values. (If you are working in Dataflow, you will have to skip the duration data type.) Follow these steps:

1. Add a new step to the MCodeValues query and create this formula:

   `=#duration(1,1,1,0)`

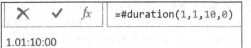

`=#duration(1,1,10,0)`

1.01:10:00

Figure 2-26 The result from the duration intrinsic function.

2. Name the query step Duration. As shown in Figure 2-26, the intrinsic function delivers a duration value in the form days:hours:minutes:seconds. In this case, the result is 1 day, 1 hour, and 10 minutes.

3. Add a new step to the MCodeValues query and create this formula:
   `= #duration(1,1,10,0) + #duration(5,0,0,0)`

4. Name the query step AddDurations. As shown in Figure 2-27, the formula adds 5 days to 1 day, 1 hour, and 10 minutes to get the result 6 days, 1 hour, and 10 minutes.

`= #duration(1,1,10,0) + #duration(5,0,0,0)`

6.01:10:00

Figure 2-27 The addition operator is defined for duration values.

5. Add a new step to the MCodeValues query and create this formula:
   `= #duration(1,1,10,0) * 2`

`= #duration(1,1,10,0) * 2`

2.02:20:00

Figure 2-28 Multiplication works between a duration value and a number value.

6. Name the query step DurationTimesNumber. As shown in Figure 2-28, the formula multiplies the number 2 by the duration 1 day, 1 hour, and 10 minutes to get the result 2 days, 2 hours, and 20 minutes.

Duration values can work with number values and all the date- and time-related values. Here are a few durations that help you see what you can enter into arguments:

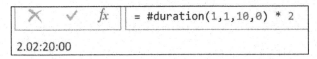

```
=#duration(0,48,0,0) = 2:00:00:00 = 2 days
=#duration(0,0,1,43) = 0:00:01:43 = 1 minute and 43 seconds
```

```
=#duration(0,40,0,0) = 1:16:00:00 = 1 day and 16 hours
=#duration(0,-8,0,0) = -0:08:00:00 = - 8 hours
```

Date Values

The format for dates depends on the regional settings for your computer. For example, in the United States a date is shown as mm/dd/yyyy, and in France a date is shown as dd/mm/yyyy. I use the US date format for all examples in this book. (Chapter 6 covers the Locale feature, which allows you to work with dates from other locales and other formats.)

M code date values are different from dates in an Excel worksheet. In the beginning of spreadsheet history, Lotus 1-2-3 and then Excel incorrectly assumed that the year 1900 was a leap year and that the day 2/29/1900 existed. This error persists in worksheets today. In addition, the earliest possible date in an Excel worksheet is 1/1/1900. M code date values remedy both deficiencies. Date values in M code do not list 2/29/1900 as a valid date. In addition, M code date values span from 1/1/0001 to 12/31/9999 (the Common Era on the Gregorian calendar).

> **Note:** Although you can perform date math calculations in Power Query on all Gregorian calendar dates, if you start with whole numbers and apply the date data type, the smallest number is -657,434, which corresponds to the date 1/1/0001.

If you are using dates before 1/1/1900 in a query and you load the query results to the Data Model in Power Pivot or Power BI, the dates will work as valid dates; however, if the same dates are loaded to the Excel worksheet, the dates before 1/1/1900 will be loaded as text dates rather than as valid date values. As in an Excel worksheet, M code date values are encoded with serial numbers that help formulas perform date math. However, M code date serial numbers are different from the date serial numbers in an Excel worksheet.

As shown in Figure 2-29, serial numbers in a worksheet and in M code are the same for dates on 3/1/1900 or after, but the dates between 1/1/1900 and 2/28/1900 are off by one. In a worksheet, dates before 1/1/1900 are considered text values, with a left alignment, and therefore they do not have serial numbers, as shown in Figure 2-29. In M code, date serial numbers are negative starting with the date 12/29/1899 and increment by -1 until the first possible date. Notice that the worksheet serial number for 2/29/1900 is 60, and the M code serial number for 2/28/1900 is 60. This bit of Microsoft cleverness allows you to import the date 2/29/1900 and have it interpreted as 2/28/1900, or you can import 2/28/1900 with the serial number 59 and have it interpreted as 2/27/1900 because its serial number is 59.

Power Query Serial Numbers	Power Query Dates	Excel Serial Numbers	Excel Dates
2958465	12/31/9999	2958465	12/31/9999
45114	7/7/2023	45114	7/7/2023
366	12/31/1900	366	12/31/1900
365	12/30/1900	365	12/30/1900
61	3/1/1900	61	3/1/1900
		60	2/29/1900
60	2/28/1900	59	2/28/1900
59	2/27/1900	3	1/3/1900
3	1/2/1900	2	1/2/1900
2	1/1/1900	1	1/1/1900
1	12/31/1899	Text	12/31/1899
0	12/30/1899	Text	12/30/1899
-1	12/29/1899	Text	12/29/1899
-2	12/28/1899	Text	12/28/1899
-102589	2/12/1619	Text	2/12/1619
-255899	5/15/1199	Text	5/15/1199
-644000	10/13/0136	Text	10/13/0136

Figure 2-29 *Some of the possible dates and serial numbers in Power Query and in a worksheet.*

Finally, in M code, the negative and positive date serial numbers allow you to make accurate date formulas, like this:

```
End Date - Start Date = Number of Days Between Two Dates
```

For example, 12/29/1899 - 12/28/1899 = -1 - -2 = 1 day. As another date calculation example, if you create an expression to calculate 12/28/1899 + 2 days, you get -2 + 2 = 0, which is the correct date, 12/30/1899.

A **date value** is encoded as a serial number that represents the number of days since epoch, starting from January 1, 0001 Common Era on the Gregorian calendar. The maximum number of days since epoch is 3652058, corresponding to December 31, 9999. There is no literal syntax for date values, but you can use an intrinsic function to hard-code date values, as shown here:

```
=#date(year, month, day)
```

Here's an example of this intrinsic function:

```
=#date(1598, 1, 15)= 1/15/1598
```

Figures 2-30 and 2-31 show the operators defined for date values.

Operation	Operator
Greater than	>
Greater than or equal	>=
Less than	<
Less than or equal	<=
Equal	=
Not equal	<>
Coalesce	??

Figure 2-30 *Operators that are defined to work between two date values.*

Operator	Left Operand	Right Operand	Meaning
x + y	date	duration	Date offset by day duration
x + y	duration	date	Date offset by day duration
x - y	date	duration	Date offset by negated day duration
x - y	date	date	Duration between dates
x & y	date	time	Merged into datetime

Figure 2-31 *These operators permit one or both of their operands to be date values.*

Whereas Figure 2-30 shows operators defined for two date values, Figure 2-31 shows the operators allowed between duration and date values, two date values, and date and time values. In Figure 2-31, the first two rows show that you can add a day duration value to a date value to get a new date value. For example, this formula would work:

```
= #date(2023,1,1) + #duration(8,0,0,0) = 1/9/2023
```

The third row of Figure 2-31 shows that you can subtract a day duration value from a date value to get a new date value. However, subtracting a date value from a duration value is not defined. For example, this formula would work:

```
= #date(2023,1,1) - #duration(8,0,0,0) = 12/24/2022
```

The fourth row of Figure 2-31 shows that when you subtract a date from a date, you get a day duration, where the result can be positive or negative. For example, this formula would work:

```
= #date(2022,12,24) - #date(2023,1,1) = -8:00:00:00
```

The last row of Figure 2-31 shows that you can merge a date value and a time value by using the join operator to create a datetime value. In a worksheet and DAX, date and time values are merged using the addition operator rather than the join operator. Also, notice that the order of operands matters. Whereas in a worksheet and DAX you can add a time to a date or a date to a time, in M code you can only merge a date value with a time value, using this formula:

```
date & time
```

Now that you have learned about date values, you can create several date expressions by following these steps:

1. Add a new step to the MCodeValues query and create this formula:

   ```
   =#date(1598, 1, 15)
   ```

2. Name the query step Date. In Figure 2-32, notice that dates from the 16th century work as valid dates in M code.

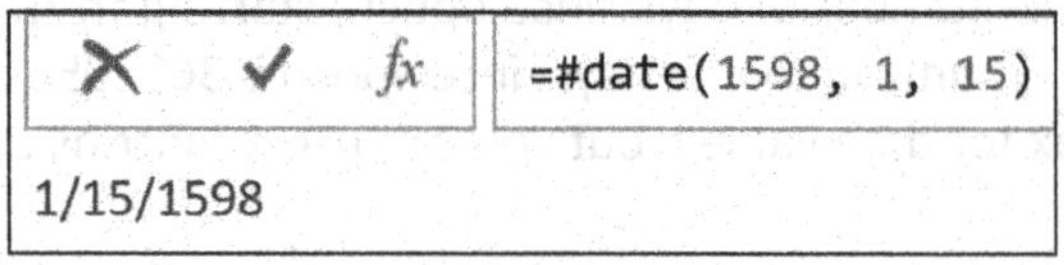

✕	✓	*fx*	=#date(1598, 1, 15)

1/15/1598

Figure 2-32 *The result from a date intrinsic function.*

1. Add two new steps to the MCodeValues query and create these two formulas, which will add 8 days to the date 1/1/2023:

   ```
   = #date(2023,1,1) + #duration(8,0,0,0)
   ```

   ```
   = Date.AddDays(#date(2023,1,1),8)
   ```

2. Name the first query step DatePlusDuration and the second query step DateAddDayFunction. Figures 2-33 and 2-34 show that both formulas deliver the same date: 1/9/2023.

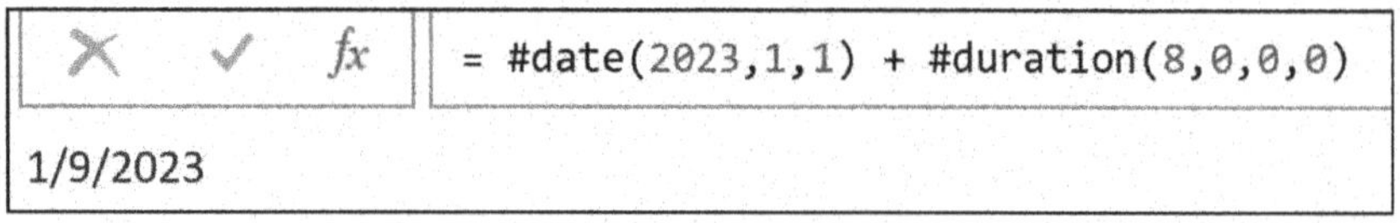

✕	✓	*fx*	= #date(2023,1,1) + #duration(8,0,0,0)

1/9/2023

Figure 2-33 *To add 8 days to a date, you can use a duration value.*

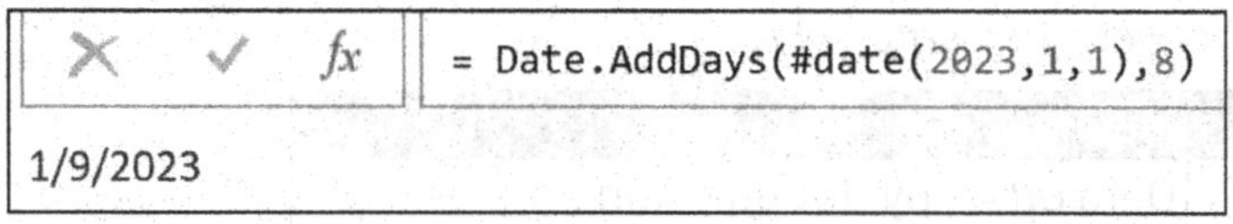

✕	✓	*fx*	= Date.AddDays(#date(2023,1,1),8)

1/9/2023

Figure 2-34 *To add 8 days to a date, you can use the Date.AddDays function.*

In a worksheet or DAX, when you want to add days to a date, you just add a number value to the date value—for example, 1/1/2023 + 8 = 1/9/2023. However, in M code, as you are learning, you must always be aware of the values and the operators. The formulas in Figures 2-33 and 2-34 both hard-code the values. Later in this chapter you will see examples that use both of these methods on a table with dates and number of day values.

Time Values

As with time values in a worksheet and DAX, an M code **time value** is encoded as a serial number between 0 and 1 that represents the proportion of a 24-hour day; for example, 8 AM = 8/24 = 1/3 =0.3333. There is no literal syntax for time values, but you can use an intrinsic function to hard-code time values as shown here:

```
=#time(hour, minute, seconds)
```

Here's an example of this intrinsic function:

```
=#time(11,10,57) = 11:10:57
```

Operation	Operator
Greater than	>
Greater than or equal	>=
Less than	<
Less than or equal	<=
Equal	=
Not equal	<>
Coalesce	??

Figure 2-35 *Operators that are defined to work between two time values.*

Figures 2-35 and 2-36 show the operators defined for time values. Time values have the same set of defined operators as date values. For example, you can offset a time value with a time duration value to get a new time value using addition and subtraction, you can calculate the difference between two time values to get a duration value, and you can merge a date and time by using the join operator.

Operator	Left Operand	Right Operand	Meaning
x + y	time	duration	Time offset by time duration
x + y	duration	time	Time offset by time duration
x - y	time	duration	Time offset by negated time duration
x - y	time	time	Duration between times
x & y	date	time	Merged into datetime

Figure 2-36 *These operators permit one or both of their operands to be time values.*

To create several time value expressions, follow these steps:

1. Add a new step to the MCodeValues query and create this formula:

   ```
   =#time(11,10,57)
   ```

2. Name the query step Time. Figure 2-37 shows that the result is 11:10:57 AM.

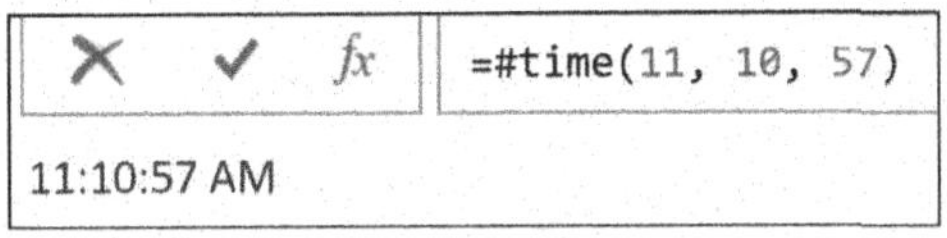

✕ ✓ *fx*	=#time(11, 10, 57)

11:10:57 AM

Figure 2-37 *The result from a time intrinsic function.*

3. Add a new step to the MCodeValues query and create the following formula, which subtracts 1:30 PM from 9 PM:

   ```
   = #time(21,0,0) - #time(13,30,0)
   ```

4. Name the query step SubtractTimeValues. Figure 2-38 shows that the difference between the two times is a duration value equal to 7 hours and 30 minutes.

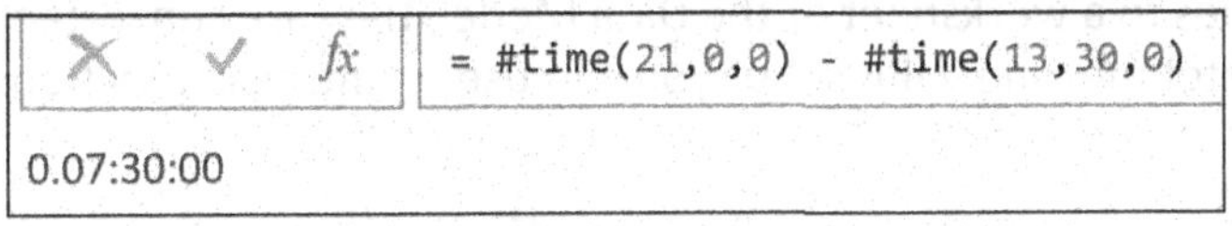

✕ ✓ *fx*	= #time(21,0,0) - #time(13,30,0)

0.07:30:00

Figure 2-38 *Subtracting two time value results in a duration value.*

5. Add a new step to the MCodeValues query and create this formula:

   ```
   = #date(2023,1,1) & #time(21,0,0)
   ```

6. Name the query step DateJoinTime. Figure 2-39 shows the merged datetime value 1/1/ 2023 9 PM.

✕ ✓ *fx*	= #date(2023,1,1) & #time(21,0,0)

1/1/2023 9:00:00 PM

Figure 2-39 *The join operator is used to merge a date value and a time value.*

Datetime Values

In M code, a **datetime value** is encoded as a serial number that represents the number of days since 1/1/0001 plus any decimal amount that represents the proportion of a 24-hour day. There is no literal syntax for datetime values, but you can use an intrinsic function to hard-code datetime values as shown here:

```
=#datetime(year, month, day, hour, minutes, seconds)
```

Here's an example of this intrinsic function:

```
=#datetime(2021,10,1,11,10,57) = 10/01/21 11:10:57 AM
```

Operation	Operator
Greater than	>
Greater than or equal	>=
Less than	<
Less than or equal	<=
Equal	=
Not equal	<>
Coalesce	??

Figure 2-40 *Operators that are defined to work between two datetime values.*

Figures 2-40 and 2-41 show the operators defined for datetime values. These operators are the same as the ones defined for date and time values except that you cannot use the join operator.

Operator	Left Operand	Right Operand	Meaning
x + y	datetime	duration	Datetime offset by duration
x + y	duration	datetime	Datetime offset by duration
x - y	datetime	duration	Datetime offset by negated duration
x - y	datetime	datetime	Duration between datetimes

Figure 2-41 *These operators permit one or both of their operands to be datetime values.*

To create a datetime value using an intrinsic function, follow these steps:

1. Add a new step to the MCodeValues query and create this formula:

   ```
   =#datetime(2021,10,1,11,10,57)
   ```

2. Name the query step Datetime. Figure 2-42 shows that the result is 11:10:57 AM on October 1, 2021.

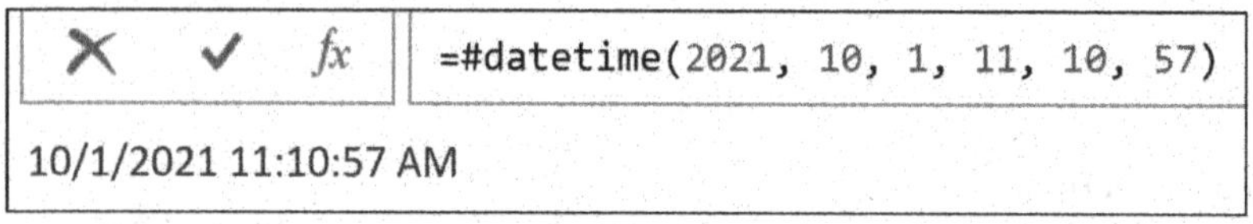

✗ ✓ *fx*	=#datetime(2021, 10, 1, 11, 10, 57)
10/1/2021 11:10:57 AM	

Figure 2-42 *The result from a datetime intrinsic function.*

Datetimezone Values

A **datetimezone value** is encoded as a serial number that represents a UTC (Universal Coordinated Time) datetime value with a time zone offset. The time zone offset is set in the last two arguments, offset-hours and offset-minutes. The offsets can be negative or positive. Datetimezone values do not exist in a worksheet or in the Data Model. If you load datetimezone values to a worksheet or the Data Model, they are converted to datetime values. There is no literal syntax for datetimezone values, but you can use an intrinsic function to hard-code datetimezone values as shown here:

```
=#datetimezone(year, month, day, hour, minute, second, offset-hours, offset-minutes)
```

Here's an example of this intrinsic function:

```
=#datetimezone(2021,10,1,11,10,57,09,0) = 10/01/21 11:10:57 AM + 9 hours
```

Figures 2-43 and 2-44 show the operators defined for datetimezone values. These operators are the same as the ones defined for date, time, and datetime values except that you cannot use the join operator.

Operation	Operator
Greater than	>
Greater than or equal	>=
Less than	<
Less than or equal	<=
Equal	=
Not equal	<>
Coalesce	??

Figure 2-43 *Operators that are defined to work between two datetime values.*

Operator	Left Operand	Right Operand	Meaning
x + y	datetimezone	duration	Datetimezone offset by duration
x + y	duration	datetimezone	Datetimezone offset by duration
x - y	datetimezone	duration	Datetimezone offset by negated duration
x - y	datetimezone	datetimezone	Duration between datetimezones

Figure 2-44 *These operators permit one or both of their operands to be datetime values.*

To create a datetimezone value using an intrinsic function, follow these steps:

1. Add a new step to the MCodeValues query and create this formula with a datetime value that is offset by 9 hours:

    ```
    =#datetimezone(2021,10,1,11,10,57,09,0)
    ```

2. Name the query step Datetimezone. Figure 2-45 shows that the result is 10/1/2021 11:10:57 + 9:00.

✕	✓	*fx*	=#datetimezone(2021, 10, 1, 11, 10, 57, 09, 0)

10/1/2021 11:10:57 AM +09:00

Figure 2-45 *The result from a datetime intrinsic function.*

Figure 2-46 shows the let expression that is created in the MCodeValues query based on the steps you've taken so far.

```
let
    Null = null,
    NullPlus5 = null+5,
    Logical = true,
    FalseLessThanTrue = false < true,
    JoinLogical = false & true,
    Text = "Quad",
    JoinText = "Quad" & " is a rad boomerang",
    AddTextNumbers = "43" + "20",
    Number = 43,
    MultiplyNumbers = 23 * 2,
    ExponentNumbers = #!"2 ^ 4",
    NumberPowerFunction = Number.Power(2, 4),
    GetDayTypeQuery = DayTypeSalesQ,
    FormulaWithValues = Table.AddColumn(GetDayTypeQuery,"IfExpression",
        each if [DayType] = "Workday" and [Max Sale] >= 3000 then true else null,type nullable logical),
    Duration = #duration(1,1,10,0),
    AddDurations = #duration(1,1,10,0) + #duration(5,0,0,0),
    DurationTimesNumber = #duration(1,1,10,0) * 2,
    Date = #date(1598, 1, 15),
    DatePlusDuration = #date(2023,1,1) + #duration(8,0,0,0),
    DateAddDayFunction = Date.AddDays(#date(2023,1,1),8),
    Time = #time(11, 10, 57),
    SubtractTimeValues = #time(21,0,0) - #time(13,30,0),
    DateJoinTime = #date(2023,1,1) & #time(21,0,0),
    Datetime = #datetime(2021, 10, 1, 11, 10, 57),
    Datetimezone = #datetimezone(2021,10,1,11,10,57,09,0)
in
    Datetimezone
```

Figure 2-46 *The let expression for the MCodeValues query.*

Working with Date- and Time-Related Values

Next, you are going to create several custom columns and work with date- and time-related values. Follow these steps:

1. In the Power Query Editor, select the query named DurationQ in the Chapter01and02 group. As shown in Figure 2-47, notice that the dates before 1/1/1900 are text values.

2. Add the following data types to the columns:
    *   Add the date data type to the StartDate column. Notice that all the dates in the column are now date values, including 1/1/0001.
    *   Add the date data type to the EndDate column.
    *   Add the whole number data type to the DaysToAddToEnd column.
    *   Add the time data type to the StartTime column.
    *   Add the time data type to the EndTime column.

3. Name the step AddDataTypes.

Figure 2-47 shows the results after you have applied all five data types. Notice that dates before 1/1/1900 are date values, which can be used in date calculations.

StartDate	EndDate	DaysToAddToEnd	StartTime	EndTime
1	1/26/2023 12:00:00 AM	1/29/2023 12:00:00 AM	2	0.333333333	0.416666667
2	12/30/9998 12:00:00 AM	1/4/9999 12:00:00 AM	10	0.385416667	0.552083333
3	1/2/1902 12:00:00 AM	5/5/1902 12:00:00 AM	55	0.28125	0.708333333
4	1/1/0001	1/2/0001	5	0.833333333	0.15625
5	1/15/1598	1/1/1600	12	0.9375	0.208333333

Figure 2-47 *Initially the dates before 1/1/1900 are considered text values.*

Extracting the Year from a Date

To extract the years from the StartDate column (refer to Figure 2-48), follow these steps:

1. Select the StartDate column, click the Add Column tab in the Ribbon, go to the From Date & Time group, click the Date dropdown, hover over Year, and click Year in the submenu.

StartDate	EndDate	DaysToAddToEnd	StartTime	EndTime
1	1/26/2023	1/29/2023	2	8:00:00 AM	10:00:00 AM
2	12/30/9998	1/4/9999	10	9:15:00 AM	1:15:00 PM
3	1/2/1902	5/5/1902	55	6:45:00 AM	5:00:00 PM
4	1/1/0001	1/2/0001	5	8:00:00 PM	3:45:00 AM
5	1/15/1598	1/1/1600	12	10:30:00 PM	5:00:00 AM

Figure 2-48 *The date data type converts the text dates to dates.*

2. Name the step ExtractYearFromStartDate.

Figure 2-49 shows the formula that is created. Because a new column is added to a table, Table.AddColumn is used, and all four arguments for the function are being used. Notice that in the third argument, where you build a formula, the Date.Year function is used.

```
= Table.AddColumn(AddDataTypes, "Year", each Date.Year([StartDate]), Int64.Type)
```

dToEnd	StartTime	EndTime	Year
2	8:00:00 AM	10:00:00 AM	2023
10	9:15:00 AM	1:15:00 PM	9998
55	6:45:00 AM	5:00:00 PM	1902
5	8:00:00 PM	3:45:00 AM	1
12	10:30:00 PM	5:00:00 AM	1598

Figure 2-49 *The year has been extracted from the date.*

These are some of the date values and what they do:

- **Date.Year** extracts a year from a date.
- **Date.Month** extracts the month number from a date.
- **Date.AddDays** adds days to a date to get a new date.
- **Day.EndOfMonth** extracts the end-of-month date from a date.
- **Date.DayOfWeekName** extracts the day-of-week name from a date.

Also notice that the fourth argument in Table.AddColumn lists the data type for the whole number Int64. Type. Usually, data types are prefaced by the keywork type (for example, type logical), but there are a few data types that do not follow this convention, such as Int64.Type. (The full list of data types is shown in Figure 2-2, near the beginning of this chapter.)

Adding and Subtracting Date Values

Now let's look at how to calculate the number of days between StartDate and EndDate as a duration. To accomplish this, follow these steps:

1. Add a custom column to the MCodeValues query, and in the Custom Column dialog box, name the column DurationBetweenStartAndEnd and create the following formula:

```
[EndDate] - [StartDate]
```

2. As shown in Figure 2-50, add the duration type to the fourth argument of Table.AddColumn and format the formula to make it easier to read by adding a line break and spaces to indent each argument. (If you are completing this step in Dataflow, because duration data types are not allowed, you can either skip this query step or trick Dataflow by adding a text data type to the fourth argument.)

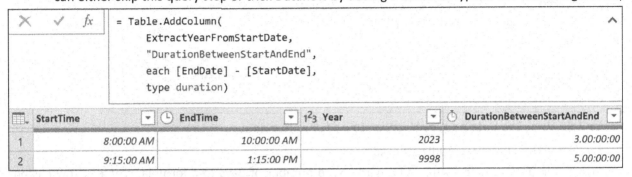

```
= Table.AddColumn(
      ExtractYearFromStartDate,
      "DurationBetweenStartAndEnd",
      each [EndDate] - [StartDate],
      type duration)
```

StartTime	EndTime	1²₃ Year	DurationBetweenStartAndEnd
1	8:00:00 AM	10:00:00 AM	2023	3.00:00:00
2	9:15:00 AM	1:15:00 PM	9998	5.00:00:00

Figure 2-50 *Subtracting dates to get a duration.*

3. Name the query step SubtractDates.

4. To use the built-in feature to subtract dates and deliver a column of whole number values, click on the EndDate column header and then hold down the Ctrl key while you click on the StartDate column header. The columns are selected in the correct order so that the start date can be subtracted from the end date. Click the Add Column tab in the Ribbon, go to the From Date & Time group, click the Date dropdown, and then click Subtract Days.

5. As shown in Figure 2-51, in the second argument of the Table.AddColumn function, change the column name from Subtraction to DaysBetweenStartAndEnd. Then format the formula to make it easier to read.

6. Name the query step SubtractDateFeature.

Figure 2-51 shows the Table.AddColumn formula result. Notice that the formula delivers the number of days as a whole number rather than as a duration. The function Duration.Days returns the days portion of a duration as a whole number.

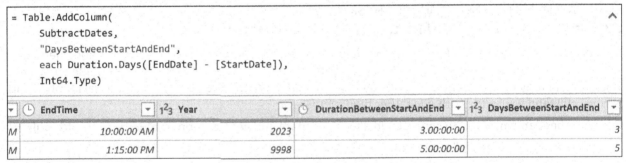

```
= Table.AddColumn(
      SubtractDates,
      "DaysBetweenStartAndEnd",
      each Duration.Days([EndDate] - [StartDate]),
      Int64.Type)
```

	EndTime	1²₃ Year	DurationBetweenStartAndEnd	1²₃ DaysBetweenStartAndEnd
M	10:00:00 AM	2023	3.00:00:00	3
M	1:15:00 PM	9998	5.00:00:00	5

Figure 2-51 *The Subtract Days feature delivers the number of days.*

These are two of the duration functions and what they do:

- **Duration.Hours** returns the hours portion of a duration.
- **Duration.TotalHours** returns the total hours as a number value from all four parts in a duration value—for example, = Duration.TotalHours(#duration(0,07,45,0)) = 7.75 hours.

Now let's look at how to add a number of days to a date. As you learned earlier, adding a number value (number of days) to a date value with an addition operator does not work because the two values do not have equivalent value types. However, the Date.AddDays function can handle the different data types and add days to a date to get a new date, where positive numbers yield a future date and negative numbers yield a past date. To create a new column, follow these steps:

1. Create a new custom column in the MCodeValues query, and in the Custom Column dialog box, name the column NewEndDate and create the following formula:

```
=Date.AddDays([EndDate],[DaysToAddToEnd])
```

2.   Add a date data type and format the formula. Figure 2-52 shows the result.

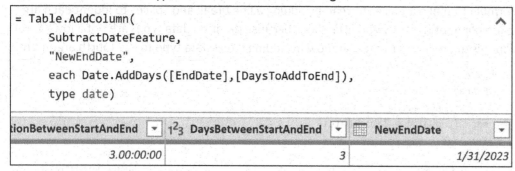

```
= Table.AddColumn(
      SubtractDateFeature,
      "NewEndDate",
      each Date.AddDays([EndDate],[DaysToAddToEnd]),
      type date)
```

tionBetweenStartAndEnd ▾	1²₃ DaysBetweenStartAndEnd ▾	NewEndDate ▾
3.00:00:00	3	1/31/2023

Figure 2-52 *Using the Date.AddDays function to add days to a date.*

3.   Name the query step AddDaysToDate.

4.   To add a new column and add a hard-coded number of days to a formula, create a new custom column, and in the Custom Column dialog box, name the column EndDatePlus20Days and create the following formula:

```
=[EndDate] + #duration(20,0,0,0)
```

5.   Add a date data type and format the formula. Figure 2-53 shows the result.

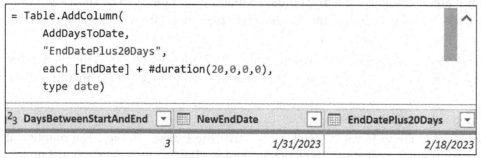

```
= Table.AddColumn(
      AddDaysToDate,
      "EndDatePlus20Days",
      each [EndDate] + #duration(20,0,0,0),
      type date)
```

²₃ DaysBetweenStartAndEnd ▾	NewEndDate ▾	EndDatePlus20Days ▾
3	1/31/2023	2/18/2023

Figure 2-53 *Using a duration intrinsic function to add hard-coded days to a date.*

6.   Name the query step AddHardCodedDays.

Adding (Merging) a Time Value to a Date Value

Now let's look at how to add a time value to a date value to get a datetime value. Microsoft's documentation for M code uses the verb *merge* rather than *add*, which is fine. But when you merge a date value and a time value, the underlying serial date and time numbers are added together to get a datetime serial number. This is why I still tend to use the verb *add* rather than *merge*.

In a worksheet and in DAX, you can just add a time to a date and get a datetime value, as in this formula:

```
="6/1/2024" + "8:00" = 6/1/2024 8 AM
```

In M code, you can add time to a date to get a datetime value, but you must use the join operator rather than the addition operator. In M code, the **join operator** (&) is more powerful than in the worksheet or DAX. In the worksheet and DAX, when you use the join operator, the result is always a text value, but in M code, you can join a date to a time to get a datetime, join a list to a list to get a combined list, and even join a table to a table to append and get a combined table, as you will see later in this chapter. To join a date to a time in M code, follow these steps:

1.   In the MCodeValues query, in the Add Column tab of the Ribbon, go to the From Date & Time group and select Combine Date and Time from the dropdown.

2.   Format the formula so it is easy to read.

3.   Name the query step JoinTimeToDate. Figure 2-54 shows the result.

```
= Table.AddColumn(
    AddHardCodedDays,
    "DateTime",
    each [EndDate] & [EndTime],
    type datetime)
```

	NewEndDate			EndDatePlus20Days			DateTime	
3	1/31/2023			2/18/2023			1/29/2023 10:00:00 AM	
5	1/14/9999			1/24/9999			1/4/9999 1:15:00 PM	

Figure 2-54 *Using the join operator and a datetime data type to add time to dates.*

Calculating Hours Elapsed from Time Values

In M code, in a worksheet, and in DAX, a time value is the proportion of a 24-hour day and is represented by a decimal serial number between 0 and 1. For example, 6 p.m. is calculated as follows: (12 + 6)/24 = 0.75.

When working with time values, a common task is to determine the number of hours that have elapsed between a start time and an end time. In M code, if you add or subtract two times, the result is a duration, so if your goal is to calculate total hours or some other unit, you can use one of many useful duration functions, such as Duration.TotalHours, to calculate the total. The M code formula for calculating total hours from a start time and an end time when both times fall on the same day is straightforward. If you are dealing with datetime values rather than time values, the formulas are also straightforward. However, if the end time value occurs on the day after the day that the start time value occurs—which we can call a **night shift calculation**—the formula is a bit tricky.

To see how to create several formulas that calculate the total hours between two times, follow these steps:

1. In the MCodeValues query, select the EndTime column and then the StartTime column. In the Add Column tab, go to the From Date & Time group, click the Time dropdown, and then select Subtract.

2. To get total hours from the resulting duration value, wrap the Duration.TotalHours function around the [EndTime] - [StartTime] formula. Change the data type from duration to number. The result is shown in Figure 2-55.

3. Name the query step SubtractTimesToGetHours.

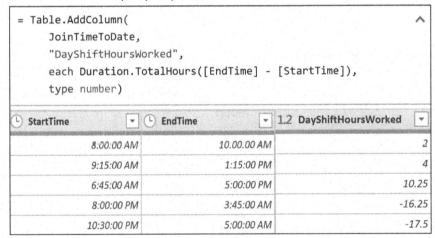

```
= Table.AddColumn(
    JoinTimeToDate,
    "DayShiftHoursWorked",
    each Duration.TotalHours([EndTime] - [StartTime]),
    type number)
```

StartTime	EndTime	DayShiftHoursWorked
8:00:00 AM	10.00.00 AM	2
9:15:00 AM	1:15:00 PM	4
6:45:00 AM	5:00:00 PM	10.25
8:00:00 PM	3:45:00 AM	-16.25
10:30:00 PM	5:00:00 AM	-17.5

Figure 2-55 *The Duration.TotalHours function delivers total hours from a duration.*

As shown in Figure 2-55, the calculated hours in the first three rows (the start and end hours that fall on the same day) are all correct, but the calculated hours in the last two rows (the night shift calculation) are not correct. If all times fall on the same day, this Duration.TotalHours formula works, but if they don't, it doesn't work. Read on to see the formula to use if the times fall on different days.

Using let Expressions to Define Variables in Formulas

When determining the hours for a night shift calculation, you can use this let expression formula in a custom column:

```
let
    EmS = Number.From([EndDate]-[StartDate])
in
    (EmS - Number.RoundDown(EmS))*24
```

This is the first time you have seen the let expression used in a formula. You use the let expression in a formula when there is a formula element that is used more than one time. The let allows you to define the formula element Number.From([EndDate] - [StartDate]) in this case as a variable and then use it throughout the formula. The advantage is that the formula element is calculated one time, and the result is stored in memory. That stored value is used every time you use the identifier that represents the variable, so it isn't necessary to recalculate the formula element each time it is used in the formula.

Using the let expression to define a variable for a formula element that is used more than one time in a formula reduces the amount of time it takes to calculate the full formula. When there are many formulas in a column, the time reduction can be significant. Because M code is notoriously slow compared to a worksheet or DAX, it is greatly beneficial to reduce formula calculation time whenever possible.

> **Note:** All three Microsoft function-based languages can define reusable variables in formulas to help reduce formula calculation time:
> - In M code, you use the let expression.
> - In a worksheet, you use the LET function.
> - In DAX, you use the VAR and RETURN keywords in an expression.

To understand the logic of the formula, you can build the custom column formula in a few steps and look at what each step delivers:

1. In the MCodeValues query, create a custom column with the formula shown in Figure 2-56.
2. Name the query step NightShiftTimesToGetHours.

```
= Table.AddColumn(
    SubtractTimesToGetHours,
    "NightShiftHours",
    each Number.From([EndTime] - [StartTime]),
    type number)
```

StartTime	EndTime	1.2 NightShiftHours
8:00:00 AM	10:00:00 AM	0.083333333
9:15:00 AM	1:15:00 PM	0.166666667
6:45:00 AM	5:00:00 PM	0.427083333
8:00:00 PM	3:45:00 AM	-0.677083333
10:30:00 PM	5:00:00 AM	-0.729166667

Figure 2-56 *The first three proportions of a 24-hour day are correct, but the last two are not.*

In the formula shown in Figure 2-56, the time difference delivers a duration, and the Number.From function converts the duration to a decimal value. The Number.From function converts to a number any value that *can* be converted to a number.

These are two of the from functions and what they do:
- **Text.From** converts to text any value that *can* be converted to text.
- **Date.From** converts to a date any value that *can* be converted to a date.

The bad news for the formula at this point is that the last two rows list negative decimal numbers that are not correct. These numbers are not correct because the formula subtracts a bigger time from a smaller time. For example, for the fourth row in the table, the incorrect calculation is 3:45 AM – 8 PM = 20/24 – 3.75/24 = -16.25/24 = -0.677083. The good news is that if you add 1 to the negative decimals, you get the correct proportion of a 24-hour day. For the fourth row, the calculation would be1 + -16.25/24 = 7.75/24 = 0.322916, which is the correct decimal for the 7.75 hours worked.

But here is the dilemma: If you add a 1 to each row in the table, the last two rows end up being correct, but then the first three are not correct. What you need is a single formula element that can deliver a 0 in the first three rows and a 1 in the last two rows. To accomplish this, you can use the existing decimals along with the Number.RoundDown function, which rounds a number down to the nearest integer.

> **Note:** In a worksheet or in DAX, the INT function behaves the same way as the M code function Number.RoundDown. A worksheet or the DAX function ROUNDDOWN does not work the same as the Number.RoundDown function. Whereas ROUNDDOWN rounds toward zero, Number. RoundDown rounds a number down to the nearest integer.

If you use the Number.RoundDown function on the column of decimal numbers, all the positive numbers will be rounded down to 0, and all the negative numbers will be rounded down to -1, which is perfect for the single formula element you want in this case. To test this, amend the formula as shown in Figure 2-57.

As shown in Figure 2-57, the formula as it sits now provides just the single formula element that you need to add to the decimal number that the Number.From formula element delivers. But now you have a new dilemma in that you need to use this formula element twice in the formula:

```
Number.From([EndDate]-[StartDate])
```

If you did this, the full formula would be as follows:

```
(Number.From([EndDate]-[StartDate])  - Number.RoundDown(Number.
From([EndDate]-[StartDate])))*24
```

```
= Table.AddColumn(
    SubtractTimesToGetHours,
    "NightShiftHours",
    each Number.RoundDown(Number.From([EndTime] - [StartTime])),
    type number)
```

StartTime	EndTime	1.2 NightShiftHours
8:00:00 AM	10:00:00 AM	0
9:15:00 AM	1:15:00 PM	0
6:45:00 AM	5:00:00 PM	0
8:00:00 PM	3:45:00 AM	-1
10:30:00 PM	5:00:00 AM	-1

Figure 2-57 *The Number.RoundDown function provides the desired single formula element.*

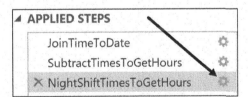

Figure 2-58 *Click the gear icon to open the Custom Column dialog box so you can edit.*

Rather than repeat the formula element, you can use the let expression to define a variable so that the formula element calculates only one time, thus reducing formula calculation time. To create the let expression in the calculated column formula, instead of editing the formula in the Formula Bar, you can use the Calculated Column dialog box. To open this dialog box and edit the formula, follow these steps:

1. As shown in Figure 2-58, in the Applied Steps list, click the gear icon on the right side of the step name NightShiftTimesToGetHours.

2. In the Custom Column dialog box, create the let expression, as shown in Figure 2-59. The let keyword allows you to define a variable. The variable name EmS stands for End minus Start. The in keyword

allows you to create the executable formula that will calculate in each row of the calculated column. In other words, everything after the keyword in is the formula.

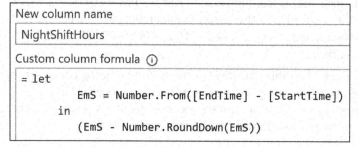

New column name

NightShiftHours

Custom column formula ⓘ

```
= let
        EmS = Number.From([EndTime] - [StartTime])
    in
        (EmS - Number.RoundDown(EmS))
```

Figure 2-59 *The let expression allows the EmS variable to be calculated just one time.*

3. In the Calculated Column dialog box, click Done. Figure 2-60 shows a column that is created with the correct decimal proportion of a 24-hour day for each row. The let expression formula works for times that occur on the same day and times that occur on two consecutive days!

```
= Table.AddColumn(SubtractTimesToGetHours, "NightShiftHours", each
    let
        EmS = Number.From([EndTime] - [StartTime])
    in
        (EmS - Number.RoundDown(EmS)))
```

DateTime	DayShiftHoursWorked	NightShiftHours
/2023	1/29/2023 10:00:00 AM	2	0.083333333
/9999	1/4/9999 1:15:00 PM	4	0.166666667
/1902	5/5/1902 5:00:00 PM	10.25	0.427083333
/0001	1/2/0001 3:45:00 AM	-16.25	0.322916667
/1600	1/1/1600 5:00:00 AM	-17.5	0.270833333

Figure 2-60 *This formula works for day shift or night shift hours.*

4. To convert the decimals to hours, as shown in Figure 2-61, multiply the formula after the keyword in by 24 hours. The figure shows the final formula with the correct elapsed hours for each row in the table.

```
= Table.AddColumn(SubtractTimesToGetHours, "NightShiftHours", each
    let
        EmS = Number.From([EndTime] - [StartTime])
    in
        (EmS - Number.RoundDown(EmS))*24)
```

DateTime	DayShiftHoursWorked	NightShiftHours
/2023	1/29/2023 10:00:00 AM	2	2
/9999	1/4/9999 1:15:00 PM	4	4
/1902	5/5/1902 5:00:00 PM	10.25	10.25
/0001	1/2/0001 3:45:00 AM	-16.25	7.75
/1600	1/1/1600 5:00:00 AM	-17.5	6.5

Figure 2-61 *Multiplying the proportional decimal by 24 yields the final hour amounts.*

Calculating Hours Elapsed from Datetime Values

If you have datetime values rather than hour values, a single simple formula works for calculating hours elapsed for both hours that fall on the same day and hours that fall on consecutive days. This formula works because a datetime value includes both the serial number date and the serial number time. If you subtract the start datetime from the end datetime, because the end datetime will always be bigger than the start datetime, you will always get the correct time, as a decimal numeral. For example, if the start time is 8 PM on 7/14/2023 and the end time is 3:45 PM on 7/15/2023, the calculation is:

```
End - Start = 07/15/2023 03:45 AM - 07/14/2023 08:00 PM =
Bigger Number - Smaller Number = 45121.8333 - 45122.1563 = 0.3229
```

0.3229 is the correct proportion of a 24-hour day that represents the 7.75 elapsed hours. Compare that result to the result from just the time portions:

```
End - Start = 3:45 AM - 8:00 PM =
Smaller Number - Bigger Number = 0.1563 - 0.8333 = -0.6771
```

-0.6771 is not the correct answer here because in this case, a bigger number was subtracted from a smaller number. To create a formula to calculate hours elapsed from two datetime values, follow these steps:

1. Select the query named DateTimeQ in the Chapter01and02 group.

2. Create the formula as shown in Figure 2-62.

3. Name this query step HoursFromDateTimes.

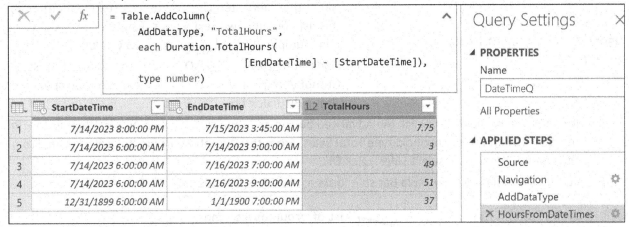

Figure 2-62 *Formula for total hours between two datetime values.*

So far in this chapter, we have studied these nine M code values: null, logical, text, number, date, time, date-time, datetimezone, and duration. These nine values are called **primitive values** because they are single-part values. Primitive values make up most of the data used to perform data analysis. In this chapter, we have also studied the type value, which allows you to define data types on columns to help provide consistent data and accurate calculations. Next, we will look at M code values that have more than one part: tables, records, and lists.

Tables, Records, and Lists

Tables, records, and lists are M code values that can hold more than one value. Most of the time, tables, records, and lists hold and store the primitive values, or data, used to perform data analysis. However, they can also hold any of the other M code values, such as functions and binary files, and they can even hold values such as tables, records, and lists. Yes, that is correct: A table can hold other tables, a list can hold other lists, and a record can even hold other records. In addition, there is an important relationship between these three M code values. If you start with a table value and look up (that is, extract, or select) a full row, the result is a record value. If you start with a table value and look up (that is, extract, or project) a full column, the result is a list value. The table itself does not contain record values and list values; the table contains rows and columns. This is an important distinction because if you try to add a table column of numbers, you will get an error; but if you look up the table column and return a list of numbers, then you can add the list of numbers without an error by using a function like List.Sum.

You will learn all about the useful table lookup process in Chapter 4. What you need to understand here is that there is a relationship between the table, record, and list values and that extracting a table column yields a list value, and extracting a table row yields a record value. Let's take a closer look at each of the three values.

List Values

A **list value** is a sequence of M code values that can contain one or more values. It can hold any of the 15 M code values and is not limited to a single value type. For example, you can have a list that contains number values, text values, date values, and even other list values. You can think of a list as a column in a table, but technically it is not a list value until the column is extracted from the table by a column lookup.

There is no intrinsic function for creating a hard-coded list. To create a hard-coded list value, you use curly brackets—known as **initialization syntax**—to enclose the list, and you use commas to separate the elements in the list. A hard-coded list is known as a **list literal**. Here is an example of a hard-coded list with two text values:

```
={"Quad","Aspen"}
```

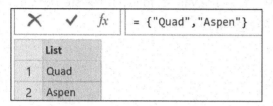

Figure 2-63 *Creating a list by using curly brackets.*

To get some practice with list values, follow these steps:

1. In the Power Query Editor, select the MCodeValues query, select the last step, Datetimezone, add a new query step, and create the list formula shown in Figure 2-63.

2. Name the query step List. As you can see in Figure 2-63, this list contains two text values. However, lists can contain multiple different value types, as you will soon see.

3. Select the DayTypeSalesQ query, select the last step, GroupByDayType, and click the gear icon to open the Group By dialog box.

4. In the Group By dialog box, click the Advanced button and then click the Add Aggregation button. In the New Column Name textbox, type Total Sales. From the Operation dropdown, select Sum. From the Column dropdown, select Sales. Click OK.

5. Edit the formula in the Formula Bar so it looks as shown in Figure 2-64.

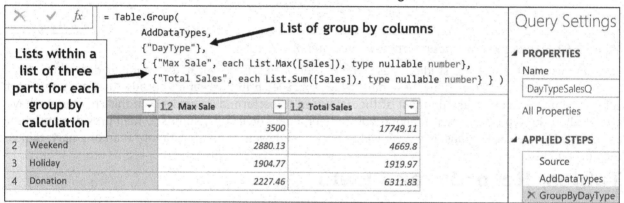

Figure 2-64 *The second and third arguments in the Table.Group function use lists.*

As shown in Figure 2-64, the Table.Group function uses two lists. In the second argument you see {"DayType"}. The DayType column is the column you used for grouping. But if only one column was used, why is it in a list? Isn't a list supposed to have more than one value? A list can have one *or more* values. And because the second argument of Table.Group allows one or more columns for grouping, the list syntax is required, even when only one column is being used for the group by calculation. Further, even if you did not know that the second argument in the Table.Group function allows more than one column for grouping, as soon as you see that the automatic feature recorded the M code as a list, you can infer that the argument allows more than one item.

List values are M's way of allowing you to enter one or more items into a location such as an argument in a function or a value location in a list. This is why a list value is required in the second argument of the Table. Group function: so that you can have one or more group by columns. It is also why a list within a list is required in the third argument of the Table.Group function: so that you can enter the three parts for each group by calculation, as a list, into a list of all the group by calculations. As shown in Figure 2-64, in the third argument of the Table.Group function, the automatic feature created a list, and then within that list there is, first, a list of the three parts for the max calculation, and then there is a list of the three parts for the sum calculation.

Microsoft has cleverly created M code with this list-within-a-list syntax to allow you to enter all the required parts for each of the group by calculations into a single location.

In addition, notice that for each of the sublists, there are three different M code values: text, function, and type. If lists weren't allowed to contain different value types, this would not work. Also notice that the names of the built-in aggregate functions are List.Max and List.Sum. These two functions are two of many self-explanatory list functions that make aggregate calculations from a list of values.

These are some of the list functions and what they do:

- **List.Max** retrieves the largest alphanumeric value from a list based on Unicode characters.
- **List.Min** retrieves the smallest alphanumeric value from a list based on Unicode characters.
- **List.Sum** sums numbers from a list.
- **List.Last** returns the last value from a list.
- **List.Zip** takes a list of lists and returns a list of lists, combining items at the same position.

You can use these list functions on a list, but you cannot use any of them on a table or a column. As you can see in Figure 2-64, the List.Max and List.Sum functions do not work unless a list of values is entered into their arguments. Therefore, for the arguments in each of the two functions, the field access operators (square brackets) are used around the Sales column name to extract the Sales column as a list from the behind-the-scenes table of grouped records. (We'll discuss this behind-the-scenes table shortly.)

Note: In Chapter 4, you will learn a different column lookup technique that will work outside a custom column.

Now let's look at how the dot-dot operator works in a list. Figures 2-65 and 2-66 show two more useful list examples. In the Formula Bar in Figure 2-65, you can see that the **dot-dot operator** in a list allows you to create a sequence of numbers between a start number and an end number. Figure 2-66 shows that you can also use a list and the dot-dot operator to create a sequence of letters. To create these two lists, follow these steps:

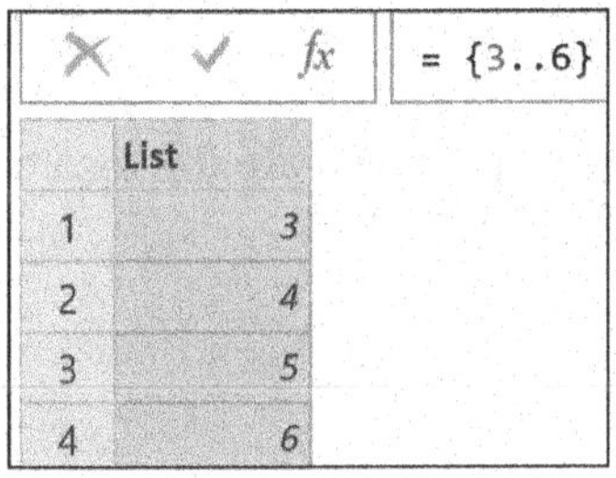

Figure 2-65 *The dot-dot operator allows you to create a list sequence of numbers.*

1. In the Power Query Editor, select the MCodeValues query and select the last query step, List.

2. Add a new query step with the list formula shown in Figure 2-65.

3. Name this query step ListSequenceNumbers.

4. Add a second new query step with the list formula shown in Figure 2-66.

5. Name this query step ListSequenceLetters.

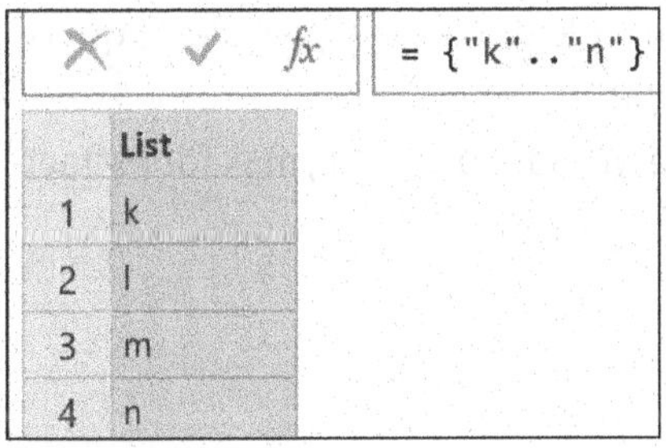

Figure 2-66 *The dot-dot operator allows you to create an alphabetical list.*

For the final list example, we will look at how to use the join operator, &, to combine two or more lists into a single list. To combine two lists, follow these steps:

1. Add a new query step with the list formula shown in Figure 2-67.

2. Name this query step JoinLists.

As shown in the Formula Bar in Figure 2-67, the first list contains a number and some text, then there is the join operator, and then the second list contains a list and a record. The result shows that a single list was created with four different M code values. Although joining two list literals like this is not very practical—because you could instead just create a single list with the four values—joining lists is a common task. For example, you might want to join two customer lists or two lists of product data.

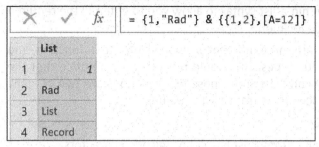

Figure 2-67 *Using the join operator to join two lists.*

As you have seen, you use lists all over the place in M code: for creating your own lists, in function arguments that require lists, for creating sequential lists, and even for joining two lists.

Record Values

A **record value** is an ordered sequence of columns with M code values entered in each column. A record can hold any of the 15 M code values, including other records. You can think of a record as a row in a table, but technically it is not a record value until the row is extracted from the table by a row lookup.

There is no intrinsic function to create a hard-coded record. To create a hard-coded record value, you use square brackets—known as initialization syntax—to enclose the record, and you use commas to separate the pairs of columns and values. A hard-coded record is known as a **record literal**. The generalized identifier for the column name does not need quotation marks or the # sign. The column name is followed by an equals sign and then the value.

Here is an example of a hard-coded record with two columns and two values:

```
=[Boom Product = "Quad", Sales = 43]
```

To try your hand at creating M code records, follow these steps:

1. In the MCodeValues query, select the last step, JoinLists, add a new query step, and create the record formula shown in Figure 2-68.

2. Name this query step Record.

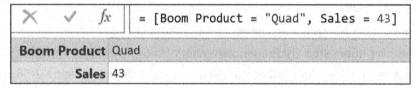

Figure 2-68 *Creating records by using square brackets.*

3. To extract a row in a table as a record value in a custom column, select the DayTypeSalesQ query, select the last step, GroupByDayType, and add a new custom column.

4. In the Custom Column dialog box, use an **underscore**, which is the M code formula syntax for extracting a row from a table as a record value, as shown in Figure 2-69.

5. Name the column Record and then click OK.

6. Name the query step ExtractRecordInCustomColumn.

Custom Column

Add a column that is computed from the other columns.

New column name

Record

Custom column formula ⓘ

= _   ◀━━━━━ **Underscore**

Figure 2-69 *An underscore is all you need to extract a record from a table in a custom column.*

As shown in Figure 2-70, the new column contains a record value in each row, with the column names from the table and the values for each column from the given row. This technique can be useful in formulas that analyze records. In the Formula Bar, notice that the underscore follows the each keyword in the third argument of the Table.AddColumn function. The each and underscore combination for extracting records only works in table functions like Table.AddColumn.

> **Note:** In Chapter 4, you will learn the row lookup method for extracting a specific record from a table rather than all records in a custom column by using each and an underscore. And in Chapter 3, you will learn that each and an underscore work together as a custom function. But for now, it is sufficient to just think of the each-and-underscore combination as the M code you use to extract each row as a record in a custom column.

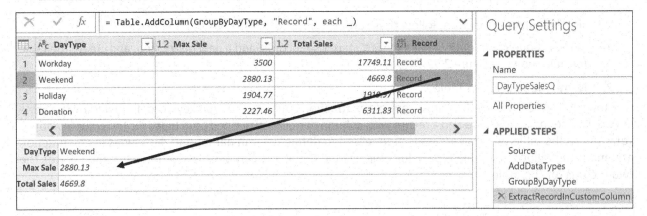

Figure 2-70 *By using an underscore after the keyword each, you can extract the row and deliver a record value.*

For the final record example, you will see how to use the join operator to combine two or more records into a single record. To combine two records, follow these steps:

1. In the MCodeValues query, select the last step, Record, add a new query step, and create the record formula shown in Figure 2-71.

2. Name the query step JoinRecords.

As shown in the Formula Bar in Figure 2-71, the first record contains a single column named Product and a "Quad" text value. Next is the join operator, and then the second record contains a pair of columns and values: the column Sales and a 43 number value and the column SalesRep and a "Chantel" text value. The result of this formula is a single record with three columns and three values.

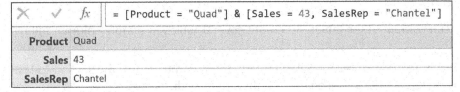

Figure 2-71 *Using the join operator to join two records.*

Throughout the rest of the book, you will see record values used often.

Table Values

A **table value** has column names in the first row and records in subsequent rows. Tables are essential to any data analysis process because they hold all the data to be analyzed. A table can hold any of the 15 M code values, including other tables. You can think of a table as being made up of record values in rows and list values in columns. However, technically a row in a table is not a record value until you extract it from the table, and a column in a table is not a list value until you extract it from the table. (Extracting rows and columns from tables is a very common task, and you will learn about it in Chapter 4.)

The table intrinsic function can have as many columns or records as you like. In the first argument of the table intrinsic function you list the column names, and in the second argument you list the records:

```
=#table(ColumnNames, Records)
```

There are two different syntactical structures for the table intrinsic function. Here is an example of a table with data types:

```
= #table(
    type table [Boom Product = text, Sales = number],
    {{"Quad",43}, {"Aspen",35}})
```

Here is an example of a table with no data types:

```
=#table(
    {"Boom Product", "Sales"},
    {{"Quad",43},{"Aspen",35}})
```

To use the table intrinsic function, follow these steps:

1. In the MCodeValues query, select the last step, JoinRecords, add a new query step, and create the table formula shown in Figure 2-72.

2. Name the query step Table.

As shown in Figure 2-72, the first argument of the function contains the type keyword, followed by the table keyword to define a table type and a record with column names and defined data types for the column names. You can use the table type and an associated record to define column names and data types in any function argument that allows the table type value. The second argument contains lists within a list and creates the two records for the table.

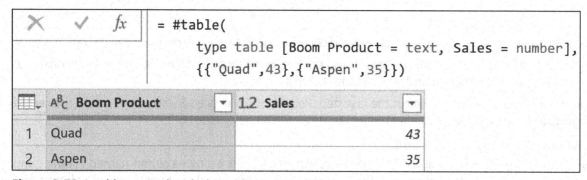

Figure 2-72 *A table created with the table intrinsic function.*

> **Note:** In later chapters, you will see that knowing how to use the table intrinsic function comes in handy for some advanced tricks.

Next, let's look at how a table can contain other tables. To create several tables in a table column, follow these steps:

1. To create a column of tables, select the DayTypeSalesQ query. Then, to the right of the second-to-last step, named GroupByDayType, click the gear icon to open the Group By dialog box.

2. In the Group By dialog box, click the Add Aggregation button. In the New Column Name textbox, type GroupedRecordsTable. Select All Rows from the Operation dropdown and then click OK.

As shown in Figure 2-73, a new column is added with a table of grouped records based on the unique list of conditions from the DayType column.

By selecting All Rows from the Operation dropdown, you can access the behind-the-scenes table of grouped records that I mentioned when we talked about list values. In addition, this technique of collecting tables of grouped data in a column is helpful in data modeling transformations, as you will see in Chapter 7. In Chapter 7 you will also learn how to use the From Folder feature to gather tables in a column when appending tables. In Power Query, columns of tables are common; they are a unique and useful characteristic of M code that the other Microsoft function-based languages do not possess.

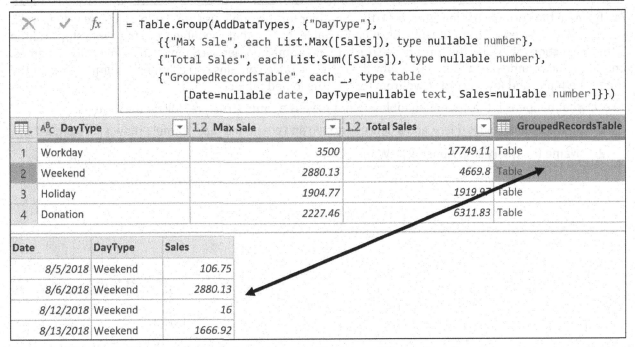

Figure 2-73 *The third group by calculation stores a table value of the grouped records.*

In Figure 2-73, you can see that the third argument in the Table.Group function shows lists within a list that contains the three group by calculations. The third group by calculation list contains the M code for the tables in each row. Notice the each-and-underscore combination. It delivers a table value rather than the record value you saw earlier with the Table.AddColumn function. This is because the Table.Group function is programmed differently than the Table.AddColumn function. With the Table.AddColumn function, the each and underscore work only with one row in each cell of the column and therefore deliver a record; with the Table.Group function, the each and underscore work with a grouped set of one or more records in each cell of the column and therefore deliver a table. Finally, in the third group by calculation list, the third section contains the type table and a record value that defines the data types for the columns. This is very convenient because if you expand the column, the original data types will remain intact for each column.

Combining (or Appending) Tables

For this final table example, we look at how to use the join operator to combine, or append, two or more tables into a single table. In M code, Microsoft treats the verbs **append** and **combine** as synonyms when referring to tables. For example, the Table.Combine function and the Append feature both append two or more tables into a single table. I tend to use the verb append rather than combine.

When you **append tables**, you take two or more tables that have the same structure (that is, the same number of columns, same column names, and same column data types) and stack them, one on top of the other, to create a single table with a single set of column names in the first row. If the tables do not have the same structure, the resulting table may contain unwanted columns and null values. In this section we look at how to append tables with the join operator; in later chapters, we will look at how to use the Table.Combine function and other features. To append two tables by using the join operator, follow these steps:

1. In the MCodeValues query, select the last step, Table, add a new query step, and create the table formula shown in Figure 2-74.

2. Name the query step JoinTables.

```
= Table & #table( type table [Boom Product = text, Sales = number], {{"Aspen",27} , {"Quad", 86}})
```

AB_C Boom Product	1.2 Sales
1 Quad	43
2 Aspen	35
3 Aspen	27
4 Quad	86

Figure 2-74 *One option for joining tables is to use the ampersand (&) join operator.*

As shown in the Formula Bar in Figure 2-74, the identifier for the previous step, Table, is a table value, and it is joined with the results from the intrinsic function table. Notice that the table from the Table step and the intrinsic function table have the same table structure: the same number of columns, the same column names, and the same column data types. This is why the resulting table contains two columns, column names at the top of the table, and four records (two from each of the joined tables).

To see what happens if the appended tables do not have the same structure, follow these steps:

1.   In the MCodeValues query, add a new query step and create the table formula shown in Figure 2-75.

2.   Name the query step AppendNotWork.

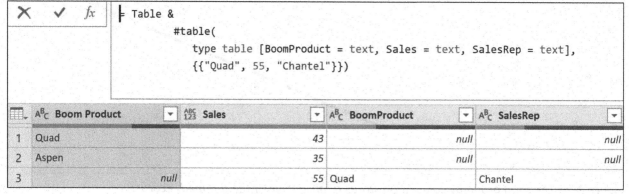

Figure 2-75 *The structure of the two tables should be the same before you append.*

As shown in Figure 2-75, the resulting table has four columns rather than two, and it contains many null values. The BoomProduct column (the third column) and the SalesRep column are created because those column names do not exist in the top table. The null values exist because the field names do not exist in the other table and therefore have no parallel values. The missing data type in the Sales column is due to the fact that the two Sales columns—one from each table—have different data types. The Sales column from the first table has a decimal data type, and the Sales column from the second table has a text data type. When this happens, the resulting column has no defined data type.

Appending tables is a very common task in data analysis, and it is crucial to understand that all the tables you want to append must have the same structure. In Chapter 7, you will learn how to build custom functions to append tables that do not have the correct structure.

Table values are the heart and soul of data analysis, and we will be using table values often throughout the rest of the book.

> **Note:** The last three M code values that we have studied—list, record, and table—are often the M code containers of primitive values (the first nine M code values that we studied). However, lists, records, and tables do not always hold primitive values. As you have learned, list values can contain component parts for a group by calculation, record values can contain the data types for a table, table values can contain other tables, and, in fact, these container values can hold any of the 15 possible M code values. You have also learned that there is a tight relationship between tables, records, and lists. If you extract a row from a table, you get a record value. Extract a column from a table, and you get a list value.

Binary Values

An M code **binary value** represents a sequence of bytes, such as an Excel file, a text file, an XML file, an image, an audio file, or another data source. It is important to have the binary value type in M code so that you can accomplish tasks such as importing multiple Excel or text files and extracting the data from within those files.

You will learn how to work with binary values in Chapters 6 and 7. As a preview of those chapters, Figure 2-76 shows a Content column that contains binary values in each row and a binary data type. This column contains Excel files. In row 2, the Excel file is named GrassValley.xlsx. As you will see in Chapter 6, M code provides great functions such as Excel.Workbook and other features to extract objects from Excel files.

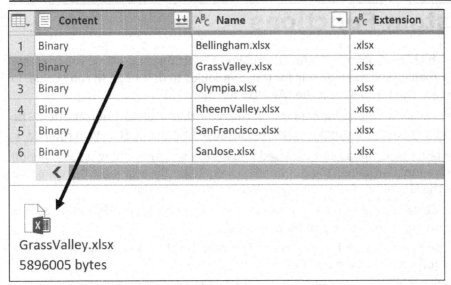

Figure 2-76 *The binary value type allows you to import Excel files that contain data.*

Summary

In this chapter, we have looked at 14 of the 15 M code value types: type, null, logical, text, number, time, date, datetime, datetimezone, duration, table, record, list, and binary. The value we haven't yet covered, the function value, is perhaps the most powerful M code value, and you'll learn about it next, in Chapter 3. Now that you have some foundational knowledge about M code values, you are ready to learn what you can do with M code, starting with custom functions in Chapter 3.

Chapter 3: Custom Functions

Perhaps the most exciting and useful M code value is the **function value**. A function value allows you to create a **custom function** that defines variables and the mapping for those variables to deliver an M code value. In Excel, the parallel function to create function values is the LAMBDA function.

In M code, function values are particularly helpful for data transformations that you must repeat often. The function-expression syntax rules for creating a custom function are listed below and illustrated in Figure 3-1:

- Variable names are separated by commas and enclosed in parentheses. They show up as function arguments when you use a function value. You can define a value type for a variable by typing the keyword as, followed by the identifier of the value type. Value types are optional.

- The rules for naming variables are the same as for naming identifiers: no keywords and no spaces (and if there are spaces, use the # symbol and quotation marks).

- The go to operator (=>) comes after the defined variables and indicates that everything after it is the mapping of the variables (or the formula to execute).

- The mapping of the variables can be any M code that delivers an M code value. The mapping almost always uses the defined variables, but it does not have to use them.

- After the closing parenthesis for the last variable name and before the go to operator, you can define value types for the output of the function by typing the keyword as followed by the identifier of the value type. Value types are optional.

- As with all other M code, you can add non-executable comments to a custom function by beginning a single-line comment with two forward slashes (//) or starting a multiline comment (with multiple hard returns) with /* and ending it with */.

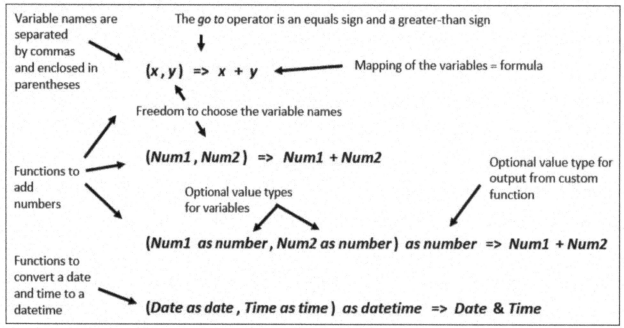

Figure 3-1 *You can create your own custom functions, using the syntax rules shown here.*

You can create custom functions in any M code, but you are most likely to create them in three places:

- **A new query that uses the let expression to deliver a reusable custom function value, called a reusable function query (or just a function query):** In this case, the function query is available throughout the Power Query Editor.

- **A function argument that requires a function:** In this case, the custom function is available only in the function argument).

- **As an intermediate step in a let expression, called a function query step:** In this case, the function query step is available throughout the let expression, but the let expression itself does not necessarily have to deliver a custom function value.

Next, you will see how to build custom functions in all three places. You will also learn about the keyword each and the underscore character (_), which together can work as syntactical shorthand for a custom function.

Creating Two Reusable Function Queries

The first reusable function query that you will create is a function to convert a date and a time to a datetime. You will create a new query that delivers a function value so that you can use the function throughout the Power Query Editor. When you create a function query, you type it directly into the Advanced Editor. The formula for this calculation is simple:

```
Date & Time = Datetime
```

A function query like this is useful if you need to send a file to a coworker who is not familiar with using the join operator to create a datetime value from date and time values.

To create your first function query, follow these steps:

1. In the Power Query Editor, create a new blank query in the Chapter03 group and name the function query DatetimeFromDateAndTime.

2. Open the Advanced Editor, type the notes and the let expression custom function shown in Figure 3-2, and then click Done.

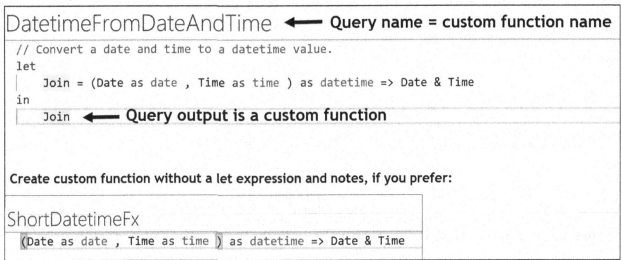

Figure 3-2 *The query delivers a function value.*

Figure 3-3 shows the result you get. To the left of the query name is a function icon, which indicates that the query output is a custom function that can be used throughout the Power Query Editor. In the middle, you can create a new query that uses the function query by entering the parameters and then clicking the Invoke button. Rather than type in a date and time as parameters to create a new query that delivers a single datetime value, you can use the function query in a custom column to create a column of datetime values. On the right you can see DatetimeFromDateAndTime, which is the name of the new reusable function query that you can invoke in a custom column.

Figure 3-3 *By entering parameters, you can create a new function query that creates a single datetime value.*

3. As shown in Figure 3-4, in the Chapter01and02 group, select the DurationQ query, click the Add Column tab in the Power Query Ribbon, and then, in the General group, click the Invoke Custom Function button.

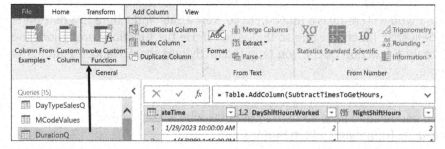

Figure 3-4 *The Invoke Custom Function button invokes the function in a new column.*

4. In the Invoke Custom Function dialog box, as shown in Figure 3-5, type DateTimeFx in the New Column Name textbook, select DatetimeFromDateAndTime from the Function Query dropdown, select EndDate from the Date text dropdown, select Column Name from the Time dropdown, select EndTime from the Time text dropdown, and then click OK.

Invoke Custom Function

Invoke a custom function defined in this file for each row.

New column name

DateTimeFx

Function query

DatetimeFromDateAndTime ▾

Date

▦ ▾	EndDate ▾

Time

▦ ▾	EndTime ▾
🕐 Time
▦ Column Name

← **Time argument dropdown allows you to type a time or use a column**

Figure 3-5 *Completing the Invoke Custom Function dialog for the DatetimeFromDateAndTime function.*

5. Name the query step InvokeDateTimeFx.

6. Format the resulting formula and add a datetime data type as shown in Figure 3-6. In the figure, after the each keyword, notice that the function query uses two arguments to generate the date-time value.

Note: A coworker might not be sophisticated enough to edit the formula by adding a datetime data type in the Formula Bar, and they would probably just add a new query step to add the data type.

```
✕  ✓  fx      = Table.AddColumn(
                  NightShiftTimesToGetHours,
                  "DateTimeFx",
                  each DatetimeFromDateAndTime([EndDate], [EndTime]),
                  type datetime)
```

▦.		1.2 DayShiftHoursWorked	▾	ABC 123 NightShiftHours	▾	▦ DateTimeFx	▾
1	3 10:00:00 AM	2		2		1/29/2023 10:00:00 AM	
2	99 1:15:00 PM	4		4		1/4/9999 1:15:00 PM	
3	02 5:00:00 PM	10.25		10.25		5/5/1902 5:00:00 PM	
4	01 3:45:00 AM	-16.25		7.75		1/2/0001 3:45:00 AM	
5	00 5:00:00 AM	-17.5		6.5		1/1/1600 5:00:00 AM	

Figure 3-6 *Your function query is used in the Table.AddColumn function.*

The second reusable function query that you will create is a function that is often used in finance. In the field of finance, it is common to calculate the effective rate (ER) based on an annual percentage rate (APR) and number of compounding periods per year (NPY). The ER is always higher than the APR when the NPY is greater than 1. ER represents the single rate that you earn or pay for the year. The math formula is:

```
ER = (1+APR/NPY)^NPY - 1
```

There is no caret symbol (^) in M code, so the M code formula looks a little different:

```
ER = Number.Power(1+APR/NPY,NPY) - 1
```

To create a reusable ER function query that rounds to the ten-thousandths position, follow these steps:

1. Create a new blank query in the Chapter03 group, name the query EffectiveRate, type the notes and let expression shown in Figure 3-7, and click Done.

```
x  Advanced Editor

EffectiveRate

/* Function to calculate the effective rate from ARP and NPY, rounded to the ten-thousandths
APR = Annual Period Rate (Year) , NPY = Number Compounding Periods per Year */
let
    ERFx = (APR as number , NPY as number ) as number =>
    Number.Round(Number.Power(1 + APR/NPY , NPY) - 1,4)
in
    ERFx
```

Figure 3-7 *Creating a function query to calculate an effective rate.*

2. To use this new effective rate function, select the query named CustomFunctionQ and, in the Add Column tab of the Power Query Ribbon, click the Invoke Custom Function button and then complete the Invoke Custom Function dialog box as shown in Figure 3-8.

3. Name the query step InvokeEffectiveRateFx.

```
Invoke Custom Function

Invoke a custom function defined in this file for each row.

New column name
ERFx

Function query
EffectiveRate               ▼

APR
⊞ ▼   APR                              ▼

NPY
⊞ ▼   PeriodsPerYear                   ▼
```

Figure 3-8 *Completing the Invoke Custom Function dialog for the EffectiveRate function query.*

4. Look at the result in Figure 3-9 and notice that it is not rounded. To fix the rounding mistake, edit the formula directly in the Formula Bar or use the Advanced Editor so that the formula looks like this:

```
Number.Round(Number.Power(1 + APR/NPY, NPY) - 1, 4)
```

Note: When you want to edit a function query, open the Power Query Editor, select the function query, and then open the Advanced Editor.

```
= Table.AddColumn(
    AddDataTypes,
    "ERFx",
    each EffectiveRate([APR], [PeriodsPerYear]),
    type number)
```

1²3 PeriodsPerYear	1²3 Invest	1.2 ERFx
12	100	0.12682503
2	25000	0.155625
365	225	0.091430819

Figure 3-9 *You can see that the EffectiveRate function does not round to the ten-thousandths position.*

5. Click Done in the Advanced Editor, and you get the correct result, as shown in Figure 3-10.

1²3 PeriodsPerYear	1²3 Invest	1.2 ERFx
12	100	0.1268
2	25000	0.1556
365	225	0.0914

Figure 3-10 *After you edit the custom function, the EffectiveRate function rounds to the ten-thousandths position, as it should.*

As you have just seen, when you edit a custom function, the calculation automatically updates. There is one universal location to edit the function. In this example, you only used the custom function a single time, but if you used it many times, the single universal location to edit the custom function would save you a lot of time.

Creating a Custom Function in a Function Argument

Now that you have created two function queries, you're ready to create a custom function in a function argument that requires a function.

In Chapter 2 you learned about the four arguments in the Table.AddColumn function:

```
Table.AddColumn(
    table as table,
    newColumnName as text,
    columnGenerator as function,
    optional columnType as nullable type) as table
```

The third argument, columnGenerator as function, requires a function value, and you can use a built-in function, a reusable function query, or a one-time custom function. Earlier you used the Invoke Custom Function button to place the EffectiveRate function query into the third argument of the Table.AddColumn function. Creating a reusable function query is the way to go when you make the same calculation multiple times. But what if you only need to make a calculation a single time? In that case, you don't need to create a reusable function query but can instead create a custom function by using the Custom Column feature, which is easier and faster than creating a function query.

> **Note:** In Chapter 7, you will create custom functions in custom columns to make many different data transformations.

To create a custom function in a custom column, follow these steps:

1. In the CustomFunctionQ query in the Chapter03 group, create a custom column with the new column name and formula, as shown in Figures 3-11 and 3-12.

2. Name the new query step CustomColumnCustomFunction.

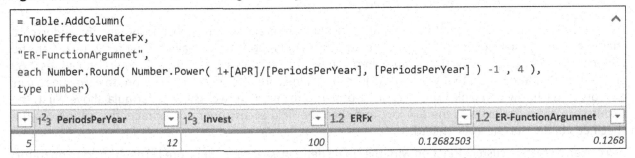

Figure 3-11 *In the Custom Column dialog box, the formula works as a custom function.*

```
= Table.AddColumn(
InvokeEffectiveRateFx,
"ER-FunctionArgumnet",
each Number.Round( Number.Power( 1+[APR]/[PeriodsPerYear], [PeriodsPerYear] ) -1 , 4 ),
type number)
```

▼ 1²₃ PeriodsPerYear	▼ 1²₃ Invest	▼ 1.2 ERFx	▼ 1.2 ER-FunctionArgumnet ▼
5	12	100	0.12682503	0.1268

Figure 3-12 *The each keyword is what allows the formula to work as a custom function.*

In Figures 3-11 and 3-12, you can see that the formula does not use variables or the go to operator. So how can this be a custom function? The answer lies in the secret power of the each keyword.

Using each and an Underscore to Create a Custom Function

As you learned back in Chapter 1, in a function argument that requires a function, such as the third argument of the Table.AddColumn function, the each keyword enables a formula to calculate in each row of a table. The each keyword also allows formulas to calculate in each row of a list value. In a function argument that requires a function, if a formula only accesses the columns from the table that is iterated, you do not need to go through the extra effort of defining variables and using the go to operator. All you need to do is type each, followed by a formula that pulls values from each row using the field access operator ([]). When you use the keyword each, the formula becomes a custom function.

In addition, as you have already seen, the underscore character (_) and the each keyword can extract a row as a record, extract a grouped set of records as a table, or extract an item from each row in a list.

Microsoft created the each-and-underscore syntax to make it easy to create custom functions. Microsoft defines this syntax like this:

The each keyword is syntactical shorthand for defining an unnamed custom function that takes a single untyped variable named _ (underscore). You can use this shorthand anywhere a function can be declared.

The each keyword is often used to pass a custom function to an argument in another function, such as Table. AddColumn, Table.SelectRows, or List.Transform. The each keyword allows you to make a calculation in each row of a table or list, and if you use the underscore character in a row in a table, it extracts everything from the row. Here are some examples of equivalent custom functions that are invoked in a custom column:

```
each [Years] * [PeriodsPerYear]
each _[Years] * _[PeriodsPerYear]
(_) => _[Years] * _[PeriodsPerYear]
(Row) => Row[Years] * Row[PeriodsPerYear]
```

To extract a row as a record in each row of a table or to extract the items in each row of a list, these are equivalent custom functions that are invoked in a custom column:

```
each _
(_) => _
(Row) => Row
```

To better understand how the each keyword and underscore character work, let's look at this custom function:

```
each [Years] * [PeriodsPerYear]
```

The Microsoft definition above says that the each keyword defines an "unnamed custom function." This means you do not use an identifier when you write the formula. Instead, you just use the each keyword and the formula. Because there is no identifier, though, you can't refer to this custom function anywhere else; you can use it only in this column.

The definition also says that the unnamed custom function "takes a single untyped variable named _ (underscore)." This means you do not have to type an underscore before each column reference (that is, before the column name in the field access operator). However, you can type the underscore character before each column reference, as shown in the following formula, and the formula works:

```
each _[Years] * _[PeriodsPerYear]
```

If you use the each keyword for a formula that uses column references, you almost never type the underscore character. This is why the definition uses the adjective "untyped." As you saw in Chapter 2, however, the underscore works with the each keyword when you want to extract a row from a table or list. Figures 2-69 and 2-70 in Chapter 2 show that you can use just the underscore after the each keyword to extract a row as a record in each row of a table. This is why the underscore character works in the formula above: First, the underscore character extracts the full row, and then the field access operator extracts the value from the specified column for the given record.

You can also create a custom function with the single defined variable underscore (_) and the go to operator:

```
(_) => _[Years] * _[PeriodsPerYear]
```

This syntactical structure is exactly the same as the each keyword syntax: a custom function taking a single variable named _ (underscore).

You don't have to use the underscore as the variable to represent a row, though; you can use any variable name that you like. In the following formula, by using the variable name Row, you explicitly name the variable based on what it does—extract the row as a record in each row of the table:

```
(Row) => Row[Years] * Row[PeriodsPerYear]
```

Say that you want to extract a row as a record in each row of a table or extract the items in each row of a list. Here are three equivalent custom functions that would all allow you to do it:

```
each _
(_) => _
(Row) => Row
```

Now say that you want to create the formulas shown earlier. To do so, you can select the query CustomFunctionQ and create formulas in a new custom column. You will have to edit the formulas in the Formula Bar after you click OK in the Custom Column dialog box to get them to match the formulas presented above. Figure 3-13 shows an example of what the formulas might look like.

```
    Each = Table.AddColumn(FormulaCF, "eachTotPeriods", each [Years] * [PeriodsPerYear], type number),
    Each_ = Table.AddColumn(Each, "eachUnderscoreTP", each _[Years] * _[PeriodsPerYear], type number),
    CF_ = Table.AddColumn(Each_, "VariableUnderscore", (_) => _[Years] * _[PeriodsPerYear], type number),
    CF = Table.AddColumn(CF_, "VariablesGoTo", (Row) => Row[Years] * Row[PeriodsPerYear], type number),
    RowEach_ = Table.AddColumn(CF, "RowEach_", each _),
    RowCF_ = Table.AddColumn(RowEach_, "RowCF_", (_) => _),
    RowCF = Table.AddColumn(RowCF_, "RowCF", (Row) => Row)
in
    RowCF
```

Figure 3-13 *Seven formulas to help illustrate how the each-and-underscore syntax works.*

Creating a Custom Function Query Step in a let Expression

You are less likely to create a custom function as a query step—called a function query step—in a let expression than to create a function query or add a custom function in a custom column. However, a reusable function query step in a let expression is perfect if you have a complex data transformation that has a repeating calculation that will be used only in the data transformation.

In this section you will not create a complex data transformation query; rather, you will create a function to calculate an effective rate as a query step in the CustomFunctionQ query's let expression. To create this function query step in the Advanced Editor, follow these steps:

1. Select the query CustomFunctionQ and then open the Advanced Editor. As you can see in Figure 3-13, there is no comma at the end of the last step of this query. You need a comma at the end so that you can add more steps. To accomplish this, click at the end of the RowCF query step, type a comma, and press Enter.

2. Type the query step name Effect, an equal sign, and then the custom function:

    ```
    (APR, NPY) => Number.Round(Number.Power(1 + APR/NPY, NPY) -1, 4)
    ```

3. Type a comma after the custom function and press Enter. The query step name Effect is now the name of a custom function that can be used throughout the let expression. The result is shown in Figure 3-14.

```
    RowCF = Table.AddColumn(RowCF_, "RowCF", (Row) => Row),
    Effect = (APR , NPY) => Number.Round( Number.Power( 1 + APR/NPY , NPY) -1 , 4)
in
    RowCF
```

Figure 3-14 *The query step named Effect delivers a custom function.*

4. To use the Effect function in a custom column, type out the query step CustomColumnEffect, as shown in Figure 3-15. Notice that in the first argument of the Table.AddColumn function, you must skip the Effect function query step and refer to the identifier two steps above, as that is the correct table value for the argument.

Figure 3-15 *Using the new function query step in the Table.AddColumn function.*

5. Change the query output after the in keyword to CustomColumnEffect and then click Done. Figure 3-16 shows the result.

Figure 3-16 *The M code you typed in the Advanced Editor adds a new column.*

Recursion with Custom Functions

You have seen some great uses for M code custom functions, but custom functions can also perform recursion. **Recursion** means that a function can call itself and is allowed to iterate over a value or loop back and forth from a value until a task is completed. For a formula to loop, it must know when the task is complete so the looping can stop.

> **Note:** The REDUCE worksheet function can simulate recursion, and the LAMBDA worksheet function can perform recursion.

The left column in Figure 3-17 shows a list of alphanumeric values, and the right column shows the result after all the digits from 0 to 9 are removed from each alphanumeric value. In this section, you will see how to build a recursive custom function to accomplish this task.

Alphanumeric Values	Values with Numerals Removed
Quad63544398106	Quad
8803456464 Sioux Radcool	Sioux Radcool
014369Carlota	Carlota
c1o43ol	cool

Figure 3-17 *The goal is to remove all numerals from the alphanumeric text.*

Figure 3-18 shows the looping-iterative process that you will program into your formula. Here is a list of the first few looping-iterative operations:

- For the first iteration, you take the left 0 from 0123456789 and use it to remove the 0 from Quad63544398106 to yield Quad6354439816. Then you remove the 0 from 0123456789 to get 123456789.
- For the second iteration, you take the left 1 from 123456789 and use it to remove the 1 from Quad63544398106 to yield Quad635443986. Then you remove the 1 from 123456789 to get 23456789.
- You continue the process until no digits are left in the alphanumeric value.

Alphanumeric Values	Digits	
Quad63544398106	0123456789	
Remove 0 ↑	↑ take left digit, 0	Iteration 1
Quad6354439816	123456789	
Remove 1 ↑	↑ take left digit, 1	Iteration 2
Quad635443986	23456789	
	↑ take left digit, 2	Iteration 3
Quad635443986	3456789	.
Quad6544986	456789	.
Quad65986	56789	.
Quad6986	6789	.
Quad98	789	.
Quad98	89	.
Quad9	9	.
Quad		.

Figure 3-18 *The formula iterates one digit at a time until all digits are removed from the text.*

Follow these steps to create a reusable recursive custom function to remove all numeric characters from a list of alphanumeric values:

1. Create a blank query and name it RemoveChar.
2. Using Figure 3-19 as a guide, create the recursive custom function.

RemoveChar **Single input for function**

```
let
    RemoveCharQS = (Text as text ,CharToRemove as text) as text =>
        if CharToRemove = "" then Text.Trim(Text)
        else RemoveChar(
                Text.Remove(Text,Text.Start(CharToRemove,1)),
                Text.End(CharToRemove,Text.Length(CharToRemove)-1)
            )
in
    RemoveCharQS
```

Trigger to stop formula and deliver result

Figure 3-19 *The RemoveChar query contains a custom function that performs recursion.*

3. As shown in Figure 3-20, invoke the new custom function in a new column in the RecursionQ query from the Chapter03 group. Name the query step InvokeRecursiveFx.

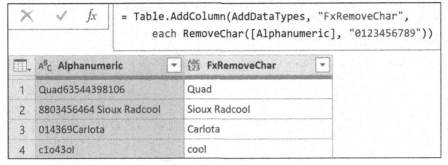

```
×   ✓   fx      = Table.AddColumn(AddDataTypes, "FxRemoveChar",
                        each RemoveChar([Alphanumeric], "0123456789"))
```

	AᴮC Alphanumeric	ABC₁₂₃ FxRemoveChar
1	Quad63544398106	Quad
2	8803456464 Sioux Radcool	Sioux Radcool
3	014369Carlota	Carlota
4	c1o43ol	cool

Figure 3-20 *Invoking the function named RemoveChar.*

These are the important parts of the reusable function shown in Figure 3-19:

- The name of the reusable function is the name of the query: RemoveChar. This name is called within the let expression that defines the function. When a function calls itself, this process is called recursion.

- The two function inputs are text, which is the text you want to remove characters from, and CharToRemove, which is the digits that you want to remove.

- When a function calls itself, it always needs to be conditional, or it will yield an infinite loop. You therefore need a trigger to stop the looping and recursion. In this case, you use an if expression that asks the logical question "Does the called function RemoveChar have no characters left"? When there are no characters left, the output is a trimmed version of the function input named Text.

- The name of the query step that creates the function is RemoveCharQS. Because this is the output for the query, the query delivers a reusable function.

- Figure 3-20 shows that when a user enters the text string "0123456789", digits are removed from the text string. However, the user can enter any set of characters that they would like to enter.

Figure 3-21 shows a second version of this type of formula, but it does not involve recursion because the function does not call itself. In addition, because this function's only purpose is to remove the digits 0 to 9, the digits are hard-coded into the formula. To try this custom function, follow these steps:

1. Create a blank query and name it RemoveNumbers.

2. Using Figure 3-21 as a guide, create the reusable custom function.

```
RemoveNumbers

let
    nums = "0123456789",

    RemoveNumbersQS = (Text as text) as text =>
        if nums = "" then Text.Trim(Text) else
            RemoveChar(
                Text.Remove(Text,Text.Start(nums,1)),
                Text.End(nums,Text.Length(nums)-1)
            )
in
    RemoveNumbersQS
```

Figure 3-21 *The iterative function removes all characters that are specified.*

Note: Alternatively, if you already defined the function as shown in Figure 3-19, you can write the RemoveNumbers custom function as follows:

```
= (Text as text) as text => RemoveChar(Text,"0123456789")
```

3. As shown in Figure 3-22, invoke the new custom function in a new column in the RecursionQ query.
4. Name the query step InvokeFx02.

```
✕   ✓   fx      = Table.AddColumn(InvokeRecursiveFx, "FxRemoveNumebrs",
                    each RemoveNumbers([Alphanumeric]), type number)
```

	A^B_C Alphanumeric	▼	ABC_123 FxRemoveChar	▼	1.2 FxRemoveNumebrs	▼
1	Quad63544398106		Quad		Quad	
2	8803456464 Sioux Radcool		Sioux Radcool		Sioux Radcool	
3	014369Carlota		Carlota		Carlota	
4	c1o43ol		cool		cool	

Figure 3-22 *When you invoke this function, you can choose the text to remove.*

As shown in Figure 3-23, you can create a simple custom column formula that uses the Text.Remove function with a list of items in the second argument to remove the digits from the text. You can try this formula in the RecursionQ query from the Chapter03 group.

```
✕   ✓   fx      = Table.AddColumn(InvokeFx02, "Formula", each
                    Text.Trim(Text.Remove([Alphanumeric], {"0".."9"})))
```

	A^B_C Alphanumeric	▼	ABC_123 FxRemoveChar	▼	1.2 FxRemoveNumebrs	▼	ABC_123 Formula
1	Quad63544398106		Quad		Quad		Quad
2	8803456464 Sioux Radcool		Sioux Radcool		Sioux Radcool		Sioux Radcool
3	014369Carlota		Carlota		Carlota		Carlota
4	c1o43ol		cool		cool		cool

Figure 3-23 *For the task of removing digits, this formula is easier than the recursion formula.*

Using List.Accumulate to Simulate Recursion

The **List.Accumulate** function can simulate recursion by iterating over a list of values. It iterates through a list of values, repeats an action at each position in the list to determine an intermediate value (the current state of the iterating variable), and delivers the value associated with the last position in the list. This function does not deliver all the intermediate values; it delivers just the last one. However, you can program a logical test into the custom function in the third argument if you want to stop the iteration before the iteration gets to the last value in the list.

Sometimes an intermediate value is a summarized value, as with a running total, or it may be a transformed value, as with a text value that gets digits removed one at a time (see Figure 3-24). It also may be a selected value, as with a discount value that is selected and replaced with each iteration until the logical test stops the process; you will see an example of this in Chapter 4.

These are the arguments for the List.Accumulate function:

```
List.Accumulate(
    list as list,
    optional seed as any,
    accumulator as function) as any
```

The **list** argument contains the list to iterate. The optional **seed** argument contains the initial value to use in the first iteration, if necessary. For example, if the repetitive operation is addition, because the first number in the list needs a number added to it, you use zero as the seed. The seed defines the data type for the current state of the iterating variable in the list. In some cases, the custom function that is defined in the third argument does not use the seed argument. In such a case, you can use a null value to skip this argument.

The **accumulator** argument contains a custom function that creates the repeating action that works on each item in the list. The custom function must have two variables, and how the two variables work is defined by the List.Accumulate function. (This is similar to how functions that use comparer functions define how the comparer functions work within each particular function. You will learn more about this in Chapter 4.) The first variable is the current state of the intermediate value, and it is automatically stored after each iteration so that it can be used in the next iteration. The second variable is the value in the current row of the list being iterated.

Figure 3-24 shows an example of how to use List.Accumulate to remove numbers from an alphanumeric value. If you want to try this example, you can create this custom column formula in the RecursionQ query from the Chapter03 group. I named the query step CCListAccumulate.

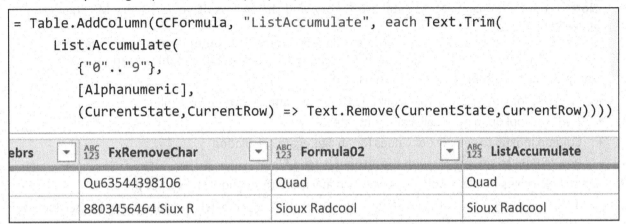

```
= Table.AddColumn(CCFormula, "ListAccumulate", each Text.Trim(
    List.Accumulate(
        {"0".."9"},
        [Alphanumeric],
        (CurrentState,CurrentRow) => Text.Remove(CurrentState,CurrentRow))))
```

ebrs		ABC 123 FxRemoveChar		ABC 123 Formula02		ABC 123 ListAccumulate
		Qu63544398106		Quad		Quad
		8803456464 Siux R		Sioux Radcool		Sioux Radcool

Figure 3-24 *The List.Accumulate function can simulate recursion.*

These are the mechanics of how this formula works:

- The list argument of the List.Accumulate function contains the list to iterate. Each row in the iteration is represented by the third argument's custom function's CurrentRow variable.
- The seed argument of the List.Accumulate function contains the alphanumeric value where you want to remove number digits. This value is represented by the custom function's CurrentState variable.
- The accumulator argument defines the custom function. The custom function must have two variables (even when you discard one). How the variables work is defined by the List.Accumulate function: The first variable is the current intermediate state, and the second variable is the current row in the list being iterated. The Text.Remove function holds the alphanumeric value as the function iterates over the list of digits that should be removed. The function keeps looping back to the list, incrementing through the list, removing all the digits one by one. When the iteration gets to the last digit in the list, 9, the Text.Trim function trims the extra spaces, and the value is delivered to the cell.

Summary

In this chapter, you have learned the syntax for creating custom functions, including the convenient each-and-underscore syntax. You have also learned about the three main locations where you build custom functions: in a let expression that delivers a reusable function query that can be used throughout the Power Query Editor, in a function argument where a function is required, and as a query step in a let expression that can be used throughout the let expression. You have also learned how to build a custom function that can perform recursion.

You now have almost all the fundamental knowledge required to build any custom function that you might need. However, there is one more topic related to custom functions that you need to understand: how to construct custom functions when you are nesting two functions that both use the each keyword and the interior function must access data from the exterior function's table. You will learn about this in Chapter 4, where I teach you how to perform approximate match lookups with M code. Based on what you've learned in this chapter, you will be able to build many custom functions throughout the rest of the book that will perform amazing data transformations.

Chapter 4: M Code Lookup Formulas

Now that you have studied the fundamental building blocks of M code—expressions, let expressions, queries, built-in functions, custom functions, M code values, and data types—you are ready to learn about M code lookups. An **M code lookup** allows you to look up a value or to look up a row as a record, a column as a list, or one or more columns as a table.

> **Note:** From relational algebra, database theory, and the Microsoft Power Query M Language Specification:
> * Projection (represented by π) involves picking a column (attribute) from a table (relation).
> * Selection (represented by σ) involves selecting a row (tuple) from a table (relation).

For example, these are some common lookups:

* Two-way lookup to get a table from an SQL Server database or an Excel file
* Two-way lookup to get a sales discount rate
* Column lookup to get a list of values for an aggregate calculation
* Row lookup to get records with the attributes for a file

You will see examples of these lookups as well as many more throughout the rest of the book.

The two lookup types that you will learn about in this chapter are exact match and approximate match lookups:

* An **exact match lookup** involves searching for an exact match to a **lookup value** in a **match column** that contains a unique list. When a match is made, a value is retrieved from the corresponding position in a return column. For example, the lookup value "Quad" would match "Quad" but not "Quad " (with extra spaces at the end).
* An **approximate match lookup** (also called an **exact match or next smaller lookup**) involves searching for an exact match to a lookup value or the next smaller value in a **match column**. When a match is made, a value is retrieved from the corresponding position in the return column. For example, in the match column {0, 500, 1000, 2500}, the lookup value 774 would match 500 because there is no exact match, and the next smaller value is 500.

In M code, there is a built-in method for performing the common task of doing an exact match lookup, but there is no built-in method for doing an approximate match lookup. Both M code and DAX lack a built-in method for doing an approximate match lookup. However, in an Excel worksheet, there are many functions that can do both. Later in this chapter, I will teach you how to build a custom function for approximate match lookups for tasks such as looking up a tax rate or looking up a commission rate.

Before you go any further in this chapter, it is important to understand that M code is base zero, which means that the first row is row 0, the second row is row 1, the third row is row 2, and so on. You must be aware of this when creating lookup formulas. Figure 4-1 illustrates base zero and base one.

M code is base zero		Worksheet and DAX are base one	
	Products		**Products**
Row 0	Quad	Row 1	Quad
Row 1	Aspen	Row 2	Aspen
Row 2	Carlota	Row 3	Carlota

Figure 4-1 *In M code, the first row in a table or list is row 0.*

Exact Match Lookups

If you already know how to perform a two-way exact match lookup with the worksheet INDEX function, you will easily understand M code lookups because they are very similar. Both methods start with a table that has rows and columns, and then you provide a row number and a column number, and the intersecting value is retrieved. Figure 4-2 shows the two-way exact match lookup formulas for M code and the INDEX function.

M code lookup:	*Table* {*RowNum* } [*Column Name*]
	Product {1} [Retail Price] = 26.95
Excel INDEX:	**INDEX(***Table* , *RowNum* , *ColNum* **)**
	INDEX(Product, 2, 3) = 26.95

Figure 4-2 *An M code lookup and the INDEX function work similarly.*

Products	Supplier	Retail Price
Quad	Gel Booms	43.69
Aspen	Colorado Inc.	26.95
Carlota	Gel Booms	27.95
Sunset	Colorado Inc.	32.95

Figure 4-3 *Product lookup table.*

Let's look at an example using the Product table shown in Figure 4-3. If you want to use an Excel worksheet to look up the retail price for the Aspen product, you start by finding the Aspen product in the Products column (row 2), and then you find the Retail Price column (column 3), and the intersecting price of 26.95 is returned. As shown in Figure 4-2, for the INDEX function, you enter the table name, the row number, and the column number into the function. The function retrieves the price at the intersection of row 2 and column 3: 26.95.

Now say that you want to use M code to do the same lookup. As shown in Figure 4-2, in M code, you start with a table, put the row number in curly brackets (called the **row positional index operator** or **row index operator**), and then put the column name in square brackets (called the **field access operator**). The M code uses this information to retrieve the price 26.95.

There are two types of M code exact match lookups: row index lookups and key match lookups (see Figure 4-4).

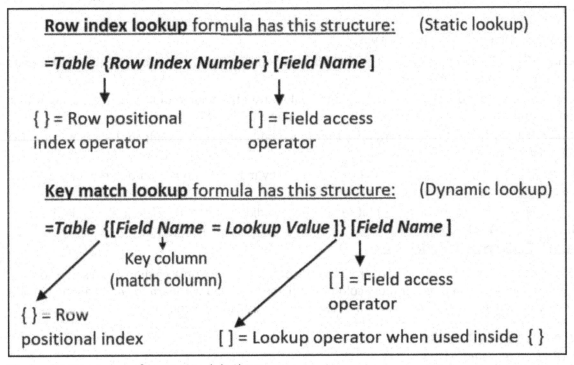

Figure 4-4 *Two types of exact match lookups.*

Row Index Lookups

A **row index lookup** is an exact match two-way lookup based on a hard-coded row number in the positional index operator and a column name in the field access operator. This lookup retrieves a value from a table at the intersection of the designated row number and column name. The hard-coded row number does not change when the sort order or content of the column changes. The lookup is static, so the row number does not change when the data changes.

Here is the syntax for a row index lookup:

```
Table {Row Index Number}[Field Name]
```

Here are some examples of row index lookups:

- Source{0}[Content] gets the first value from the Source table's Content column.
- Source{0} gets the first row from the Source table as a record value.
- Source[Content] gets the Content column from the Source table as a list value.
- Source[[Content]] gets the Content column from the Source table as a table.
- {43,86}{0} gets the first item from the list, 43.
- {43,86}{2} yields an error because there is no third item.
- {43,86}{2}? delivers a null instead of an error (because it uses the optional operator, ?).
- {43,86}{2}?? 5 delivers 5 instead of an error (because it uses the coalesce operator, ??).

Key Match Lookups

A **key match lookup** performs an exact match two-way lookup based on an equality logical test between a lookup value and a match column (key column) that contains a unique list of values. The equality test must be inside square brackets, called the **lookup operator**. The lookup operator must be inside the positional index operator. The logical test dynamically determines the row position when the column is sorted or when the data changes. The field name in the field access operator determines the column position. When you enter the field name, you enter it as a generalized identifier, with no quotation marks and no #. Then the intersecting value is retrieved from the table.

With a key match lookup, if there are duplicate values in the key column, an error is produced.

Here is the syntax for a key match lookup:

```
Table{[Field Name = LookupValue]}[Field Name]
```

Here are some examples of key match lookups:

- Source{[File="DD"]}[Content] gets the value from the Source table's Content column that corresponds to the row position DD in the File column.
- Source{[File="DD",Col="G"]}[Content] gets the value from the Source table's Content column that corresponds to the row position DD in the File column and G in the Col column.
- Source{[File="DD"]} gets the record from the Source table that corresponds to the row position DD in the File column.
- Source{[POP="Z"]} yields an error that reads "The key matched more than one row in the table" because there was more than one Z in the POP column.
- Source{[File="YY"]} yields an error that reads "The key didn't match any rows in the table" because there was no YY value in File column.

Row and Column Lookups

Figure 4-5 shows the syntax for looking up a row as a record, for looking up a column as a list, for looking up a column, and for looking up one or more columns. I this section, you will learn to create all the M code lookups shown in Figures 4-4 and 4-5, as well as a few other helpful M code lookups.

Look up a row to return a record
=Table {Row Index Number}
=Table {[Field Name = Lookup Value]}

Look up a column to return a list
=Table [Field Name]

Look up a column to return a one-column table
=Table [[Field Name]]

Look up columns to return a table
=Table [[Field Name], [Field Name2]]

Figure 4-5 *Common lookup tasks.*

Here are the types of lookups you will work with in the upcoming examples:

- Row index lookup to retrieve a record
- Row index two-way lookup to retrieve a value
- Key match lookup to retrieve a record
- Key match two-way lookup to retrieve a value
- Key match lookup that yields an error when there are duplicates in the column
- Key match lookup that yields an error when there is no match
- Column lookup to return a list
- Column lookup to return a one-column table
- Drill-down lookup when there is no primary key
- Drill-down lookup when there is a primary key
- Check for a primary key
- Addition of a primary key to a table

Figure 4-6 shows the table that you will use for most of the lookup formula examples in this chapter.

ABc Products	ABc Supplier	1.2 Retail Price
1 Quad	Gel Booms	43.69
2 Aspen	Colorado Inc.	26.95
3 Carlota	Gel Booms	27.95
4 Sunset	Colorado Inc.	32.95

Figure 4-6 *Query step table with the identifier AddDataTypes.*

Row Index Lookup to Retrieve a Record or a Value

To create a row index lookup, follow these steps:

1. In the Power Query Editor, select the LookupExamplesQ query.

2. Select the query step AddDataTypes.

3. To do a row index lookup to retrieve the first record in the table, add a new query step and create the formula shown in Figure 4-7. Name the step RowIndexLookupRecord.

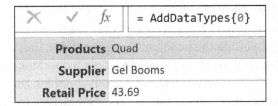

Figure 4-7 *Row index lookup to retrieve the first record in the table.*

As shown in Figure 4-7, when you use a table with a positional index operator, a row is extracted from the table as a record value. The zero inside the positional index operator represents the first row, and therefore the Quad record is extracted from the table in this case. However, the zero is hard-coded into the formula. This means that if you sort the table, the row position will remain the first row, but a different record will be retrieved.

4. To sort the table, select the AddDataTypes step and then, from the Product column dropdown arrow, select A to Z Sort Ascending. When the dialog box asks if you want to insert a new step, click Insert. Name the step SortAscending and then select the RowIndexLookupRecord query step.

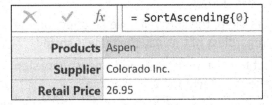

Figure 4-8 *After the sort, a new record is retrieved from the table.*

Because you have performed a row index lookup, as shown in Figure 4-8, this formula always retrieves the first row, even when the data changes. Sometimes hard-coding is what you want, and sometimes it is not. (Later in this chapter, you will see that hard-coding a row value is the best way to extract a list of the names of the primary keys in a table but that it is not the best way to look up a supplier name for a product.)

5.   To create a two-way lookup to retrieve the supplier name from the first record in the table, in the Applied Steps list, click the red x to delete the SortAscending query step.

6.   Select the query step RowIndexLookupRecord, add a new query step with the new formula shown in Figure 4-9, and name the step RowIndex2WayLookup. Be sure to refer to the table named AddDataTypes.

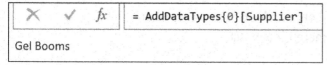

```
✕    ✓    fx    = AddDataTypes{0}[Supplier]
```
Gel Booms

Figure 4-9 *Row index two-way lookup to get the supplier's name from the first row.*

As shown in Figure 4-9, the lookup formula uses a table, the positional index operator, and the field access operator to retrieve the supplier's name, Gel Booms. However, because the row number is hard-coded into the formula, if the table is sorted, you will get a different supplier name. A key match lookup is not affected by sorting, as you will see next.

Key Match Lookup to Retrieve a Record or a Value

With a key match lookup, you can use a lookup value to try to get an exact match in the match column to determine the row number for the lookup. However, just as with exact match lookup formulas in DAX and an Excel worksheet, in order to avoid errors, the match column must almost always contain a unique list of values. To see how this works, follow these steps:

1.   To do a key match lookup to retrieve the Quad record from the table, select the last query step and add a new query step with the formula shown in Figure 4-10. (Notice that this lookup formula, like the one in the previous section, is referring to the table named AddDataTypes.) Name the step KeyMatchLookupRecord.

```
✕    ✓    fx    = AddDataTypes{[Products = "Quad"]}
```
Products	Quad
Supplier	Gel Booms
Retail Price	43.69

Figure 4-10 *Key match lookup to retrieve the product Quad record from the AddDataTypes table.*

As you can see in Figure 4-10, the formula uses a table with a key match positional index operator to extract the Quad record from the table. In the formula, the square brackets are inside the positional index operator—that is, {[]}. When the square brackets are inside the positional index operator, they function as the **lookup operator** rather than as the field access operator. Inside the lookup operator, the logical test matches the lookup value, Quad, against the match column named Products to determine the row position. As I have mentioned several times, when you use square brackets to create records, field access operators, or lookup operators, the identifier for the column does not need to be in quotation marks. This is why the Products column name is not in quotation marks. But the lookup value, "Quad", is a text value, and so it must be in quotes.

After the key match lookup, if you sort the AddDataTypes table, the sort will have no effect on the lookup formula. The Quad record will still be retrieved, regardless of the way the table is sorted.

2.   To look up the supplier's name for the Quad record, select the last query step, add a new query step with the new formula shown in Figure 4-11, and name the step KeyMatch2WayLookup.

```
✕    ✓    fx    = AddDataTypes{[Products = "Quad"]}[Supplier]
```
Gel Booms

Figure 4-11 *The key match two-way lookup to get the supplier's name from the Quad record.*

As shown in Figure 4-11, the key match two-way lookup formula uses a table with the lookup operator inside the positional index operator and the field access operator to retrieve the Quad record supplier's name, Gel Booms.

A key match can fail in some situations. To see one type of error you can get with a key match lookup, select the last query step, add a new query step with the formula shown in Figure 4-12, and name the step KeyMatchDupsDontWork.

```
X    ✓    fx    = AddDataTypes{[Supplier = "Gel Booms"]}
```
```
⚠    Expression.Error: The key matched more than one row in the table.
```

Figure 4-12 *An error occurs because Gel Booms occurs twice in the Supplier column.*

You get the error message "The key matched more than one row in the table" because there are duplicate values in the Supplier column. To avoid errors, a key match lookup should only be performed on a column that contains a unique set of values.

> **Note:** Although a key match lookup can work on a column with duplicate values when that column contains a single occurrence of the lookup value, it is best practice to perform a key match lookup on a column that contains a unique set of values.

To see another type of error you can get with a key match lookup, select the last query step, add a new query step with the formula shown in Figure 4-13, and name the step KeyMatchNoMatch.

```
X    ✓    fx    = AddDataTypes{[Products = "Sunspot"]}
```
```
⚠    Expression.Error: The key didn't match any rows in the table.
```

Figure 4-13 *There is no Sunspot in the Products column.*

Just as with worksheet and DAX exact match lookup formulas, if the lookup value does not exist in the lookup column, you get an error. As you can see in Figure 4-13, the error message in M code is "The key didn't match any rows in the table." To avoid this error and get a null value instead, you could use the optional operator, like this:

```
AddDataTypes{[Products = "Sunspot"]}? = null
```

To yield a value rather than an error, you could use the coalesce operator, like this:

```
AddDataTypes{[Products = "Sunspot"]}? ?? "No Match" = "No Match"
```

Column Lookup to Return a List or a Column

So far, you have seen how to look up a record and a value by using either a row index or a key match lookup. Now you will see how to look up a column to return a list or a single-column table. The type of lookup you will do is called a **column lookup**. The good news is that there is only one type of column lookup (not two types, as is the case with row lookups). This is because the field names in a table are always unique in Power Query. There are no duplicate field names in a table. When you place a column name inside the field access operator for a lookup, the order of the columns in the table will never adversely affect the accuracy of the column lookup. With a column lookup, you never have to deal with duplicates. To experiment with column lookups, follow these steps:

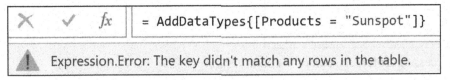

1. To see how to look up a column as a list, in the LookupExampleQ query, select the last query step, add a new step with the formula shown in Figure 4-14, and name the step LookupColumnAsList.

Figure 4-14 *Looking up a column and returning a list.*

As shown in Figure 4-14, to look up a column and return a list, you use the table identifier followed by a column name inside the field access operator. This is one of the most common types of lookups because many functions require lists of values rather than columns of values. For example, an aggregate function such as List.Sum or List.

Average requires a list of values. As another example, list transformation functions like List.Last, List. Zip, and Table.Combine also require lists of values.

2.   To use a list of values in an aggregate function, select the last query step, add a new query step with the formula shown in Figure 4-15, and name the step AverageRetailPrice. As shown in the figure, the average retail price for the boomerang products is 32.885.

✕	✓	*fx*	= List.Average(AddDataTypes[Retail Price])

32.885

Figure 4-15 *Looking up a column and returning a list inside an aggregate function.*

3.   Sometimes, you do not want a column lookup to be returned as a list of values. To look up a column and return a single-column table, you use double field access operators rather than a single field access operator. To see how this is done, select the last query step, add a new query step with the formula shown in Figure 4-16, and name the step LookupColumnAsColumn.

✕	✓	*fx*	= AddDataTypes[[Retail Price]]

⊞	1.2 **Retail Price** ▼
1	43.69

Figure 4-16 *Using double field access operators to look up a column.*

4.   When you look up a column, a table with a single column is returned. Sometimes this is all you need for your analysis. Other times, you may want a few columns from a larger table. To see how to look up two columns, select the last query step, add a new query step with the formula shown in Figure 4-17, and name the step LookupColumnsToTable.

✕	✓	*fx*	= AddDataTypes[[Products],[Retail Price]]

⊞	A^Bc **Products** ▼	1.2 **Retail Price** ▼
1	Quad	43.69

Figure 4-17 *Looking up two columns and returning a two-column table.*

As shown in Figure 4-17, to look up two or more columns, you use field access operators for each column that you want to extract, place a comma between the field access operators, and then start and end the formula with square brackets. Using the following formula is another way to return a table with the extracted columns:

```
Table.SelectColumns(AddDataTypes,{"Products", "Retail Price"})
```

> **Note:** The lookup formula and the Table.SelectColumns formula return the same two-column table. I have noticed no performance differences between the two formulas. When I am typing a formula and I want to look up columns, I tend to use the lookup formula. However, if I am using the user interface, I tend to use the Table.SelectColumns method (which involves selecting columns, right-clicking, and selecting Remove Other Columns).

Now that you know how to use row index and key match lookups to look up a record, a list, a column, or a value, you have the fundamental skills you need to perform M code exact match lookups. Figure 4-18 shows the 13 lookup formulas that you created in the LookupExampleQ query, along with 2 drill-down formulas that you'll create in the next section.

```
// LookupExampleQ query
let
    Source = Excel.CurrentWorkbook(),
    GetExcelTableLookupExamples = Source{[Name="LookupExample"]}[Content],
    AddDataTypes = Table.TransformColumnTypes(GetExcelTableLookupExamples,
        {{"Products", type text}, {"Supplier", type text},
            {"Retail Price", type number}}),
    RowIndexLookupRecord = AddDataTypes{0},
    RowIndex2WayLookup = AddDataTypes{0}[Supplier],
    KeyMatchLookupRecord = AddDataTypes{[Products = "Quad"]},
    KeyMatch2WayLookup = AddDataTypes{[Products = "Quad"]}[Supplier],
    KeyMatchDupsDontWork = AddDataTypes{[Supplier = "Gel Booms"]},
    KeyMatchNoMatch = AddDataTypes{[Products = "Sunspot"]},
    OptionalToGetNull = AddDataTypes{[Products = "Sunspot"]}?,
    CoalesceToGetNoMatchText = AddDataTypes{[Products = "Sunspot"]}? ??"No Match",
    LookupColumnAsList = AddDataTypes[Retail Price],
    AverageRetailPrice = List.Average(AddDataTypes[Retail Price]),
    LookupColumnAsColumn = AddDataTypes[[Retail Price]],
    LookupColumnsToTable = AddDataTypes[[Products],[Retail Price]],
    DrillDownOnTableNoKey = LookupColumnsToTable{0}[Products]
in
    DrillDownOnTableNoKey
```

Figure 4-18 *A variety of different lookup formulas.*

Drill-Down Lookup Formulas and Primary Keys

Drill Down is a user interface command that allows you to look up a value from a table, list, or record. When you drill down on a particular cell or column, the M code value is extracted as a new step in the query. It works like this:

- When you drill down on a cell in a table with no primary key, the row index lookup is used to extract the value.
- When you drill down on a cell in a table with a primary key, a key match lookup is used to extract the value.
- When you drill down on a column in a table, a column lookup is used to exact a list from the column.
- When you drill down on a cell in a record, a column lookup formula is used to extract the value from the record.
- When you drill down on a value in a list, a row index lookup is used to extract a value from the list.

Note: We will talk about determining whether a table has a primary key later in this section.

To try drilling down in these various ways, follow these steps:

1. In the DrillDownQ query in the Chapter04 group, select the query step named TableWithoutKey, right-click the Quad cell in the Product column, and then, as shown in Figure 4-19, select Drill Down from the dropdown list. Name the new query step ExtractQuadRowIndex.

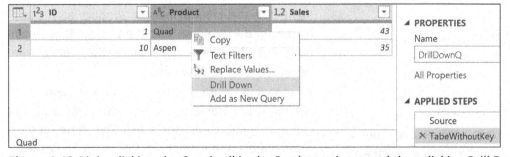

Figure 4-19 *Right-clicking the Quad cell in the Product column and then clicking Drill Down.*

As shown in Figure 4-20, when there is no primary key on the table and you drill down on a cell, the Drill Down feature uses a row index lookup. The value delivered is the text item Quad. This lookup is not dynamic. The first row value, 0, is hard-coded into the formula. If the source table is sorted, the lookup formula retrieves the Aspen value rather than the Quad value.

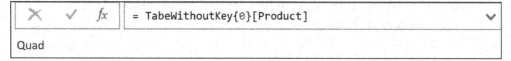

Figure 4-20 *Drilling down on a table with no key involves using a row index lookup.*

2. To drill down on a table with a primary key, as shown in Figure 4-21, create a new query step in the current query and create a reference to the query named TableHasKey. The table TableHasKey that is pulled into the query has a primary key on the ID column. Name the new query step TableWithKey.

1²₃ ID	ᴬᴮ𝒸 Product	1.2 Sales
1	Quad	43
10	Aspen	35

`= TableHasKey`

Figure 4-21 *Referencing the TableHasKey query.*

3. Right-click the Quad cell in the Product column and select Drill Down from the dropdown list. Name the new query step ExtractQuadKeyMatch.

    As shown in Figure 4-22, when there is a primary key on the table and you drill down on a cell, the Drill Down feature uses a key match lookup. The value delivered is the text item Quad. This lookup is dynamic and will always look up the row with the ID 1, regardless of how the table is sorted or how the data changes. Notice that the automatic formula uses the primary key column for the lookup, even though you drilled down on the Quad cell. This is by design so that only a single matching item is available for the lookup and retrieval process. Just as with worksheet and DAX lookup formulas, a key match lookup finds one and only one matching item and is immune to sorting and other data changes.

`= TableWithKey{[ID=1]}[Product]`

Quad

Figure 4-22 *Drilling down on a table with a key involves a key match lookup.*

4. As shown in Figure 4-23, create a new query step that references the first query step, named Source. The Source table that is pulled into the query step does not have a primary key. Name the new query step GetSourceTable.

`= Source`

1²₃ ID	ᴬᴮ𝒸 Product	1.2 Sales
1	Quad	
10	Aspen	

Figure 4-23 *Referencing the first query step, named Source.*

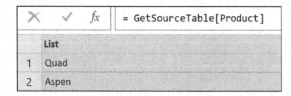

`= GetSourceTable[Product]`

List
Quad
Aspen

Figure 4-24 *Drilling down on a column from a table involves using a column lookup to retrieve a list of values.*

5. Right-click the column header Product at the top of the Product column and then select Drill Down from the dropdown list. Name the query step ExtractProdcutFieldColumnL.

    As shown in Figure 4-24, when you drill down on a column from a table, the Drill Down feature uses a column lookup to extract a list. The same type of column lookup to extract a list works on tables with or without primary keys. This is because the column names in a table are always unique in Power Query. There can be no duplicate column names, and so a column lookup will work on either type of table.

6. To do a record drill-down, create a new query step with the record literal, as shown in Figure 4-25. Name the new query step CreateRecord.

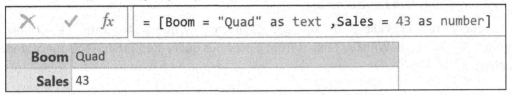

Figure 4-25 *Typing out the M code for this record literal.*

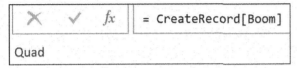

Figure 4-26 *Drilling down for a value in a record involves using a column lookup to retrieve the value.*

7. Right-click the Quad cell in the Product column and then select Drill Down from the dropdown list. Name the query step ExtractQuadFromRecord.

    As shown in Figure 4-26, when you drill down on the value in a column in a record, the Drill Down feature uses a column lookup to extract the value. Because records contain columns and values within a column, a column lookup is used to extract the column value.

8. To do a list drill-down, as shown in Figure 4-27, create a new query step named Create List and type the following list literal as your formula:
    ={1,"Quad",null}

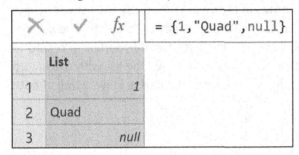

Figure 4-27 *You can type out the M code for this list literal.*

9. Right-click the Quad item in the list and then select Drill Down from the dropdown list. Figure 4-28 shows the result. Name the query step ExtractQuadFromList.

    As shown in Figure 4-28, when you drill down on an item in a list, the Drill Down feature uses a row index lookup. Because lists cannot have primary keys, drilling down for a list always involves using a row index lookup.

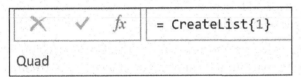

Figure 4-28 *Drilling down for a value in a list involves using a row index lookup.*

Determining if a Table Has a Primary Key

What if you have a table, and you are not sure whether it has a primary key? Is there a way to check? The crazy thing is that Microsoft did not put a button or command in the user interface to determine if a table has a primary key. The only way to check whether there is a primary key in a table is to use the **Table.Keys function**. This function takes a table as its only argument and reports whether there is a primary key; if there is a primary key, the function reports the name(s) of the column(s) making up the primary key. To see how the Table.Keys function works, follow the steps:

1. Select the last query step, ExtractQuadFromList, and create a new query step with the formula shown in Figure 4-29. (The TableWitoutKey table is from a previous query step.) Name the query step CheckKeyButNoKey.

    As shown in Figure 4-29, the Table.Keys function delivers an empty list, which indicates that there is no primary key in the TabeWithoutKey table.

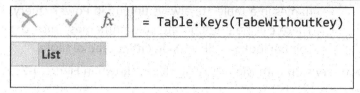

Figure 4-29 *The empty list indicates that there is no key.*

2.   Select the last query step, CheckKeyButNoKey, and create a new query step with the formula shown in Figure 4-30. (The TableWithKey table is from a previous query step.) Name the query step CheckKeyAndYesKey.

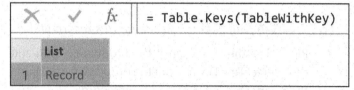

Figure 4-30 *The list contains a single record value and indicates that there is a key.*

3.   To extract the record from the first row in the list generated by the Table.Keys function, edit the formula in the query step CheckKeyAndYesKey, as shown in Figure 4-31. Because the list will always have a single row, there is no need to use a key match lookup; it is easier to create a row index lookup with a zero for the first row. (Alternatively, you could click the green hyperlinked record to drill down and get the list of column names, but that action would remove the list with the record and replace it with a list of column names. I did not do that because I wanted to leave a trail of both steps.)

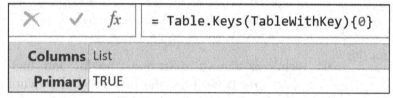

Figure 4-31 *The list in the Columns column contains the key column names.*

As shown in Figure 4-31, the record contains two columns and two values. The Columns column contains a list with the key column names. The Primary column contains the Boolean value true to indicate that there is a primary key in the table.

4.   To extract the list from the Columns column, click the green hyperlinked list to drill down. Name the query step ExtractFieldNames.

Note: Tables, records, and lists that are contained in other tables, records, or lists show green hyperlinks that allow you to click and extract the value by drilling down.

As shown in Figure 4-32, after you click the green hyperlinked list, a list with the primary key column ID is extracted. This table had a single column to define its primary key. As you will see in the next two examples, a key can be made up of one or more columns.

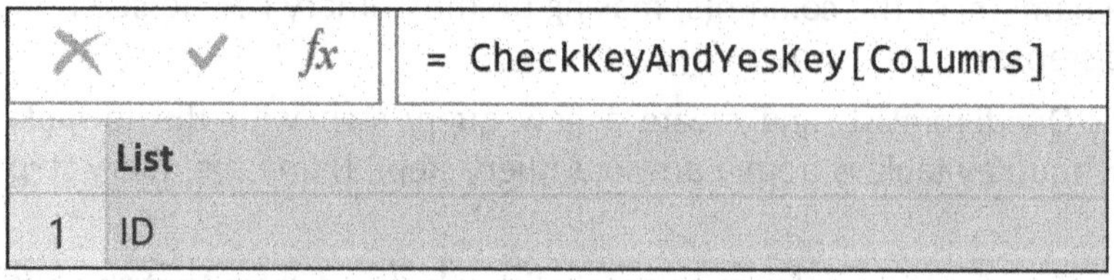

Figure 4-32 *The primary key column in the TableWithKey table is the ID column.*

Functions That Create a Primary Key

The next two examples look at the data connector functions Excel.CurrentWorkbook and Sql.Database to show how they use primary keys. (Chapter 6 covers these two functions in full detail.)

The **Excel.CurrentWorkbook function** returns the contents of the current Excel workbook, including objects such as Excel tables, defined names, and dynamic arrays. The **Sql.Database** function returns the selected database objects from an SQL Server database.

> **Note:** The example of the Excel.CurrentWorkbook function is only in the Excel file MCodeBook-Start.xlsx. The example of the Sql.Database function is in both the Excel and Power BI Desktop files. If you want to try the Sql.Database function example in Dataflows, you can use the SQL Server database data connector button and log in with these credentials:
> - Server: pond.highline.edu
> - Database: BoomData
> - UserName: excelisfun
> - Password: ExcelIsFun!

To see how to use the Excel.CurrentWorkbook function, follow these steps:

1. In the Excel file MCodeBook-Start.xlsx, select the query named ExcelCurrentWorkbookImport. As shown in Figure 4-33, the Excel.CurrentWorkbook function returns a table with objects from the current workbook. The Name column holds the name of each object, and the Content column holds the data for each object and a green table hyperlink to drill down. Because names for objects in an Excel file are unique, the Excel.CurrentWorkbook function assigns a primary key to the Name column, which causes the Drill Down feature to use a key match lookup.

☓ ✓ _fx_	= Excel.CurrentWorkbook()	
Content	**Name**	
1 Table	DayTypeSales	
2 Table	Duration	
3 Table	DateTime	
4 Table	CustomFunctionT	
5 Table	LookupExample	
6 Table	fSalesAprox	
7 Table	disDiscountAprox	
8 Table	FolderPath	

Figure 4-33 *Excel.CurrentWorkbook returns a table of Excel file objects.*

2. To extract the disDiscountAprox table from the Content column, click the green hyperlinked table in row 7 to drill down. The query step is automatically named Navigation.

> **Note:** When you drill down on the first Source step in a query, the new query step is automatically named Navigation. Although the name always shows as Navigation in the Applied Steps list, you can change it in the Advanced Editor.

As shown in Figure 4-34, a key match lookup is used to do a two-way lookup to extract the disDiscountAprox table. This lookup happens automatically when you click the green hyperlink to drill down. Notice that this automatic lookup formula has the correct structure for a key match two-way lookup as it includes the following:
- Positional row index operator (curly brackets)
- Lookup operator (square brackets inside the curly brackets)
- Name of the column to match with the table name and determine the row position
- Field access operator (square brackets after the row index operator) to determine the column position

```
X   ✓   fx      = Source{[Name="disDiscountAprox"]}[Content]
```

	ABC 123 Sales	▼	ABC 123 Discount	▼
1	0		0	
2	500		0.025	
3	1000		0.045	
4	2500		0.075	

Figure 4-34 *A drill-down key match lookup is automatic when a table has a primary key.*

Extracting a table is a common task for a key match lookup because of the primary key on a table.

Another common task where a primary key causes a key match lookup is with the Sql.Database function. To use the Sql.Database function, follow these steps:

3.　In the Power Query Editor in the Excel or Power BI Desktop file, select the query SQLImport. As shown in Figure 4-35, the Sql.Database function returns a table with objects from the SQL Server database. The first two arguments of this function list the name of the server and the name of the database. The Name column contains the name of the database objects, the Data column contains the data and a green table hyperlink to drill down, the Schema column contains the locations of the objects, the Item column contains the actual references to the objects (they are the same as the names in the Name column in this example, but they could be different), and the Kind column indicates the type of object in the Data column, such as a table, view, or function.

```
X   ✓   fx      = Sql.Database("pond.highline.edu", "BoomData")
```

	A^B_C Name	▼	ABC 123 Data	⇔	A^B_C Schema	▼	A^B_C Item	▼	A^B_C Kind
1	dCalendar		Table		dbo		dCalendar		Table
2	dCountry		Table		dbo		dCountry		Table
3	dProduct		Table		dbo		dProduct		Table
4	fTransactions		Table		dbo		fTransactions		Table

Figure 4-35 *The Sql.Database function returns a list of database objects.*

When you looked at the Excel.CurrentWorkbook function, you saw that it assigned a single-column primary key to the returned table. The Sql.Database function also assigns a primary key, but because a database can contain multiple locations for objects, the assigned primary key uses the two columns Name (for the name of the object) and Schema (for the location of the object). This two-column primary key causes the Drill Down feature to use a key match lookup.

4.　To extract the dProduct table from the Data column, click the green hyperlinked table in row 3 to drill down. The query step is automatically named Navigation.

As shown in Figure 4-36, a key match lookup based on two columns is used to do a two-way lookup to extract the dProduct table.

```
X   ✓   fx      = Source{[Schema="dbo",Item="dProduct"]}[Data]
```

	A^B_C Product	▼	1.2 Retail Price	▼	1.2 Standard Cost	▼	A^B_C Category	▼	fTr
1	Alpine		23.95		10.09	Beginner		Table
2	Aspen		23.95		9.48	Beginner		Table
3	Bellen		26.99		10.75	Beginner		Table

Figure 4-36 *A drill-down key match lookup uses two columns for the primary key.*

Note: This is a second example where a drill-down key match lookup occurs because of the primary key on the table. Other data connector functions, such as Excel.Workbook and Pdf.Tables, also use primary keys and drill-down key match lookups to retrieve data.

Finally, if you want to add a primary key to a table, you can use the **Table.AddKey function**, whose arguments are shown here:

```
Table.AddKey(
    table as table,
    key column/columns as list,
    isPrimary as logical) as table
```

To try this function, follow these steps:

1. In the DrillDownQ query, select the last step, ExtractFieldNames, add a new query step, and create the formula shown in Figure 4-37. Name the step AddKeyToTableWithoutKey.

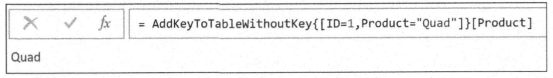

= Table.AddKey(TabeWithoutKey,{"ID","Product"},true)

1²₃ ID	ᴬᴮ꜀ Product	1.2 Sales
1	1 Quad	43
2	10 Aspen	35

Figure 4-37 *Adding a primary key based on two columns.*

2. To test whether the table has a primary key, you could use the Table.Keys function as you did earlier, or you could try to drill down and see if the lookup formula uses a key match lookup with two columns as the primary key. Figure 4-38 shows the drill-down result I got when I tried it. I named my step ExtractQFrom2KeyTable.

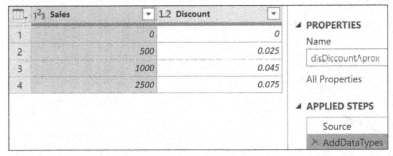

= AddKeyToTableWithoutKey{[ID=1,Product="Quad"]}[Product]

Quad

Figure 4-38 *After adding a primary key, a drill-down uses a key match lookup based on two columns.*

Approximate Match Lookups

As you have seen, M code has built-in methods for create exact match lookup formulas, but there is no built-in method for an approximate match lookup. However, using your knowledge of how to build custom functions, you can build a function to complete an approximate match lookup.

As you first learned at the beginning of this chapter, an **approximate match lookup**, or **exact match or next smaller lookup**, involves taking a **lookup value** and searching for an exact match or the next smaller value in a **match column**, and when a match is made, a value is retrieved from the corresponding position in a **return column**.

The Table.Buffer Function

Figure 4-39 shows the lookup table that is used for the following examples.

1²₃ Sales	1.2 Discount	
1	0	0
2	500	0.025
3	1000	0.045
4	2500	0.075

▲ PROPERTIES

Name

disDiscountAprox

All Properties

▲ APPLIED STEPS

Source

✕ AddDataTypes

Figure 4-39 *The disDiscountAprox query is the sales discount lookup table.*

As you'll see shortly (in Figure 4-41), in the fSalesAproxQ table, the formula that you create must use the disDiscountAprox query as the lookup table in each row. This means that your formula will have to execute the disDiscountAprox query in each row to go back to the disDiscountAprox query and retrieve the whole lookup table. If you have a large dataset, this can take a long time to process and can significantly increase formula calculation time. To significantly reduce formula calculation time, you can use the **Table.Buffer** function to run the query a single time and then store the values in memory so that the formula does not have to retrieve the query in each row. Although the Table.Buffer function does not improve processing time, for a lookup table like this, it can help significantly.

This is Microsoft's full definition of the Table.Buffer function:

> Buffers a table in memory, isolating it from external changes during evaluation. Buffering is shallow. It forces the evaluation of any scalar cell values, but leaves non-scalar values (records, lists, tables, and so on) as-is. Note that using this function might or might not make your queries run faster. In some cases, it can make your queries run more slowly due to the added cost of reading all the data and storing it in memory, as well as the fact that buffering prevents downstream folding. If the data doesn't need to be buffered but you just want to prevent downstream folding, use Table.StopFolding instead.

Note: Chapter 6 discusses query folding.

To sort and then buffer the lookup table, follow the steps:

1. In the disDiscountAprox query in the Chapter04 group, select the query step AddDataTypes and then use the filter and sort dropdown arrow at the top of the Sales field to sort the column in ascending order. Name the new query step SortSalesAtoZ.

2. With the SortSalesAtoZ step selected, add a new query step and create the formula shown in Figure 4-40. Name the step BufferTable.

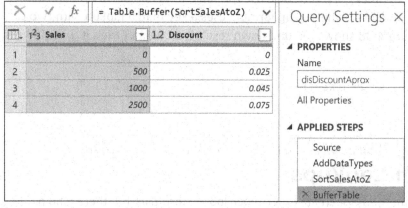

Figure 4-40 *Table.Buffer buffers a table into memory.*

Creating a Custom Column with a Custom Function

To create your first approximate match lookup formula in a custom column, follow these steps:

1. Select the fSalesAproxQ query in the Chapter04 group, select the query step AddDataTypes, click the Custom Column button in the Add Column tab in the General group, and create this formula:

```
= disDiscountAprox
```

2. Name the new column DiscountIT. Click OK.

3. Name the step CCAproxMatchQ (where CC stands for custom column). Figure 4-41 shows the full sales discount table in the first row.

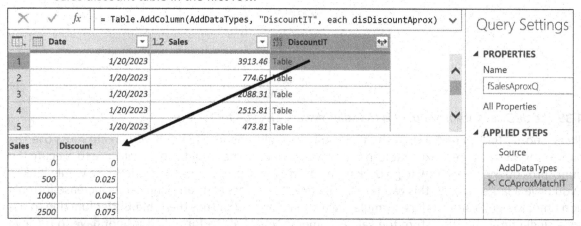

Figure 4-41 *The custom column formula pulls the buffered table into each row.*

Before you create the new lookup formula, you need to think about how the lookup table, as shown in the bottom of Figure 4-41, works and how you might create the formula. This lookup table is used to look up a customer sales amount in the Sales column (which is the match column) and retrieve a discount for a sales amount from the Discount column (which is the return column).

For example, in the second row of the fSalesAproxQ table, if you need to retrieve the discount for a $774.61 sales amount, the lookup value $774.61 is used to search from top to bottom through the Sales column (which is sorted ascending) until it finds an exact match or the next smaller value. Looking through the Sales column, you can see that there is no exact match, and the next smaller value is 500. Because 500 is in the second position in the column, when you then jump over to the Discount column (which is the return column), you take the second value, 0.025, and that becomes the discount for the $774.61 sales amount. If you need to retrieve the discount for a $2800 sales amount, because the value is greater than any value in the Sales column, the last value, $2500, becomes the matching value. Because the matching value is in the fourth position, the discount 0.075 is retrieved from the fourth position in the Discount column. If there are potentially negative sales amounts, the first value in the Sales column of the lookup table would have to be smaller than any possible sales value. In this way, the first category would catch all values less than 500 and assign a discount of zero.

Sales	Discount	Categories
0	0	0 >= Sales < 500
500	0.025	500 >= Sales < 1,000
1000	0.045	1,000 >= Sales < 2,500
2500	0.075	2,500 >= Sales

Figure 4-42 *Categories for the sales discount lookup table.*

The categories for the disDiscountAprox query lookup table are shown in Figure 4-42.

When you build a custom function to look up a discount, you need to run a logical test on the entire Sales column to return a logical value for each row. If you were looking up the sales amount of $774.61, for example, the logical test would look like this:

```
{0,500,10,00,2500}<=774.61
```

and the result would look like this:

```
{true,true,false,false}
```

The corresponding values from the Sales column would be:

```
{0,500}
```

Then, as you will see, the last value, 500, determines the row position of the returned discount.

To filter the lookup table with a full-column logical test, you can use the **Table.SelectRows function**, which is similar to the FILTER function in both worksheet and DAX function-based languages. All three functions require a full-column logical test to filter a table. The arguments for the Table.SelectRows function are shown here:

```
Table.SelectRows(table as table, condition as function) as table
```

4. To filter the lookup table, you need to edit the formula in the Custom Column dialog box, so in the Applied Steps task pane, click the gear icon to the right of the query step name CCAproxMatchQ and edit the formula so it becomes:

```
Table.SelectRows(disDiscountAprox, each [Sales]<=[Sales])
```

As shown in Figure 4-43, the discount table in row 2 should be filtered down to just the first two rows, but instead the row contains the full discount table.

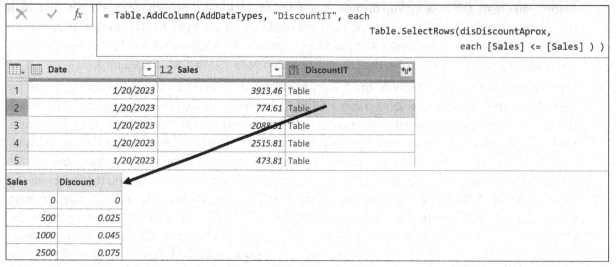

Figure 4-43 *The formula did not filter the disDiscountAprox table.*

The problem is coming from the formula element that is supposed to be filtering the sales discount table:

```
each [Sales] <= [Sales]
```

Because this formula element is inside the Table.SelectRows function, and its first argument contains the disDiscountAprox table, the formula thinks that both [Sales] references are from the same table: the disDiscountAprox table. The formula as it sits now sees this:

```
{0,500,1000,2500}<={0,500,1000,2500} = {true,true,true,true}
```

Somehow, you need to get the first [Sales] reference to jump back out to the AddDataTypes table inside the Table.AddColumn function and get the second [Sales] reference to look at the disDiscountAprox table inside the Table.SelectRows function. In row 1, you want this:

```
{0,500,10,00,2500}<=774.61 = {true,true,false,false}
```

To be even more explicit, you really need the logical test to look like this:

```
each disDiscountAprox[Sales] <= AddDataTypes[Sales]
```

This would give you the correct Sales columns from the correct tables. However, you are not allowed to preface your column references with table references in this situation.

The cause of this problem comes from back-to-back each keywords inside nested iterator functions, like Table.AddColumn and Table.SelectRows. The solution is to define variables within the scope of a particular function. This way, the variables know where they came from: They know which function to work within and which table they should be referencing. You can define variables in arguments that expect a function value in two ways:

- You can eliminate the each keyword, which works as a substitute for a custom function, and define your own custom function.
- You can keep all the each keywords and use the let expression to define variables.

5. To try the first method, defining a custom function, edit the formula in the Custom Column dialog box so it becomes:

```
Table.SelectRows(disDiscountAprox, (IT) => IT[Sales]<=[Sales])
```

6. As shown in Figure 4-44, inside the Table.SelectRows function, replace the each keyword with a custom function and a variable name that can represent each row in the isDiscountAprox table. I chose the variable name IT, for "inside table," since I saw the table as being inside each cell in the column, but you can name the variable whatever you would like.

7. To designate the Sales column as coming from the disDiscountAprox table, place the name of your variable in front of the field access operator, like this: IT[Sales]. Once you do this, the [Sales] reference

will be able to reference the AddDataTypes table back in the Table.AddColumn function. As shown in Figure 4-44, the two Sales columns can find the appropriate tables, and the Table.SelectRows function can filter the table in each row of the AddDataTypes table.

Another alternative for the variables is to not use any each keywords and to define a custom function in both functions. In this example, I use the variable name OT to refer to the outside table:

```
= Table.AddColumn(AddDataTypes, "DiscountIT", (OT) =>
        Table.SelectRows(disDiscountAprox, (IT) =>
        IT[Sales] <= OT[Sales]))
```

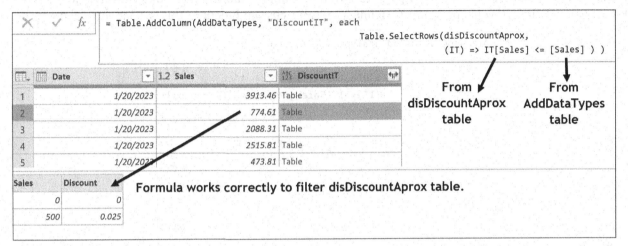

Figure 4-44 *Replacing the each keyword with a custom function to avoid the back-to-back each keyword conflict.*

8. Extract the Discount column from the filtered table as a list so you can get the last discount. Notice that the Table.SelectRows function is delivering a filtered table value. Also, as you learned in Chapter 3, the generalized lookup formula for looking up a list from a column in a table is:
    Table[ColumnName]

    This means you can simply place your field access operator after the Table.SelectRows function to extract your discount list.

9. To create the next iteration of the formula, edit the formula in the Custom Column dialog box so it becomes:
    ```
    Table.SelectRows(disDiscountAprox, (IT) =>
            IT[Sales]<=[Sales])[Discount]
    ```

    As shown in Figure 4-45, there is a filtered list in each row of the table.

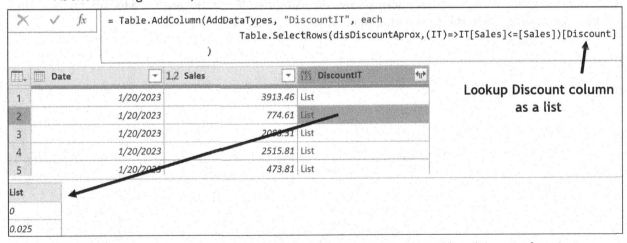

Figure 4-45 *The field access operator works on the table delivered by the Table.SelectRows function.*

The last step in the formula is to get the last discount in the list. To do this, you can use the **List.Last function**, which is another of Microsoft's self-explanatory functions: It extracts the last value from a list.

10. To get the last discount, edit the formula in the Custom Column dialog box so it becomes:

```
List.Last(
        Table.SelectRows(disDiscountAprox, (IT) =>
        IT[Sales]<=[Sales])[Discount])
```

11. Click OK in the Custom Column dialog box and then edit the formula in the Formula Bar to add the data type number in the fourth argument of the Table.AddColumn function.

Figure 4-46 shows the finished approximate match formula. This sort of custom column formula is great if the lookup is a one-time task. But if you are going to do multiple approximate match lookup formulas in the same Power Query Editor, it would be better to define a reusable custom function. This is what you will do next.

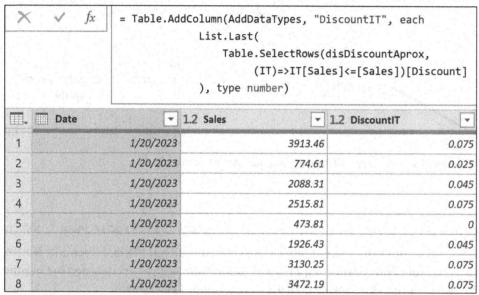

```
= Table.AddColumn(AddDataTypes, "DiscountIT", each
            List.Last(
                Table.SelectRows(disDiscountAprox,
                    (IT)=>IT[Sales]<=[Sales])[Discount]
            ), type number)
```

Date	1.2 Sales	1.2 DiscountIT
1	1/20/2023	3913.46	0.075
2	1/20/2023	774.61	0.025
3	1/20/2023	2088.31	0.045
4	1/20/2023	2515.81	0.075
5	1/20/2023	473.81	0
6	1/20/2023	1926.43	0.045
7	1/20/2023	3130.25	0.075
8	1/20/2023	3472.19	0.075

Figure 4-46 *The List.Last function is the last addition to complete the formula.*

Creating a Reusable Custom Function

Figure 4-47 shows the complete approximate match lookup custom function query that you are going to create in this section. Notice that this custom function defines a single external sales column as a variable in the first row before the let keyword. Also notice that the sales discount lookup table is hard-coded into the custom function using a table intrinsic function. The advantage of hard-coding the lookup table into the query is that the lookup table will be treated as a constant and will not be recalculated in each row of the table that the custom function iterates. Like the Table.Buffer function you saw earlier, this can benefit the formula's performance. The disadvantage when hard-coding any value into a formula or query is that it is harder to change later, and it makes tracking down errors more difficult. However, if a lookup table like this will not change often, then this is a great option.

```
SalesDiscount

(Sales as number) as number =>
let
    // Hard code discount table. Sales = match column. Discount = return column.
    DiscountTable =
    #table(type table [Sales = number, Discount = number],
        {{0,0},{500,0.025},{1000,0.045},{2500,0.075}})
in
    // Function to lookup discount based on sales with external sales column input
        List.Last(
            Table.SelectRows( DiscountTable, each [Sales] <= Sales) [Discount]
        )
```

Figure 4-47 *A custom function query with a hard-coded lookup table.*

To create this reusable approximate match lookup formula, follow these steps:

1. In the Power Query Editor, create a new blank query in the Chapter04 group and name the function query SalesDiscount.

2. Open the Advanced Editor, type the notes and the let expression custom function query as shown in Figure 4-47, and then click Done.

3. To invoke the new reusable query, select the last query step in the fSalesAproxQ query, use Invoke Custom Function in the Add Column tab to invoke the SalesDiscount function, and name the new column DiscountFx. Now, when you click OK, you should see a new column, as shown in Figure 4-48.

✕	✓	fx	= Table.AddColumn(CCAproxMatchIT, "DiscountFx", each SalesDiscount([Sales]),type number)	

	Date	1.2 Sales	DiscountIT	1.2 DiscountFx
1	1/20/2023	3913.46	0.075	0.075
2	1/20/2023	774.61	0.025	0.025
3	1/20/2023	2088.31	0.045	0.045
4	1/20/2023	2515.81	0.075	0.075
5	1/20/2023	473.81	0	0
6	1/20/2023	1926.43	0.045	0.045
7	1/20/2023	3130.25	0.075	0.075
8	1/20/2023	3472.19	0.075	0.075

Figure 4-48 *Invoking the SalesDiscount function query in the fSalesAproxQ table.*

Creating a Custom Column Using the let Expression

Now let's look at how to use the let expression to avoid the back-to-back each keyword conflict you saw in your approximate match formula. As you learned in Chapter 2, you can use the let expression to define variables in formulas. But whereas in Chapter 2, you defined a variable to avoid recalculation of a repeated formula element, in this chapter, you will define a variable in the scope of the first of two nested functions so that the variable output will always come from the first function.

As shown in Figure 4-49, you have the nested functions Table.AddColumn and Table.SelectRows. The goal is to define a variable for the Sales column in the Table.AddColumn function so that you can use the variable in the Table.SelectRows function.

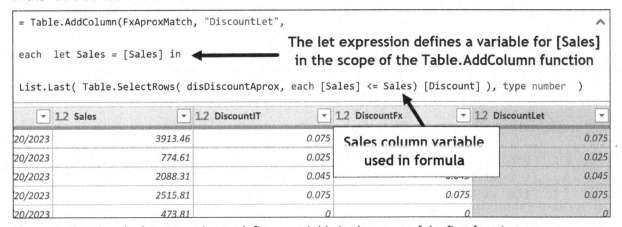

Figure 4-49 *Using the let expression to define a variable in the scope of the first function.*

In the third argument of the Table.AddColumn function, after the each keyword, you can define a let expression variable for the formula element [Sales]: Sales = [Sales]. This will allow the Sales variable to be used throughout the rest of the formula, and the variable evaluation will always occur inside the scope of the Table.AddColumn function. This will work perfectly so that as Table.AddColumn iterates down the Sales column inside the FxAproxMatch table, the Sales variable will see the value 3913.46 in row 1, 774.61 in row 2, and so on. Further, when you define the variable Sales inside the first of the nested functions, when you get to the third argument in the second function, Table.SelectRows, you can use the formula element [Sales], and there will be no conflict with the first function's Sales column. The [Sales] reference will correctly get the values from the disDiscountAprox table.

To create an approximate match lookup formula using the let expression, select the last query step in the fSales-sAproxQ query and create the custom column as shown in Figure 4-49. Name the query step CCAproxMatchLet.

Using the List.Accumulate Function to Perform an Approximate Match Lookup

As an alternative to using the Table.SelectRows function to filter the sales discount table, you can use the List.Accumulate function and the if expression. (I originally learned this lookup formula from my friend Geert Delmulle.) For large datasets, the List.Accumulate function may calculate more quickly than the Table.SelectRows function. When I timed the two formulas based on an 8 million row SQL dataset, I found the List.Accumulate formula to be about 15% faster.

You studied the List.Accumulate function in detail in Chapter 3. This function is perfect for performing an approximate match lookup because it can iterate through the list of sales values, and when it finds a match, the if expression that you use in the List.Accumulate function stops the iteration, and the discount value is delivered. In contrast, the Table.Select function must iterate through all rows in the Sales column every time the lookup formula tries to deliver a discount. Because this iterative process happens in each row of the column that contains the lookup formula, the savings in iterations results in a performance benefit: The formula does not take as long to calculate. This is the reason for the difference between the two formulas when I timed them on the 8 million row SQL dataset.

Figure 4-50 shows an example of how to use the List.Accumulate function and the if expression to build an approximate match lookup formula. To try building this formula, follow these steps:

1. Start a blank query and name it SalesDiscountAcc. Using Figure 4-50 as a guide, create a reusable custom function query to perform an approximate match lookup using the List.Accumulate function and the if expression.

```
//SalesDiscountAcc
(Sales as number) as number =>
let
    // Hard coded DiscountTable = sales/discount lookup table
        DiscountTable =
        #table(type table [Sales = number, Discount = number],
        {{0,0},{500,0.025},{1000,0.045},{2500,0.075}}),
    // Rows in table minus one becasue M Code is base zero
        Rows = Table.RowCount(DiscountTable)-1
in
    List.Accumulate(
        {0..Rows},
        null,
        // cs = Current state of discount selection
        // cr = Current row in list iteration
        (cs, cr) =>
            if
                DiscountTable{cr}[Sales]  <=  Sales
                then DiscountTable{cr}[Discount]
                else cs )

/* List.Accumulate is like the Excel worksheet REDUCE function.
   Parallel formula:
   =REDUCE(
        "",
        SEQUENCE(ROWS(DiscountTable[Sales])),
        LAMBDA(cs,cr,
            IF(  INDEX(DiscountTable[Sales],cr)<=E5,
                INDEX(DiscountTable[Discount],cr),
                cs))) */
```

Figure 4-50 *The List.Accumulate function may perform better than the Table.SelectRows function.*

2. Select the CCAproxMatchLet query step in the fSalesAproxQ query and then invoke the new function to calculate the discount based on the sales values in each row of the Sales column (see Figure 4-51). Name the query step CCAproxMatchAcc.

```
= Table.AddColumn(CCAproxMatchLet, "DiscountAcc", each SalesDiscountAcc([Sales]),type number)
```

1.2 Sales	1.2 DiscountIT	1.2 DiscountFx	1.2 DiscountAcc
3913.46	0.075	0.075	0.075
774.61	0.025	0.025	0.025
2088.31	0.045	0.045	0.045
2515.81	0.075	0.075	0.075
473.81	0	0	0
1926.43	0.045	0.045	0.045
3130.25	0.075	0.075	0.075
3472.19	0.075	0.075	0.075

Figure 4-51 *The reusable SalesDiscountAcc function used in the fSalesAproxQ query.*

This is how the formula works:

- The list argument in the List.Accumulate function contains the formula element {0..Rows}. The custom function row variable counts the rows in the lookup table and subtracts 1 to get a count of 3. The list generated is {0, 1, 2, 3}, which represents each row position in the lookup table. The if expression in the accumulator argument uses the row positions to look up values in the lookup table.

- The seed argument in the List.Accumulate function is not needed for this function, so you use a null value to skip the argument.

- The accumulator argument of the List.Accumulate function is where you define a two-variable custom function. The first variable is the current state of the intermediate value, which I named cs. The second variable is the value in the current row of the list being iterated, which I named cr. The if expression is used to define the repeating action for each row in the list, and it is the mechanism used to stop the iteration before it reaches the last row in the list. In addition, the array from the first argument, {0,1,2,3}, represents each row in the lookup table, with each row in the iteration represented by the variable cr. In row 2 of the CCAproxMatchLet table, this is how the if expression was evaluated to get the final discount of 0.025:

  - **If 0 <= 774.61 then 0 else cs:** Because this evaluates to true, the cs (current state) is a 0 discount that is available to be used in the next iteration.

  - **If 500 <= 774.61 then 0.025 else cs:** Because this evaluates to true, the cs is a 0.025 discount that is available to be used in the next iteration.

  - **If 1000 <= 774.61 then 0.045 else cs:** Because this evaluates to false and the cs is a 0.025 discount, the iteration stops, and the discount is delivered to the cell.

Summary

This chapter covers M code lookup formulas. You have seen how to do two types of exact match lookups: row index lookups and key match lookups. You have also seen how to look up columns and rows, learned about primary keys and how they relate to lookup formulas, and seen several different types of approximate match lookup formulas.

Now that you have learned about the fundamental M code building blocks—expressions, let expressions, queries, built-in functions, custom functions, M code values, data types, and M code lookups—you're ready to look at four common data transformation tasks: unpivot, append, join/merge, and group by.

Chapter 5: Unpivot, Append, Join, and Group By

The data transformation tasks unpivot, append, join/merge, and group by are common tasks used to transform data. Most of the time you use the user interface to accomplish these tasks. However, it is helpful to understand the M code functions that these features use when writing the code for you, and occasionally you will have to enhance the generated code by writing some code of your own code. First, we will look at the unpivot feature.

Unpivot and the Table.UnpivotOtherColumns Function

The unpivot feature can covert a cross-tabulated table that contains data into a proper table of data. This is an important transformation because tables are easy to analyze, and cross-tabulated tables are not. Cross-tabulated tables rarely come from databases or structured data environments; instead, they come from data situations where proper table structure is not understood.

For example, Figure 5-1 shows a cross-tabulated table with student names in the first column, class name attributes as column headers, and grades in the interior of the cross-tabulated table. With data like this, data analysis tasks such as sorting and creating PivotTables are very difficult—and may even be impossible. With this table, how could you use the sort feature to sort grades from biggest to smallest? Or how could you use a PivotTable to calculate the GPA for each student? You would need to unpivot the cross-tabulated table and create a proper table.

Student	Busn216	Busn135	Busn218	BI348
Abdi Hyde	3.7	3	3.9	3.6
Dean Washington	3.6	3.4	4	3.6
Chantel Mims	3.8	3.5	3.7	3.8
Earnestine Graff	3.9	4	1.7	2.9
Jim Jones	2.1	1.1	2.3	0.5

Figure 5-1 *Cross-tabulated tables are hard to analyze.*

Figure 5-2 shows the mechanics of how an unpivot is performed if the goal is to create a proper table with records that contain the fields student, class, and grade. Because the cross-tabulated table uses four class names as column headers, the resulting table will contain four records for each original row. For example, in Figure 5-2, you can see that the first row in the cross-tabulated table is converted to four records for the student Abdi Hyde—one for each class.

Cross tabulated table with four class attribute columns

Student	Busn216	Busn135	Busn218	BI348
Abdi Hyde	3.7	3	3.9	3.6
Dean Washington	3.6	3.4	4	3.6
Chantel Mims	3.8	3.5	3.7	3.8
Earnestine Graff	3.9	4	1.7	2.9
Jim Jones	2.1	1.1	2.3	0.5

Student	Class	Grade
Abdi Hyde	Busn216	3.7
Abdi Hyde	Busn135	3
Abdi Hyde	Busn218	3.9
Abdi Hyde	BI348	3.6
Dean Washington	Busn 216	3.6
Dean Washington	Busn135	3.4
Dean Washington	Busn218	4
Dean Washington	BI 348	3.6
⋮		

Figure 5-2 *The unpivot feature converts each row into four records.*

The unpivot feature can be found in the Transform tab in the Any Column group, or you can right-click a column or columns to get to the feature. You have these three unpivot options:

- **Unpivot Columns:** Creates table records from selected columns and leaves other columns intact.
- **Unpivot Other Columns:** Creates table records from columns not selected and leaves the selected column or columns intact.
- **Unpivot Only Selected Columns:** Creates table records from the selected column or columns and ignores columns that are not selected.

The first two options, Unpivot Columns and Unpivot Other Columns, are the most frequently used options, and they both use the same function, Table.UnpivotOtherColumns. The arguments for the **Table. UnpivotOtherColumns function** are shown here:

```
Table.UnpivotOtherColumns(
    table as table,
    pivotColumns as list,
    attributeColumn as text,
    valueColumn as text) as table
```

The **table** argument contains the table to unpivot, the **pivotColumns** argument contains a list of one or more columns that you do not want to unpivot, the **attributeColumn** argument contains the column name for the attribute column (or column names from the unpivoted columns), and the **valueColumn** argument contains the column name for the value column (which contains values from the unpivoted columns).

To try using the Table.UnpivotOtherColumns function, follow these steps:

1. Select the StudentGradesQ query in the Chapter05 group. (Figure 5-1 shows the table output for this query.) Right-click the Student column header and select Unpivot Other Columns. Name the query step UnpivotClassColumns.

> **Note:** Notice that you had to select only a single column before invoking the Unpivot Other Columns command. This will be important later.

As shown in Figure 5-3, the table records are created from the columns you did not select (Busn216, Busn135, Busn218, and BI348), and the selected Student column is left intact. The Formula Bar shows the Table.UnpivotOtherColumns function's four arguments:

- The first argument lists the table output from the previous query step.
- The second argument lists the name of the selected column when the unpivot was performed—in this case, Student. Notice that the column name is text, as required, but it is housed in a list. As I mentioned earlier, any time a function argument requires a list, you can infer that multiple elements are allowed in that argument. This is correct because you can unpivot based on multiple columns.
- The third and fourth arguments contain the Attribute and Value column names, which are not very informative.

`= Table.UnpivotOtherColumns(AddDataTypes, {"Student"}, "Attribute", "Value")`

Student	Attribute	Value
1 Abdi Hyde	Busn216	3.7
2 Abdi Hyde	Busn135	3
3 Abdi Hyde	Busn218	3.9
4 Abdi Hyde	BI348	3.6
5 Dean Washington	Busn216	3.6

Figure 5-3 *The Unpivot Other Columns feature uses the Table.UnpivotOtherColumns function.*

2. To change the Attribute and Value column names, in the Formula Bar change "Attribute" to "Class" and "Value" to "Grade" (see Figure 5-4).

`= Table.UnpivotOtherColumns(AddDataTypes, {"Student"}, "Class", "Grade")`

Student	Class	Grade
1 Abdi Hyde	Busn216	3.7
2 Abdi Hyde	Busn135	3

Figure 5-4 *Editing the formula in the Formula Bar to add informative column names.*

As shown in Figure 5-5, if you were to highlight the four attribute columns and then use the Unpivot Columns option, you would get the same result and the same formula shown in Figure 5-3. The Unpivot Other Columns and Unpivot Columns options both use the Table.UnpivotOtherColumns function. This is by design so that if you add more attribute columns to the source table, the formula will still work to unpivot the table.

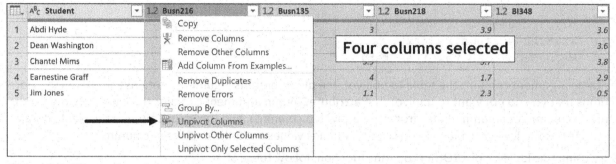

Figure 5-5 *The Unpivot Columns feature accomplishes the same goal as Unpivot Other Columns but is not as easy to use.*

> **Note:** If you had to choose between using the Unpivot Other Columns and Unpivot Columns options for this example, it might be quicker to use the Unpivot Other Columns option because you have to select only one column before invoking the command.

The Table.UnpivotOtherColumns Function in a Custom Column

It is common to get a column filled with tables that you need to append into a single table. (Chapter 7 covers this topic in greater detail.) Figures 5-6 and 5-7 show a column filled with cross-tabulated tables. You might want to append them into a single table, but it is not possible to do that until you unpivot each table. To unpivot each table, you can create a custom column and use the Table.UnpivotOtherColumns function.

Notice that the cross-tabulated tables in Figures 5-6 and 5-7 do not have the same number of class attribute columns. This is no problem if you unpivot with the Student column selected.

CrossTab
1   Table
2   Table
3   Table
4   Table

Student	Busn216	Busn135	Busn218	BI348
Abdi Hyde	3.7	3	3.9	3.6
Dean Washington	3.6	3.4	4	3.6
Chantel Mims	3.8	3.5	3.7	3.8
Earnestine Graff	3.9	4	1.7	2.9
Jim Jones	2.1	1.1	2.3	0.5

Figure 5-6 *The first row contains a cross-tabulated table with four class attribute columns.*

CrossTab
1   Table
2   Table
3   Table
4   Table

Student	Math101	Math146	Math148
Abdi Hyde	3.5	4	2.9
Dean Washington	4	3.5	4
Chantel Mims	3.9	3.8	3.9
Earnestine Graff	3.3	2.7	0.6
Jim Jones	3.7	2.7	0

Figure 5-7 *The second row contains a cross-tabulated table with three class attribute columns.*

To create a custom column, follow these steps:

1. Select the CrossTabsInColumn query in the Chapter05 group, go to the Add Column tab, go to the General group, and click the Custom Column button.

2. Create the formula and new column name as shown in Figure 5-8 and click OK. Name the query step CCUnpivotCrossTabTables. Figure 5-9 shows the result.

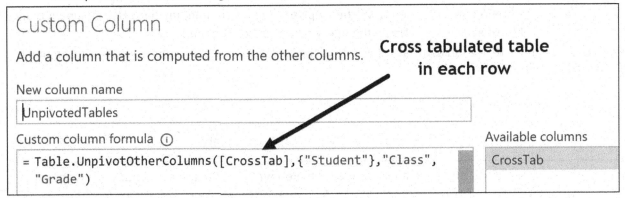

Figure 5-8 *The Table.UnpivotOtherColumns function in a custom column.*

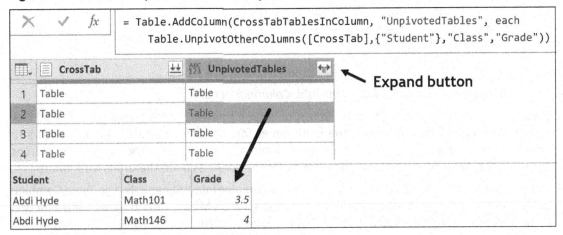

Figure 5-9 *Each row has an unpivoted table.*

As shown in Figure 5-9, the formula created a proper table of data in each row, with the same three column names for each table. Once you have a column with tables that all have the same structure (that is, the same number of columns, same column names, and same data types), you can append the tables into a single table of data. If the structure is not the same for all tables—for example, if a column name is spelled incorrectly—the append will not work. (You will learn how to deal with tables that do not have the same structure in Chapter 7.)

Appending: Table.Combine vs. Table.ExpandTableColumn

When you have a column of tables, you can append in two ways:

-   **Invoke the Table.ExpandTableColumn function by using the expand button at the top of the column of tables:** This method is fast and easy to use. It hard-codes column names into the formula. (Hard-coding default or internally generate names is okay, but hard-coding column names coming from external sources can cause problems.) On large datasets, it may take longer to execute. In addition, the function does not infer and apply data types from source tables.

-   **Type your own M code formula using the Table.Combine function:** This method requires that you write your own M code, and column names are not hard-coded into the formula. On large datasets, the Table.Combine function may execute slightly faster than the Table.ExpandTableColumn function. (I tested the two functions on 1.2 million rows of data that came from six Excel file tables and found this to be the case.) The function can infer and apply data types from source tables when source tables have data types applied.

I usually use the Table.Combine function, but sometimes I just use the expand button at the top of the column of tables because it is fast and easy. You will try both methods so you can see for yourself.

To append the tables by using the expand button, follow these steps:

1. Right-click the UnpivotedTables column header and click Remove Other Columns. Name the query step RemoveOtherColumns.

2. Click the expand button at the top of the UnpivotedTables column, uncheck Use Original Column Name as Prefix, and click OK. Name the query step ExpandedColumns.

As shown in Figure 5-10, the tables are appended using the Table.ExpandTableColumn function. The arguments for this function are shown here:

```
Table.ExpandTableColumn(table as table,
     column as text,
     columnNames as list,
     optional newColumnNames as nullable list) as table
```

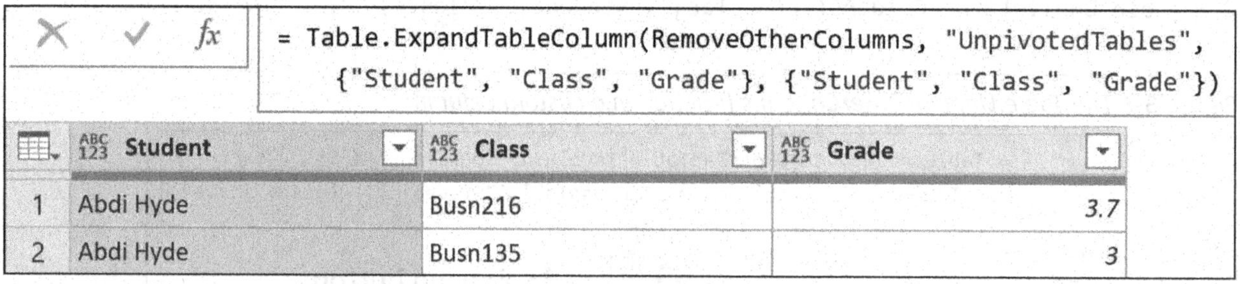

```
= Table.ExpandTableColumn(RemoveOtherColumns, "UnpivotedTables",
     {"Student", "Class", "Grade"}, {"Student", "Class", "Grade"})
```

Student	Class	Grade
1 Abdi Hyde	Busn216	3.7
2 Abdi Hyde	Busn135	3

Figure 5-10 *The expand button uses the Table.ExpandTableColumn function.*

Figure 5-10 shows that the table from step 1, RemoveOtherColumns, is listed in the **table** argument, the column to expand is recorded in the **column** argument, the field names for the table are hard-coded as a list into the **columnNames** argument, and the optional list of new column names is listed in the **newColumnNames** argument. Notice that this function did not infer data types for the columns from the underlying tables.

Recall from Chapter 2 that Microsoft uses the terms *append* and *combine* interchangeably. The Table.Combine function really does an append, rather than a combine operation; I wish Microsoft had named this function Table.Append. The **Table.Combine function** appends a list of tables with the same structure. The arguments for this function are shown here:

```
Table.Combine(tables as list, optional columns as any) as table
```

The **tables** argument requires the tables to be in a list. This is by design because when you use the field access operator to look up a column, a list is returned. The **columns** argument allows you to specify a list of column names to define the correct column names for the append process and how many columns must be in the final appended table. Microsoft says that the Table.Combine function "returns a table that is the result of merging a list of tables. The resulting table will have a row type structure defined by columns or by a union of the input types if columns is not specified."

To append the tables by using the Table.Combine function, follow these steps:

1. As shown in Figure 5-11, add a new query step to pull the CCUnpivotCrossTabTables query step table down to this new step. Name the query step CombineTables.

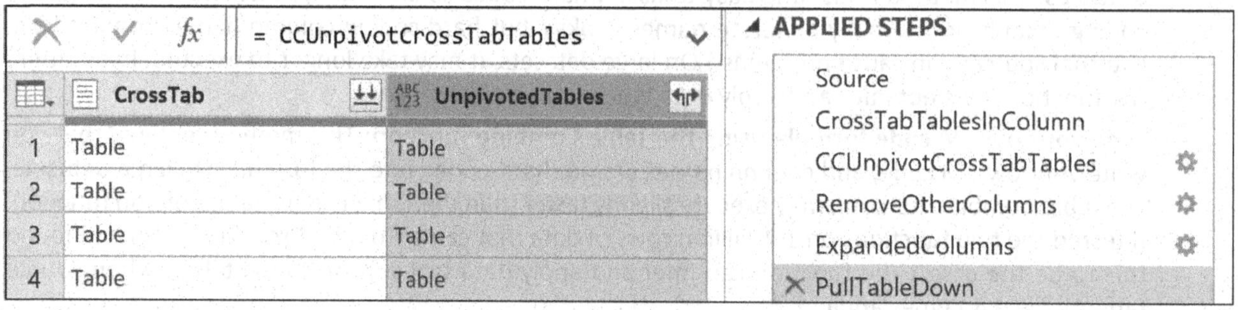

Figure 5-11 *Pulling the previous query step table down to the current step.*

2.   Use the Formula Bar to edit the formula you just created so that it matches what Figure 5-12 shows. Notice that the column lookup formula returns a list of tables.

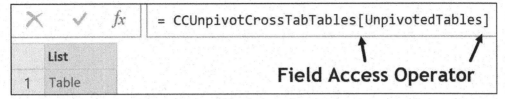

= CCUnpivotCrossTabTables[UnpivotedTables]

Field Access Operator

List

1   Table

Figure 5-12 *This is the column lookup formula that you learned about in Chapter 4.*

3.   Continue editing the formula, as shown in Figure 5-13, by wrapping the Table.Combine function around the column lookup formula.

= Table.Combine(CCUnpivotCrossTabTables[UnpivotedTables])

	A^B_C Student	A^B_C Class	1.2 Grade
1	Abdi Hyde	Busn216	3.7
2	Abdi Hyde	Busn135	3
3	Abdi Hyde	Busn218	3.9
4	Abdi Hyde	BI348	3.6
5	Dean Washington	Busn216	3.6

Figure 5-13 *Appending the table and correct data types in a single step.*

As shown in Figure 5-13, the append process is completed in a single query step, the field names are not hard-coded into the formula, and the data types are inferred from the underlying table and applied to the three columns. As you've seen, with some knowledge of M code, you can avoid using a user interface method and instead create a streamlined append formula yourself.

Now let's look at the second argument of the Table.Combine function. This example can be found in the TableCombine2ndArgument query in the Chapter05 group. Figure 5-14 shows three tables that you need to append by using the Table.Combine function. Notice that the first table has a misspelled column name and has an extra column that the other two tables don't have.

Product	Sles	Extra
Q	3	2
S	4	6
Q	2	5
A	9	9

Product	Sales
Q	3
S	4
Q	2
A	9

Product	Sales
Q	3
S	4
Q	2
A	9

Figure 5-14 *The first table has a misspelled column name and an extra column.*

As shown in Figure 5-15, if you use the Table.Combine function without the second argument, for each unique column name in the original set of tables, there is a designated column in the final appended table. The Table.Combine function does not know which column names are correct, so it chooses them all.

```
fx    = Table.Combine(FilteredRows[Content])
```

Product	Sles	Extra	Sales
1 Q	3	2	null
2 S	4	6	null
3 Q	2	5	null
4 A	9	9	null
5 Q	null	null	3
6 S	null	null	4
7 Q	null	null	2
8 A	null	null	9
9 Q	null	null	3
10 S	null	null	4
11 Q	null	null	2
12 A	null	null	9

Figure 5-15 *The Table.Combine function does not use the second argument.*

As shown in Figure 5-16, if you use the Table.Combine function with a list of the correct column names, the resulting table will contain only matching columns. The list of column names, {"Product","Sales"}, ensures that the resulting table has only two columns—Product and Sales—and ignores columns that do not have matching column names. In addition, the function lists null values when it does not find a matching column. In Figure 5-16, null values are listed in the first four rows to indicate that a Sales column was not found in the first table.

```
fx    = Table.Combine(FilteredRows[Content],{"Product","Sales"})
```

Product	Sales
1 Q	null
2 S	null
3 Q	null
4 A	null
5 Q	3
6 S	4
7 Q	2
8 A	9
9 Q	3
10 S	4
11 Q	2
12 A	9

Figure 5-16 *Using the Table.Combine function with the second argument.*

If you use Table.Combine with and without the second argument, which resulting table will be more helpful? If you do not use the second argument, the resulting table shows all columns that the function found. This might be helpful for tracking down misspelled field names. If you use the second argument, the resulting table contains only the desired columns. If you just want to ignore columns that do not match, this table might be more useful. Finally, notice that data types are not inferred with the use of Table.Combine in these examples. This is because the tables came from the Excel environment, where data types cannot be applied.

Join Operations Used by the Merge Feature

When making data transformations, join operations are commonly used to merge tables. A **join operation** connects two tables based on a primary key column and a foreign key column to merge the two tables into a new table. The primary key table has a primary key column with a unique list of values, and the rest of the columns contain attributes for each value in the primary key.

You have probably already experienced a join operation like the **left outer join** in Figure 5-17. This figure shows a Product table as an example of a primary key table. The ProductID column is the primary key, and the attribute columns are Product, Cost, and Price. The figure also shows a Sales Transaction table as an example of a foreign key table. The ProductID column is the foreign key, and the remaining columns provide details about the transactions, such as date of sale, customer ID, and units sold. In this left outer join, all records from the left are joined with only matching Price column records from the right to create a new merged table.

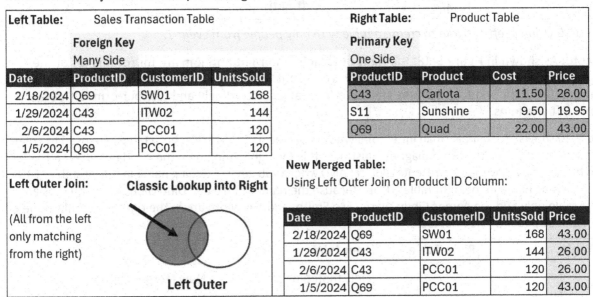

Figure 5-17 *Using a left outer join to create a sales transaction table with a price column.*

Figure 5-18 uses Venn diagrams to illustrate the six types of joins commonly used in data analysis to determine the structure of the merged table. The Venn diagram shown in Figure 5-17 illustrates the left outer join occurring in this example by highlighting the full circle on the left and only the intersection of the left and right circles on the right. Only product prices that have product IDs on the left are in the merged table. The one Sunshine record on the right has no matching product ID on the left, so the price for that product is not in the merged table.

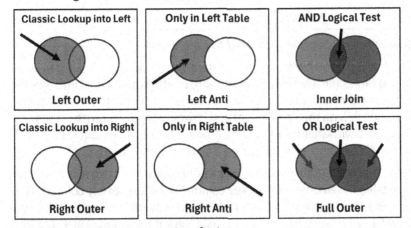

Figure 5-18 *Six common types of joins.*

Figure 5-19 illustrates a **left anti join**, where only records from the left table that are not in the right table are used to create the new merged table. The Venn diagram illustrates this by highlighting the left table without the overlap (names that are in both). Because the names Sioux Noline, Chantel Xo, and Ty Mims are in both tables, those names do not appear in the merged table.

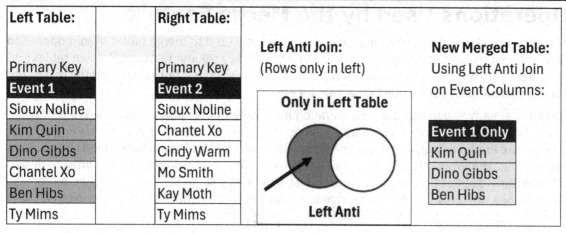

Figure 5-19 *Using a left anti join to create a table with only people from event 1.*

> **Note:** As shown in Figure 5-18, the **right outer join** and **right anti join** are mirror images of the **left out join** and **left anti join**, respectively. Because it is easy to switch tables from right to left and left to right, most of the time people orient tables accordingly and just perform left outer and left anti joins.

Figure 5-20 shows an example of an **inner join**, where only records that are in both tables are used to create the new merged table. The Venn diagram illustrates this by highlighting only the overlap between the left and right circles. The overlap represents a logical AND where you get a matching name in the left table, TRUE, and a matching name in the right table, TRUE. Because the names Kim Quin, Dino Gibbs, and Ben Hibs are in the left table only and the names Cindy Warm, Mo Smith, and Kay Moth are in the right table only, none of those names appear in the final table.

Left Table:		Right Table:	Inner Join:		New Merged Table:
			(Only matching rows in both tables.)		Using Inner Join on Event Columns:
Primary Key		Primary Key			
Event 1		**Event 2**	**AND Logical Test**		
Sioux Noline		Sioux Noline			**Both Events**
Kim Quin		Chantel Xo			Sioux Noline
Dino Gibbs		Cindy Warm			Chantel Xo
Chantel Xo		Mo Smith			Ty Mims
Ben Hibs		Kay Moth			
Ty Mims		Ty Mims	**Inner Join**		

Figure 5-20 *Using an inner join to create a table with people who went to both events.*

In my data analysis experience, the left outer join is the most common join in data transformations. This is because it is common to have to pull data from lookup tables (also known as dimension, or attribute, tables) into a table that contains the data to be summarized, often called a fact table. The left outer join is similar to the worksheet functions XLOOKUP and VLOOKUP and to relationships in the Power Pivot and Power BI Data Model (the semantic model). Whether you are working in M code, the worksheet, or the Data Model, the left outer join is the most common type of join. However, I also use the left anti and inner joins regularly in data transformations.

The least common join is the full outer join. Figure 5-21 illustrates a full outer join, where all records from the left and right tables are merged into a single table based on a primary key column and a foreign key column. The Venn diagram illustrates this by highlighting everything in both tables, including the overlap. The three distinct parts to the Venn diagram represent a logical OR, where you can have an item in the left table only (TRUE, FALSE), an item in both tables (TRUE, TRUE), or an item in the right table only (FALSE, TRUE). As shown in the merged table in Figure 5-21, the Kangaroo record is associated with a null record because the supplier ID, CC, is in the left table but not in the right table. Also in the merged table, the Darnell Booms record is associated with a null record because the supplier ID, DB, is in the right table but not in the left table. The records in the merged table that have records from both tables represent a match made on both sides during the joining process.

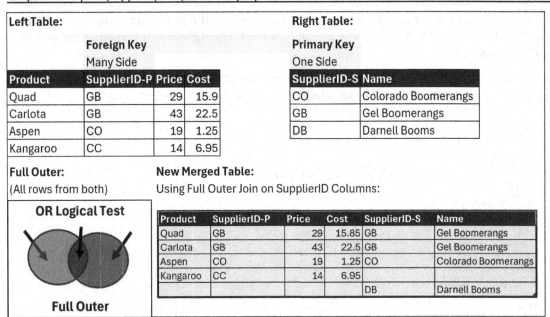

Left Table:

	Foreign Key Many Side		
Product	**SupplierID-P**	**Price**	**Cost**
Quad	GB	29	15.9
Carlota	GB	43	22.5
Aspen	CO	19	1.25
Kangaroo	CC	14	6.95

Right Table:

	Primary Key One Side
SupplierID-S	**Name**
CO	Colorado Boomerangs
GB	Gel Boomerangs
DB	Darnell Booms

Full Outer:
(All rows from both)

OR Logical Test

Full Outer

New Merged Table:

Using Full Outer Join on SupplierID Columns:

Product	SupplierID-P	Price	Cost	SupplierID-S	Name
Quad	GB	29	15.85	GB	Gel Boomerangs
Carlota	GB	43	22.5	GB	Gel Boomerangs
Aspen	CO	19	1.25	CO	Colorado Boomerangs
Kangaroo	CC	14	6.95		
				DB	Darnell Booms

Figure 5-21 *Using a full outer join to merge two tables into one table that contains all records from both of the original tables.*

Merging Using Left Outer and Left Anti Joins

Now that we have looked at common types of joins, you're ready to try using the merge feature to do a left outer join and a left anti join. Most of the time when you want to merge two tables, you use the user interface rather than type M code. The **merge feature** allows you to create a join between two tables. When you use the merge feature, the tables used must be queries. You cannot merge tables directly from the worksheet or the Data Model.

Figure 5-22 lists the six joins available with the merge feature. In the first example, you will see how to use the user interface to write most of the code for a join. Figure 5-23 shows the left and right tables that you will merge using a left outer join. After you merge the tables, you will add a few custom columns to get the final table shown on the right side of Figure 5-23.

Join Kind
Left Outer (all from first, matching from second)
Right Outer (all from second, matching from first)
Full Outer (all rows from both)
Inner (only matching rows)
Left Anti (rows only in first)
Right Anti (rows only in second)

Figure 5-22 *Six join types available in the Merge dialog box.*

Left Table = fUnitSales

Date	ProductID	UnitsSold
3/3	A51	168
2/28	Q69	60
3/3	A51	228
2/28	A51	108
3/1	S11	120
2/29	Q69	24
2/28	C43	168
3/3	A51	12
3/3	A51	60
2/28	C43	264
2/29	S11	180
2/29	S11	240
3/3	S11	216

Right Table = dProduct

ProductID	Product	Cost	Price
C43	Carlota	11.50	26.00
S11	Sunshine	9.50	19.95
Q69	Quad	22.00	43.00
A51	Aspen	11.75	24.00

Merged Table with custom columns

Date	Product	Revenue	COGS	GrossProfit
3/3	Aspen	4,032	1,974	2,058
3/3	Aspen	5,472	2,679	2,793
2/28	Aspen	2,592	1,269	1,323
2/28	Quad	2,580	1,320	1,260
3/1	Sunshine	2,394	1,140	1,254
2/29	Quad	1,032	528	504
2/28	Carlota	4,368	1,932	2,436
3/3	Aspen	288	141	147
3/3	Aspen	1,440	705	735
2/28	Carlota	6,864	3,036	3,828
2/29	Sunshine	3,591	1,710	1,881
2/29	Sunshine	4,788	2,280	2,508
3/3	Sunshine	4,309	2,052	2,257

Figure 5-23 *Left, right, and merged tables for a left outer join.*

Follow these steps to merge the left and right tables in Figure 5-23 using a left outer join and then add a few custom columns:

1. Select the fUnitSalesQ query in the Chapter05 group and select the last query step, AddDataTypes. Then, on the Home tab, go to the Combine group, click the Merge Queries dropdown arrow, and click Merge Queries as New.

2. In the Merge dialog box (see Figure 5-24), use the first dropdown arrow to select the left, or top, table. Use the second dropdown arrow to select the right, or bottom, table.

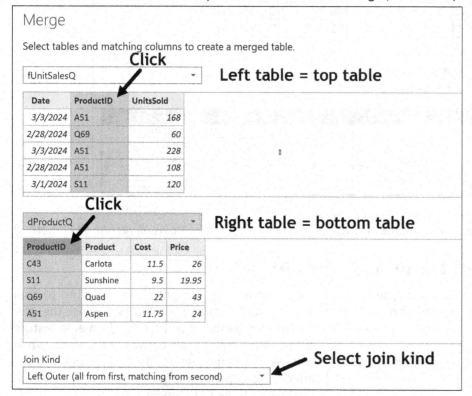

Figure 5-24 *The Merge dialog box for the left outer join.*

3. To connect the two tables using a join operation, click the ProductID column in both tables.

4. From the Join Kind dropdown, select Left Outer.

5. Click OK to merge the tables and close the dialog box. Name the new query LeftOuterGrossProfitReport. Figure 5-25 shows the merged table. As you can see in this figure, the Merge feature returns a one-row table in each row of the column with the attributes for the matching product ID. For example, in row 2, the matching product ID, Q69, brought back the name Quad, the cost 22, and the price 43. You can expand the column to get one or more of these attributes (and you will do so in just a moment).

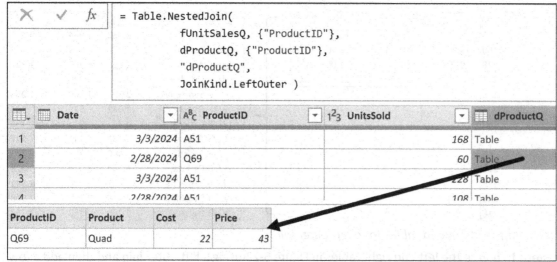

Figure 5-25 *Using the Table.NestedJoin function to retrieve the attributes for product ID Q69.*

In Figure 5-25, the Formula Bar reveals that the Merge feature uses the **Table.NestedJoin** function. This function has six arguments:

```
Table.NestedJoin(
      table1 as table, key1 as any,
      table2 as any, key2 as any,
      newColumnName as text,
      optional joinKind as nullable number) as table
```

The **table1** argument contains the left table, the **key1** argument contains the key column for the left table, the **table2** and **key2** arguments contain the table and key column, respectively, for the right table, the **newColumnName** argument contains the name of the new column, and the **joinKind** argument contains the join kind. Figure 5-26 shows a table with the different join kinds and a number equivalent for each of them. For example, you can substitute the number 1 for JoinKind.LeftOuter in the joinKind argument, and this formula will work:

Name	Number Equivalent
JoinKind.Inner	0
JoinKind.LeftOuter	1
JoinKind.RightOuter	2
JoinKind.FullOuter	3
JoinKind.LeftAnti	4
JoinKind.RightAnti	5

```
Table.NestedJoin(
fUnitSalesQ, {"ProductID"},
dProductQ, {"ProductID"}
"dProductQ", 1)
```

In addition, because the left outer join is so common, you can omit the sixth argument, and the function will perform a left outer join by default. For example, this formula would work for the left outer join in this case:

Figure 5-26 *Six types of joins for the sixth argument of the Table.NestedJoin function.*

```
Table.NestedJoin(
fUnitSalesQ, {"ProductID"},
dProductQ, {"ProductID"}
"dProductQ")
```

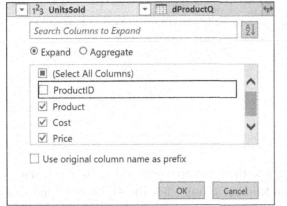

6. To expand the column and add the related Product, Cost, and Price columns to the table, click the expand column button in the top-right corner of the dProductQ column and then, as shown in Figure 5-27, uncheck the Use Original Column Name as Prefix checkbox, uncheck the ProductID column checkbox, and click OK. Name the query step ExpandProductQ.

As shown in Figure 5-28, three new columns are added to the table, with the correct product ID attributes. Because this is a left outer join, all records from the Sales tables are listed with the matching records from the Product table. It is as if three worksheet lookup formulas have all appeared at once!

Figure 5-27 *Expanding the column to get product attributes.*

```
Table.ExpandTableColumn(Source, "dProductQ", {"Product", "Cost", "Price"}, {"Product", "Cost", "Price"})
```

	Date	ProductID	UnitsSold	Product	Cost	Price
1	3/3/2024	A51	168	Aspen	11.75	24
2	3/3/2024	A51	228	Aspen	11.75	24
3	2/28/2024	A51	108	Aspen	11.75	24
4	2/28/2024	Q69	60	Quad	22	43

Figure 5-28 *A merged table using a left outer join.*

7. As shown in Figure 5-29, select the Price and UnitsSold columns and then, to add a new column that calculates revenue, in the Add Column tab, go to the From Number group, click the Standard dropdown arrow, and then click Multiply. Name the query step CalculateRevenue.

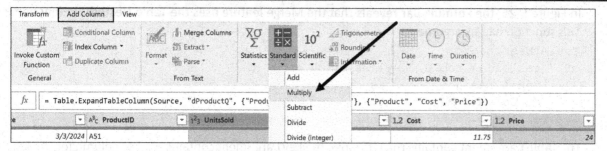

Figure 5-29 *Selecting the columns to multiply and then using the Multiply feature.*

8.   As shown in Figure 5-30, edit the second argument of the Table.AddColumn function and change the name from "Multiplication" to "Revenue". As you can see in the figure, the Multiply feature writes the formula for you, using the Table.AddColumn function. You can also see that, because there was a number data type on at least one of the columns selected, the feature conveniently applied the number data type. (If both columns were whole numbers, the whole number data type, Int64.Type, would instead be applied.)

```
= Table.AddColumn(ExpanddProductQ, "Revenue", each [UnitsSold] * [Price], type number)
```

AᴮC Product	1.2 Cost	1.2 Price	1.2 Multiplication
168 Aspen		11.75	24	4032
228 Aspen	**Edit New Column Name**	11.75	24	5472
108 Aspen		11.75	24	2592

Figure 5-30 *The Multiply feature used the Table.AddColumn function.*

9.   Again using the Multiply feature, select the Cost and UnitsSold columns and then add a new column to calculate cost of goods sold (COGS). Edit the formula in the Formula Bar to change the column name from "Multiplication" to "COGS". Name the query step CalculateCOGS. Figure 5-31 shows the result.

```
= Table.AddColumn(#"Inserted Multiplication", "COGS", each [UnitsSold] * [Cost], type number)
```

1.2 Cost	1.2 Price	1.2 Revenue	1.2 COGS
11.75	24	4032	1974
11.75	24	5472	2679
11.75	24	2592	1269

Figure 5-31 *Using the Multiply feature to calculate COGS.*

10.   Select the Revenue column, select the COGS column, and then, to add a new column that calculates gross profit, in the Add Column tab, go to the From Number group, click the Standard dropdown arrow, and select Subtract (see Figure 5-32). The order of the subtraction will always be first column selected minus second column selected.

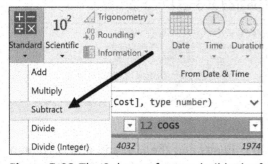

Figure 5-32 *The Subtract feature builds the formula for you.*

11.   Edit the formula in the Formula Bar to change the column name from "Subtraction" to "Gross Profit", as shown in Figure 5-33. Name the query step CalculateGrossProfit.

```
= Table.AddColumn(CalculateCOGS, "GrossProft", each [Revenue] - [COGS], type number)    ⌄
```

1.2 Price	1.2 Revenue	1.2 COGS	1.2 GrossProft
11.75	24	4032	1974	2058
11.75	24	5472	2679	2793

Figure 5-33 *Using the Subtract feature to calculate gross profit.*

12. To remove the unnecessary columns, select the following five columns, in this order: Date, Product, Revenue, COGS, and GrossProfit. (The order of selection determines the order, from left to right, of the resulting table.) Right-click one of the selected columns and select Remove Other Columns. Name the query step KeptReportColumns. Figure 5-34 shows the finished report.

```
✕  ✓  fx    = Table.SelectColumns(CalculateGrossProfit,{"Date", "Product", "Revenue", "COGS", "GrossProft"})    ⌄
```

	Date	A^B_C Product	1.2 Revenue	1.2 COGS	1.2 GrossProft
1	3/3/2024	Aspen	4032	1974	2058
2	3/3/2024	Aspen	5472	2679	2793
3	2/28/2024	Aspen	2592	1269	1323
4	2/28/2024	Quad	2580	1320	1260
5	3/1/2024	Sunshine	2394	1140	1254
6	2/29/2024	Quad	1032	528	504
7	2/28/2024	Carlota	4368	1932	2436
8	3/3/2024	Aspen	288	141	147
9	3/3/2024	Aspen	1440	705	735
10	2/28/2024	Carlota	6864	3036	3828
11	2/29/2024	Sunshine	3591	1710	1881

Query Settings ✕

▲ PROPERTIES
Name
LeftOuterGrossProfitReport

All Properties

▲ APPLIED STEPS
Source ⚙
ExpandProductQ ⚙
CalculateRevenue ⚙
CalculateCOGS ⚙
CalculateGrossProfit ⚙
✕ KeptReportColumns ⚙

Figure 5-34 *A report created mostly via the user interface (and with some M code).*

13. If you are working in Excel, load this table as a connection only. If you are working in Power BI Desktop or Dataflows, right-click the query and uncheck Enable Load.

Comparing Two Lists of Values

Almost everyone needs to compare lists at some point. There are different questions you can answer by comparing lists. For example, say that you have a table that contains a list of people who went to one event and another table that contains a list of people who went to another event. You can compare these lists to answer the following questions:

- **What people went to the first event but not the second event?** To answer this question, you would use a left anti join to get the names from the first table that are not in the second table.
- **What people went to both events?** To answer this question, you would use an inner join to find the names that appear in both tables.
- **What people went to the second event but not the first event?** To answer this question, you would use a right anti join, or you could just switch the order of the tables and do a left anti join.

In this section, you're going to work through an example of answering the first question, using a left anti join. As shown in Figure 5-35, the goal of this merge is to determine who went to Event01 but did not go to Event02. In other words, you want the names in the Event01 table that are not in the Event02 table.

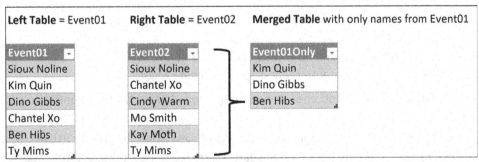

Figure 5-35 *Left, right, and merged tables for a left anti join.*

To use a left anti join, follow these steps:

1. Select the Event01 query in the Chapter05 group, select the last query step, AddDataTypes, and then, in the Home tab, go to the Combine group, click the Merge Queries dropdown arrow, and select Merge Queries as New.

2. As shown in Figure 5-36, select the Event01 query as the left, or top, table and select the Event02 query as the right, or bottom, table. Choose Left Anti in the Join Kind dropdown and click OK to merge the tables and close the dialog box. Name the new query LeftAntiEvent01Only.

Figure 5-36 *The Merge dialog box for the left anti join.*

3. As shown in Figure 5-37, in each row of the Event02 column, the retrieved table contains a null value because there was no matching record. Because you do not need this column, right-click the column header and select Remove. Name the query step RemoveEvent02Column.

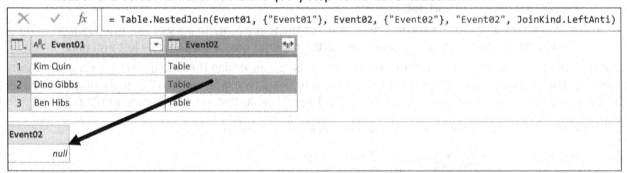

Figure 5-37 *The left anti join returns null values because there are no matching records.*

4. Double-click the Event01 column name and change the name from "Event01" to "Event01Only". Name the query step NameColumn.

5. If you are working in Excel, load this table as a connection only. If you are working in Power BI Desktop or Dataflows, right-click the query and uncheck Enable Load. Figure 5-38 shows the resulting query.

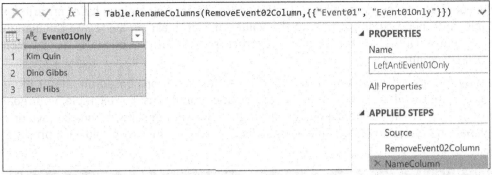

Figure 5-38 *The finished report shows names of people who went to only Event 01.*

> **Note:** In this section we have looked at left outer and left anti joins. The other common join kind is the inner join. If you would like, you can try an inner join on the Event01 and Event02 queries.

The Table.Group Function and the Group By Feature

You are probably already familiar with four ways you can perform the group by operation, illustrated in Figure 5-39: using a standard PivotTable, a Power BI matrix visual, worksheet formulas, or a DAX Data Model PivotTable. Using the Power Query Group By feature is a fifth way to perform this operation. Figure 5-39 shows four examples in which a product report is made from the SalesT table, with two or three aggregate calculations for each product. This is the essence of the group by operation.

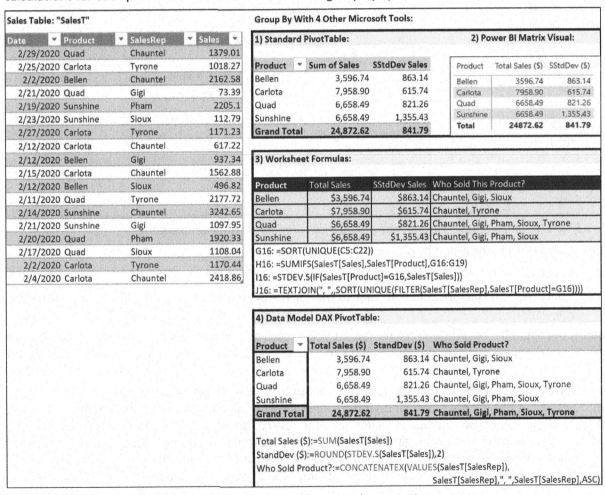

Figure 5-39 *You are probably already familiar with the group by operation.*

In a standard PivotTable, you drag one or more fields to the Rows area to create a unique list of criteria for each row in the PivotTable, and then you drag a field to the Values area to make an aggregate calculation based on the row criteria. In Power Query, you can simulate this process by using the Group By feature, which is based on the SQL GROUP BY command.

The Power Query **Group By feature** creates a unique set of row header conditions based on one or more fields and then makes aggregate calculations based on the row header conditions. For example, your goal might be to create a product report with three aggregate calculations for sum of sales, standard deviation for sales (a measure of variation in sales numbers), and a joined list a sale rep names who sold each product, as shown in Figure 5-40.

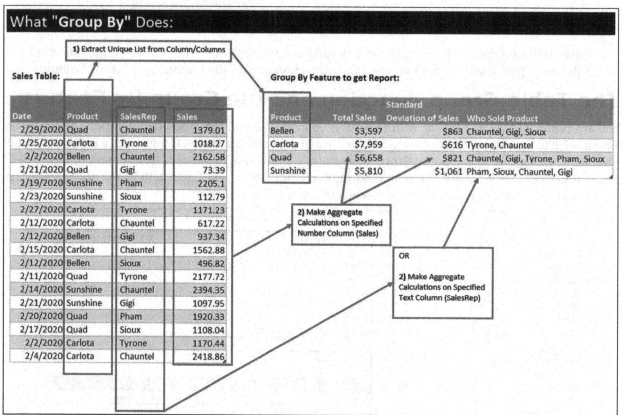

Figure 5-40 *Creating a unique list and performing a calculation for each unique item.*

There are two steps in the group by process:

1. Select the column for row conditions and then extract a unique list.

2. Select the two columns that you want to use for the aggregate calculations and then perform the calculations.

If you choose a number column, you can make calculations such as sum and standard deviation. If you choose a text column, you can perform operations like join or count (although Figure 5-40 does not show a count operation).

The Power Query Group By feature offers seven built-in aggregate calculations: sum, median, min, max, count rows, count distinct rows, and all rows (for subtables with matching records). As illustrated in Figure 5-41, behind the scenes, every group by action uses the row conditions to gather all matching records into a subtable that can be used for aggregate calculations. For the product report you will create in this section, the standard deviation and the join calculations are not in the list of built-in calculations. But don't worry: I will show you a great hack that allows you to create any type of aggregate calculations you might need.

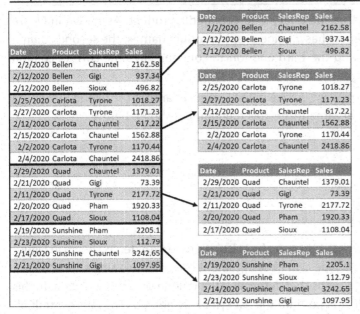

Figure 5-41 *A group by operation groups related records together into subtables.*

You can access the Group By feature in three ways: on the Home tab in the Transform group, on the Transform tab in the Table group, or by right-clicking the column(s) you want to group by and selecting Group By.

To try the example shown in Figure 5-40, follow these steps:

1. Select the GroupByProductReport query in the Chapter05 group, select the last query step, AddDataTypes, right-click the Product column header, and select Group By.

2. In the Group By dialog box (shown in Figure 5-42), select the Advanced button, click the Add Aggregation button twice, type the three new column names in the New Column Name textboxes, select the three operations from the Operation dropdowns, and then select the Sales column under Column for the first two columns. (The last column will not have an operation because the All Rows option pulls the grouped set of records into each row of the grouped report.)

   Notice in Figure 5-42 that the second operation is not standard deviation, and the third operation is not join. The selected operations—Sum and All Rows—are temporary selections that serve as placeholders that will allow the Group By feature to write most of the M code for you. You will edit the M code later to complete this hack.

Group By

Specify the columns to group by and one or more outputs.

○ Basic   ◉ Advanced

| Product ▾ |

[Add grouping]

New column name	Operation	Column
Total Sales	Sum ▾	Sales ▾
Standard Deviation for Sales	Sum ▾	Sales ▾
Who Sold Product	All Rows ▾	▾

[Add aggregation] ←

Figure 5-42 *The second and third operations are placeholders until you can edit the M code.*

3. Click OK in the Group By dialog box. Name the query step GroupedByProduct. As shown in Figure 5-43, the first column in the group by report has a unique list of product names, the second column has the correct total sales calculation, and the third and fourth columns have the correct column header name but not the correct aggregate calculation.

Before you fix the M code to get what you want, notice in the Formula Bar that the Group By feature uses the Table.Group function. The five arguments for this function are shown here:

```
Table.Group(
        table as table,
        key as any,
        aggregatedColumns as list,
        optional groupKind as nullable number,
        optional comparer as nullable function) as table
```

The **table** argument contains the table where the group by calculations are made. As shown in Figure 5-43, in this example, the table is AddDataTypes. The **key** argument can contain a single text column name or a list of column names for the columns that determine the unique set of row criteria. In this example, the single column name Product is put into the list syntax by default. The **aggregatedColumns** argument contains a list within a list, where each sublist details the three components for each aggregate calculation: column name, function, and data type. In the third argument in Figure 5-43, there are three sublists. The first list contains the correct details for the total sales calculation. The second list contains the correct column name and data type, but the placeholder List.Sum function will have to be changed. The third list contains the correct column name, but everything else will have to be changed. Notice that in the third list, after the keyword each, the underscore retrieves a table with all matching records. In Figure 5-43, you can see that the third row contains a subtable with all the Bellen records. Later, you will use this table to look up the names for the sales reps who sold the product. The optional **groupKind** argument allows you to choose the type of grouping, and the optional **comparer** argument allows you to test equality and determine inclusion for the grouping action. (You will see details and examples of these last two arguments later in this chapter.)

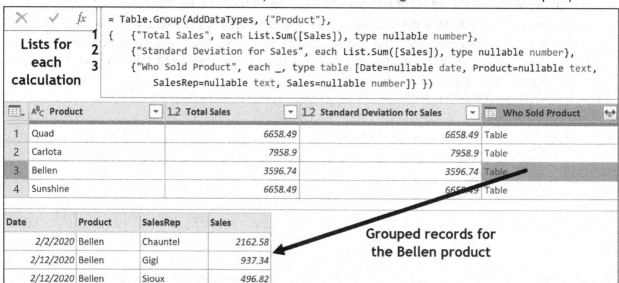

Figure 5-43 *Using the Table.Group function to make three aggregate calculations for each product.*

4. To edit the formula so that it makes a standard deviation calculation rather than a sum calculation, in the Formula Bar, in the second list in the third argument, change the list function from List.Sum to List.StandardDeviation. Figure 5-44 shows the result. Notice that by using the placeholder function, you have avoided typing some of the M code for this third aggregate calculation.

```
= Table.Group(AddDataTypes, {"Product"},
{    {"Total Sales", each List.Sum([Sales]), type nullable number},
     {"Standard Deviation for Sales", each List.StandardDeviation([Sales]), type nullable number},
     {"Who Sold Product", each _, type table [Date=nullable date, Product=nullable text,
         SalesRep=nullable text, Sales=nullable number]} })
```

▼ 1.2 Total Sales	▼ 1.2 Standard Deviation for Sales	▼ ⊞ Who Sold Product ⁴ᵗ⁾
6658.49	821.2553204	Table

Figure 5-44 *Changing List.Sum to List.StandardDeviation.*

5. In the Formula Bar, in the third argument, retype the third list so that it becomes:
    ```
    {"Who Sold Product", each _[SalesRep], type text}
    ```

    Figure 5-45 shows the result from the new third list in the Who Sold Product column. The lookup column formula element _[SalesRep] extracts a list of sales rep names in each row. Notice that there are duplicate names in the list. To remove duplicates from a list and sort the result, you can use the List.Distinct and List.Sort functions, respectively. The **List.Distinct** function removes duplicates from a list and returns a unique list. The **List.Sort** function sorts ascending, A–Z, by default. We will look at both of these functions in more detail later in this chapter.

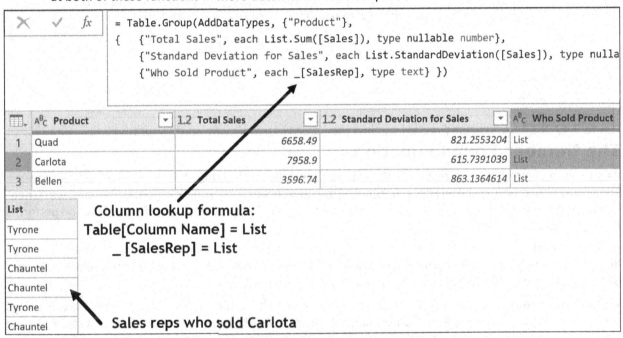

Figure 5-45 *The underscore gets the whole table, and the field access operator gets the list.*

6. As shown in Figure 5-46, to remove the duplicate names and sort the unique list, use the List.Sort and List.Distinct functions so the formula becomes:
    ```
    List.Sort(List.Distinct(_[SalesRep]))
    ```

    In Figure 5-46, notice that the list of names for the Carlota product has only two unique names. To combine the names, you can use the **Table.Combine** function by entering the text items to be joined as a list in the first argument, the **texts** argument, and the delimiter to separate the text items in the second argument, the **separator** argument.

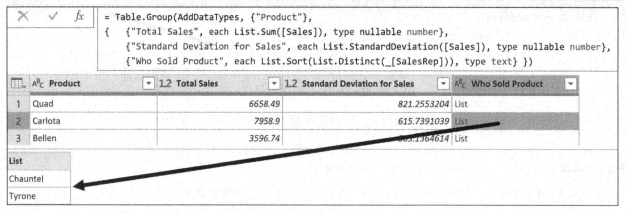

Figure 5-46 *Adding List.Sort and List.Distinct to the formula.*

7. To combine the names into a single text string, as shown in Figure 5-47, use the Text.Combine function with the delimiter comma and a space (", ") so the formula becomes:

```
Text.Combine(List.Sort(List.Distinct(_[SalesRep])),", ")
```

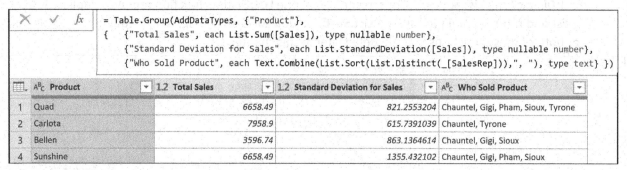

Figure 5-47 *The Text.Combine function can join the names of people who sold the product.*

The Number.Round Function

As shown in Figure 5-47, the result for the standard deviation calculation has many extra decimal places. The report would be less cluttered if you rounded the numbers to the penny position. In DAX and worksheet formulas, the ROUND function performs standard rounding; in M code, the Number.Round function performs banker's rounding by default.

In school, most of us learned standard rounding, where if the digit is 5 or more, you add 1 to the previous digit, and if the digit is 4 or less, you do not add 1 to the previous digit; either way, you then remove all extra digits to the right. With this method, there is a slight upward bias.

With banker's rounding, also called Gaussian rounding or half-even rounding, there is less bias. Banker's rounding works the same way as standard rounding except when it comes to the digit 5. At 5, it rounds to the nearest even number. This means that with the digit 5, the function will sometimes round up and sometimes round down, thereby eliminating some of the upward bias associated with standard rounding, which always rounds up. Industries such as banking, manufacturing, and software development use banker's rounding.

Figure 5-48 shows the slight upward bias of the DAX and worksheet ROUND function as compared to M code's Number.Round function.

Formula →	Number.Round([Sales], 2)	Number.Round([Sales], 2, 2)	ROUND([@Sales],2)
Sales	The default For Number.Round in M Code is Banker's Rounding	How To Simulate Excel ROUND function in M Code	ROUND Function in Worksheet & DAX perform Standard Rounding
1097.915	1097.92	1097.92	1097.92
1098.925	1098.92	1098.93	1098.93
1098.935	1098.94	1098.94	1098.94
1098.945	1098.94	1098.95	1098.95
1098.955	1098.96	1098.96	1098.96
1098.965	1098.96	1098.97	1098.97
1098.975	1098.98	1098.98	1098.98
1098.985	1098.98	1098.99	1098.99
1098.995	1099	1099	1099
9,889.595	**9,889.600**	**9889.640**	**9,889.640**

Figure 5-48 *There is a slight upward bias with the ROUND function in DAX and worksheet formulas.*

The M code **Number.Round** function performs rounding based on a specified number of digits and rounding mode. The arguments for this function are shown here:

```
Number.Round(
    number as nullable number,
    optional digits as nullable number,
    optional roundingMode as nullable number) as nullable number
```

The **number** argument contains the number to round. The **digits** argument allows you to specify the position to round to, as shown in Figure 5-49. The default for this argument is the ones position. The **roundingMode** argument allows you to specify the type of rounding to perform, as shown in Figure 5-50. RoundingMode. ToEven performs banker's rounding and is the default; RoundingMode.AwayFromZero performs the ROUND function's standard rounding.

2nd Argument for Number.Round →	Millions	Hundred Thousands	Ten Thousands	Thousands	Hundreds	Tens	Ones	Decimal Point	Tenths	Hundredths	Thousandths	Ten-Thousandths	Hundred-Thousandths	Millionths
	...-6	-5	-4	-3	-2	-1	0	.	1	2	3	4	5	6...

Figure 5-49 *The position to round to in the digits argument of the Number.Round function.*

Options	Value	Description
RoundingMode.Up	0	Round up when there is a tie between the possible numbers to round to.
RoundingMode.Down	1	Round down when there is a tie between the possible numbers to round to.
RoundingMode.AwayFromZero **(sames as worksheet & DAX ROUND function)**	2	Round away from zero when there is a tie between the possible numbers to round to.
RoundingMode.TowardZero	3	Round toward zero when there is a tie between the possible numbers to round to.
RoundingMode.ToEven **(same as banker's rounding)**	4	Round to the nearest even number when there is a tie between the possible numbers to round to.

Figure 5-50 *Rounding options in the roundingMode argument of the Number.Round function.*

Note: By default, Power Query stores numbers using a double-precision floating-point system. This means that sometimes a number like 3/10, or 0.3, is stored as 0.30000000000000001. The rounding that happens before you make any calculations with the number can lead to small errors. Although there are a number of Value functions (Value.Subtract, Value.Multiply, Value.Divide, Value.Compare, and Value.Equals) and List aggregating functions (List.Average, List.Sum, and List. Product) that allow you to specify decimal precision rather that double precision in order to avoid this problem, these solutions do not work in all situations. An alternative to switching from double precision to decimal precision is to round a number by using the Number.Round function to remove the unwanted digits. This same floating-point system can cause issues in an Excel worksheet and in the DAX Data Model. I use the ROUND function in those situations.

To round the standard deviation numbers to the penny position, in the Formula Bar, wrap the Number.Round function around the List.StandardDeviation function, as shown here:

```
Number.Round(List.StandardDeviation([Sales]),2)
```

Figure 5-51 shows the result of completing the product group by report with a mix of user interface M code and some handwritten M code.

```
= Table.Group(AddDataTypes, {"Product"},
{   {"Total Sales", each List.Sum([Sales]), type nullable number},
    {"Standard Deviation for Sales", each Number.Round(List.StandardDeviation([Sales]),2), type nullable number},
    {"Who Sold Product", each Text.Combine(List.Sort(List.Distinct(_[SalesRep])),", "), type text} })
```

1.2 Total Sales	1.2 Standard Deviation for Sales	A^B_C Who Sold Product
6658.49	821.26	Chauntel, Gigi, Pham, Sioux, Tyrone
7958.9	615.74	Chauntel, Tyrone
3596.74	863.14	Chauntel, Gigi, Sioux
6658.49	1355.43	Chauntel, Gigi, Pham, Sioux

Figure 5-51 *Number.Round helps make the report less cluttered.*

The Fourth Table.Group Argument: groupKind

The fourth argument in the Table.Group function is **groupKind**. The two options for this argument are shown in Figure 5-52:

- **GroupKind.Local, or 0:** Extracts a set of records based on a consecutive sequence of repeating items from the specified key column(s) and uses the set as the grouping categories.
- **GroupKind.Global, or 1:** Extracts a unique set of records from the specified key column(s) and uses the set as the grouping categories.

Option	Value	Description
GroupKind.Local	0	A local group is formed from a consecutive sequence of rows from an input table with the same key value.
GroupKind.Global	1	A global group is formed from all rows in an input table with the same key value.

Figure 5-52 *Options for the groupKind argument in the Table.Group function.*

Say that you have the table of baseball game records shown in Figure 5-53, and your goal is to create a report on consecutive wins/losses. In this case, you can use the GroupKind.Local option. In addition, there is a great hack for listing the start and end dates for each win or loss streak.

→   Goal: group by consecutive loss/win streaks   →

Baseball results table = **AsBaseballQ**   Oakland A's Consecutive Win/Loss Report

Date	Team	Opponent	Result	As Runs	O Runs
4/8/2022	OAK	PHI	Loss	5	9
4/9/2022	OAK	PHI	Loss	2	4
4/10/2022	OAK	PHI	Win	4	1
4/11/2022	OAK	TBR	Win	13	2
4/12/2022	OAK	TBR	Loss	8	9
4/13/2022	OAK	TBR	Win	4	2
4/14/2022	OAK	TBR	Win	6	3
4/15/2022	OAK	TOR	Loss	1	4
4/16/2022	OAK	TOR	Win	7	5
4/17/2022	OAK	TOR	Loss	3	4
4/18/2022	OAK	BAL	Win	5	1
4/19/2022	OAK	BAL	Win	2	1
4/20/2022	OAK	BAL	Loss	0	1
4/21/2022	OAK	BAL	Win	6	4
4/22/2022	OAK	TEX	Loss	1	8
4/23/2022	OAK	TEX	Loss	0	2

Result	Count	Dates
Loss	2	4/8/2022 to 4/9/2022
Win	2	4/10/2022 to 4/11/2022
Loss	1	4/12/2022 to 4/12/2022
Win	2	4/13/2022 to 4/14/2022
Loss	1	4/15/2022 to 4/15/2022
Win	1	4/16/2022 to 4/16/2022
Loss	1	4/17/2022 to 4/17/2022
Win	2	4/18/2022 to 4/19/2022
Loss	1	4/20/2022 to 4/20/2022
Win	1	4/21/2022 to 4/21/2022
Loss	2	4/22/2022 to 4/23/2022
Win	1	4/24/2022 to 4/24/2022
Loss	1	4/26/2022 to 4/26/2022
Win	1	4/27/2022 to 4/27/2022
Loss	9	4/29/2022 to 5/8/2022
Win	2	5/9/2022 to 5/10/2022

Figure 5-53 *The goal is to count consecutive wins or losses.*

To create the baseball win/loss report, follow these steps:

1. Select the AsBaseballQ query in the Chapter05 group, select the last query step, AddDataTypes, right-click the Results column header, and select Group By.

2. In the Group By dialog box, shown in Figure 5-54, click the Advanced radio button, click the Add Aggregation button once, and then complete the dialog box as shown in the figure. (Notice that there is no dialog box option to set the group kind.) Click OK.

3. Name the query step LocalGrouping.

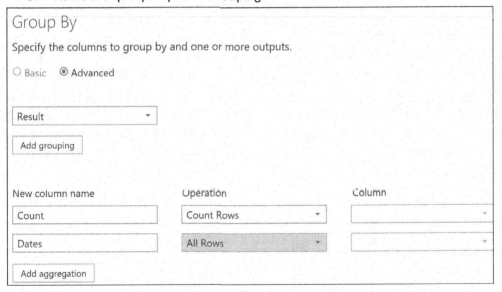

Figure 5-54 *When the operation is on the subtable, no column is needed.*

Figure 5-55 shows the result of this query: a unique list with just the two words Win and Loss.

	A^B_C Result	1²₃ Count	Dates
1	Loss	11	Table
2	Win	10	Table

Figure 5-55 *GroupKind.Global yields a unique list of losses and wins.*

4. To switch from the default GroupKind.Global to GroupKind.Local, edit the formula as shown in Figure 5-56, typing **, type text** after the second occurrence of the each keyword and typing **0** in the fourth argument of the Table.Group function.

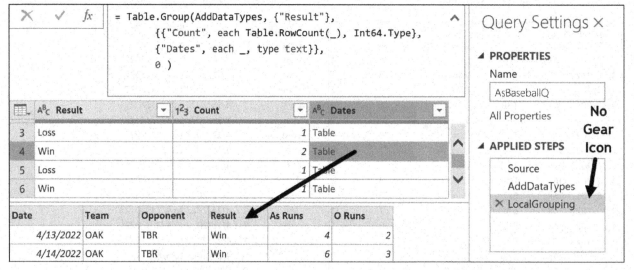

Figure 5-56 *The number 0 in the fourth argument created consecutive occurrence categories.*

In Figure 5-56, the Results column has a new set of grouping categories showing a single win or loss for each given streak, the Count column shows the correct count for each streak, and the Dates column contains a table of grouped records with a Date field that you can use for the date label.

Note: Notice that once you add the fourth argument (or fifth argument) to the Table.Group function, the editing gear icon next to the LocalGrouping step in the Applied Steps list disappears. This is because there is no option for the fourth or fifth arguments in the dialog box. All functions that use dialog boxes follow this rule: Add an argument that is not in the dialog box, and the editing gear icon disappears.

5. To create a date span label, you need to extract the minimum and maximum dates from each list of dates. The **List.Min** and **List.Max** functions can extract the minimum and maximum values, respectively, from an alphanumeric list of values that contains values such as numbers, dates, times, and even text values. To extract the minimum and maximum dates, start by editing the formula by replacing the underscore character after the second occurrence of the each keyword with _[Date]. The query will now extract a list of dates from the subtable.

6. As shown in Figure 5-57, wrap the List.Min function around the list of dates. Notice that when the formula is complete, the column is filled with the minimum date for the streak.

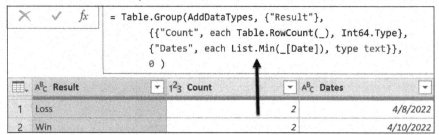

Figure 5-57 *List.Min extracts the minimum date from the list of grouped dates.*

As shown in Figure 5-58, if you try to join date values with text values, you get the error message "We cannot apply operator & to types Date and Text." As you saw back in Chapter 2, each data type has its own set of operators, and an operator rarely works with more than one data type. To amend the formula and convert the dates into text that can be joined with other text values, you can use the **Text.From** function to convert values such as numbers, dates, times, and other values into text representations of those values.

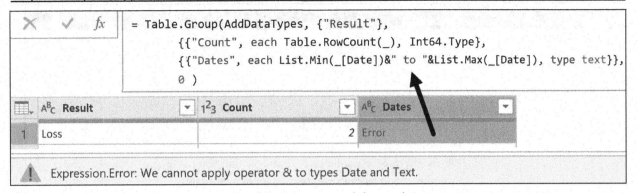

```
= Table.Group(AddDataTypes, {"Result"},
        {{"Count", each Table.RowCount(_), Int64.Type},
        {{"Dates", each List.Min(_[Date])&" to "&List.Max(_[Date]), type text}},
        0 )
```

ABC Result	123 Count	ABC Dates
1 Loss	2	Error

⚠ Expression.Error: We cannot apply operator & to types Date and Text.

Figure 5-58 *The join operator does not work to join text and date values.*

7. To create the correct date label for each streak, edit the formula for the label so it becomes:
    `Text.From(List.Min(_[Date])) & " to " & Text.From(List.Max(_[Date]))`

Figure 5-59 shows the finished formula and the finished report. The report shows that the Oakland A's had a nine-game losing streak between April 29, 2022, and May 8, 2022.

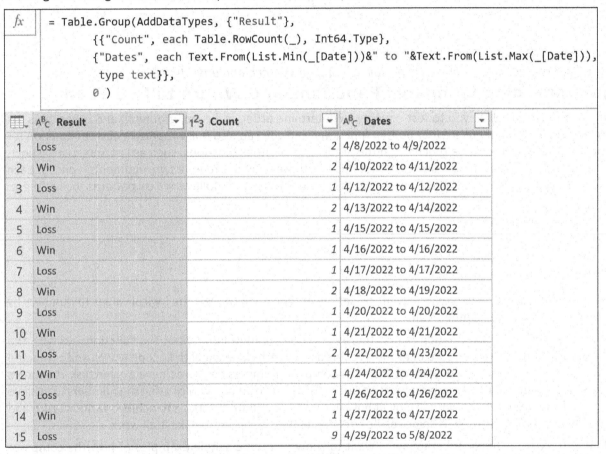

```
= Table.Group(AddDataTypes, {"Result"},
        {{"Count", each Table.RowCount(_), Int64.Type},
        {{"Dates", each Text.From(List.Min(_[Date]))&" to "&Text.From(List.Max(_[Date])),
         type text}},
        0 )
```

	ABC Result	123 Count	ABC Dates
1	Loss	2	4/8/2022 to 4/9/2022
2	Win	2	4/10/2022 to 4/11/2022
3	Loss	1	4/12/2022 to 4/12/2022
4	Win	2	4/13/2022 to 4/14/2022
5	Loss	1	4/15/2022 to 4/15/2022
6	Win	1	4/16/2022 to 4/16/2022
7	Loss	1	4/17/2022 to 4/17/2022
8	Win	2	4/18/2022 to 4/19/2022
9	Loss	1	4/20/2022 to 4/20/2022
10	Win	1	4/21/2022 to 4/21/2022
11	Loss	2	4/22/2022 to 4/23/2022
12	Win	1	4/24/2022 to 4/24/2022
13	Loss	1	4/26/2022 to 4/26/2022
14	Win	1	4/27/2022 to 4/27/2022
15	Loss	9	4/29/2022 to 5/8/2022

Figure 5-59 *Text.From converts the date values to text values.*

The Fifth Table.Group Argument: comparer

The **comparer** argument in the Table.Group function allows you to test equality and determine grouping categories with the comparer functions, as shown in Figure 5-60.

Function	Description
Comparer.Equals	Returns a logical value based on the equality check over the two given values.
Comparer.FromCulture	Returns a comparer function based on the specified culture (local in Regional settings) and case-sensitivity.
Comparer.Ordinal	Returns a comparer function which uses ordinal Unicode characters to compare values.
Comparer.OrdinalIgnoreCase	Returns a case-insensitive comparer function which uses ordinal Unicode characters to compare values.

Custom function	Allows you to build your own two variable function to compare values.
	Example: group by rows where date is not a null value:
	= Table.Group(AddDataTypes, {"Date"},
	    {{"Total Sales", each List.Sum([Amount]), type number}},
	    0, (InitialValue,CurrentRow) => Number.From(CurrentRow[Date]<>null))

Some of the functions that have arguments that can use these comparer functions are: List.Contains, List.ContainsAll, List.ContainsAny, List.Difference, List.Distinct, List.Intersect, List.IsDistinct, List.Max, List.MaxN, List.Min, List.MinN, List.Mode, List.Modes, List.PositionOf, List.PositionOfAny, List.RemoveMatchingItems, List.ReplaceMatchingItems, List.Sort, List.Union, Table.Contains, Table.ContainsAll, Table.ContainsAny, Table.Distinct, Table.Group, Table.PositionOf, Table.PositionOfAny, Table.RemoveMatchingRows, Table.ReplaceMatchingRows, Text.Contains, Text.EndsWith, Text.PositionOf, Text.StartsWith...

Figure 5-60 *Comparer functions used in Table.Group, List.Distinct, and other functions.*

Understanding Comparer Functions and Where to Use Them

Comparer functions allow you to test equality to determine order, inclusion, grouping, and other tasks. As shown in Figure 5-60, there are four built-in functions, and you can also build your own custom function for comparing. You can use these functions in the arguments of other functions, such as List.Sort, List.Distinct, and Table.Group. Microsoft's documentation states that these functions require two arguments—one for each value being compared—and that the number output for these functions follows logical patterns such as these:

```
If x > y then 1 else if x < y then -1 else 0
If x = y then 1 else 0
If x <> y then 1 else 0
If x > y then 1 else 0
If x < y then 1 else 0
```

If you build a custom function that delivers logical values, you must convert the logical values to numbers by using functions such as Number.From.

The problem with this explanation is that there is no documentation on what the functions do with the numbers 1, -1, and 0 to order, sort, or group. I scoured the internet, talked with M code MVPs, and contacted Microsoft, but I was not able to figure out how the comparer numbers help to achieve a given task. It appears that each function that uses comparer function output has its own unique way of using the numbers to achieve the given task. Nevertheless, we will look at how to use these helpful functions to achieve various tasks, and we will just assume that there is some magic going on under the hood to make it all work.

Before you try some hands-on examples, I want to show you three simple examples of how the comparer functions can be helpful for grouping. (Figures 5-61 to 5-69 help illustrate these three examples.) These examples can be found in the queries ComparerFromLocal, ComparerOrdinalIgnoreCase, and CustomFunction, in the Chapter05 group.

The **Comparer.FromCulture** function compares characters based on a culture or the locations determined by the regional setting on your computer. Its arguments are listed here:

```
Comparer.FromCulture(
    culture as text,
    optional ignoreCase as nullable logical) as function
```

The codes for the **culture** argument (called locale, or language, codes) are listed on the worksheet named Locale in the Excel file MCodeBook-Start.xlsx and at https://msdn.microsoft.com/en-us/library/cc233982.aspx. Three examples are en-US for US English, nn-NO for Norwegian, and zu-ZA for South African Zulu.

The culture argument uses the specified culture code to equate a character not in the specified culture to a character from the specified culture. **ignoreCase** allows you to specify true for ignore case and false for do not ignore case. For example, this function would equate the Norwegian Æ with the English characters AE if you used the code en-US or nn-NO. This function can be useful, for example, when you want to treat the company names Aerial Surveyor and Ærial Surveyor as equal for a grouping process. Figure 5-61 shows a simple table with a Text column that contains the letter Æ or the letters Ae. As shown in Figure 5-62, the Group By feature would treat the characters as different, but if you use the Comparer. FromCulture function in the Table.Group comparer function, as shown in Figure 5-63, the characters will be treated as equal. It is necessary to use true in the second argument to ignore case because of the English lowercase letter e.

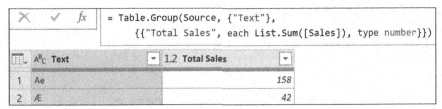

Figure 5-61 *The Norwegian character Æ and the English characters Ae.*

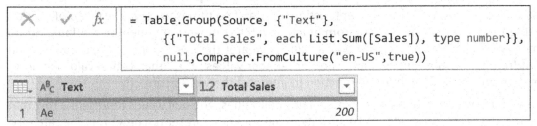

Figure 5-62 *The Group By feature treats the characters as different.*

```
= Table.Group(Source, {"Text"},
        {{"Total Sales", each List.Sum([Sales]), type number}},
        null,Comparer.FromCulture("en-US",true))
```

A^B_C Text	1.2 Total Sales
1 Ae	200

Figure 5-63 *Comparer.FromCulture treats the characters as the same.*

Comparer.OrdinalIgnoreCase can equate Unicode characters and ignore case. If you use this function in other function arguments, such as the comparer argument in the Table.Group function, you can use the function without arguments or the open and close parentheses (as you will see a little later on, in Figure 5-66). However, if you use it with the two values as functions arguments, you use the arguments shown here:

```
Comparer.OrdinalIgnoreCase(x as any, y as any) as number
```

When x > y, the function delivers 1; when x < y, the function delivers -1; and when x => y, the function delivers 0. When you use it with two items, the results are easy to interpret. Here are three examples:

```
= Comparer.OrdinalIgnoreCase("b","a") = (98 > 97) = 1
= Comparer.OrdinalIgnoreCase("a","b") = (97 < 98) = -1
= Comparer.OrdinalIgnoreCase("a","A") = (65 = 65) = 0
```

Remember that the function compares Unicode numbers. As mentioned earlier, however, when the function is used in arguments of other functions to compare columns of values, the results are correct, but it is difficult to interpret the number output.

Comparer Function Example: Using the Comparer.OrdinalIgnoreCase Function

Let's look at an example (which you can find in the ComparerFromLocal query in the Chapter05 group). Figure 5-64 shows a simple table with a Text column that contains the letter A and the letter a. As shown in Figure 5-65, the standard Group By feature would treat these characters as being different, but if you use the Comparer.OrdinalIgnoreCase function, as shown in Figure 5-66, the characters are treated as equal.

A^B_C Text	1.2 Sales
1 A	22
2 a	88

Figure 5-64 *A column containing the letter A and the letter a.*

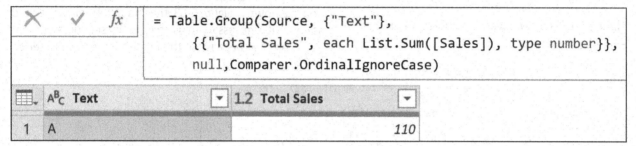

```
        ✗   ✓   fx     = Table.Group(Source, {"Text"},
                               {{"Total Sales", each List.Sum([Sales]), type number}})
```

⊞▾	A^B_C Text	▾	1.2 Total Sales	▾
1	A			22
2	a			88

Figure 5-65 *The Group By feature treats the A and a characters as being different.*

```
        ✗   ✓   fx     = Table.Group(Source, {"Text"},
                               {{"Total Sales", each List.Sum([Sales]), type number}},
                               null,Comparer.OrdinalIgnoreCase)
```

⊞▾	A^B_C Text	▾	1.2 Total Sales	▾
1	A			110

Figure 5-66 *Comparer.OrdinalIgnoreCase treats the characters A and a as being the same.*

Comparer Function Example: Building a Custom Comparer Function

Now let's look at how to build a custom comparer function. You can find this example in the CustomFunction query in the Chapter05 group. You can use a **custom function** in the comparer argument of the Table.Group function to equate two values or to check whether a value is greater than, less than, or equal to a second value. The output from the custom function must deliver number values rather than logical values in order for the comparer argument in the Table.Group function to interpret the values correctly.

Figure 5-67 shows a table with a Date column that contains null values. The null values represent a row that should be grouped with the previous date, and each date in the column represents a new grouping category. (This scenario happens in invoicing, as you will see later on.) There are two problems with grouping in this scenario.

⊞▾	▦ Date	▾	1.2 Sales	▾
1	2/22/2024			22
2	null			88
3	2/22/2024			70
4	null			20

Figure 5-67 *The null values should be grouped with the previous date.*

The first problem is that null and date values are different, and so they cannot be grouped together directly. You can solve this problem by building a custom function in the comparer argument that checks whether the value in the column is not a null value, where 1 (for true) indicates that the row is the start to a new grouping category and 0 (for false) indicates that the row is not the start to a new grouping category.

The second problem is that the two instances of the date 2/22/2024 in the Data column would normally be grouped together, rather than in different grouping categories. You can solve this second problem by using a 0 (for local grouping) in the groupKind argument, and the two dates will be treated as different grouping categories.

Figure 5-68 shows that the standard Group By feature does not group null values with previous dates. However, as shown in Figure 5-69, with a local grouping in the fourth argument and a custom function in the fifth argument, you can accomplish the complex grouping task.

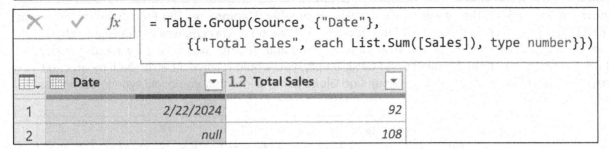

Figure 5-68 *The Group By feature treats the null and date values as being different.*

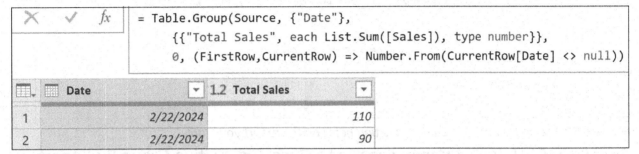

Figure 5-69 *The fourth and fifth arguments work to group nulls with previous dates.*

Comparer Function Example: Creating a Report with Characters from Different Cultures

Next, we're going to look at how to create a supplier cost report from a list of supplier names with characters from different cultures.

Figure 5-70 shows a table with supplier names and costs. The goal is to use grouping to get total costs and ignore the cultural differences in the letters in the Supplier column. To try this grouping task, follow these steps:

1. Select the SurveyCostsQ query in the Chapter05 group, select the last query step, AddDataTypes, and group by the Supplier column to get total costs. Figure 5-71 shows the result.

	ABC Supplier	1.2 Costs
1	Cœur Work Landscape	2100
2	Coeur Work Landscape	1522.36
3	Aerial Surveyor	3582.44
4	Ærial Surveyor	550.75
5	Æsthetic Landscape	1992.25
6	Cœur Work Landscape	481.26
7	Ærial Surveyor	1005.75
8	Coeur Work Landscape	250.99

Figure 5-70 *The Norwegian character Æ and the French character œ might cause problems.*

```
= Table.Group(AddDataTypes, {"Supplier"},
        {{"TotalCosts", each List.Sum([Costs]), type nullable number}})
```

	ABC Supplier	1.2 TotalCosts
1	Cœur Work Landscape	2581.26
2	Coeur Work Landscape	1773.35
3	Aerial Surveyor	3582.44
4	Ærial Surveyor	1556.5
5	Æsthetic Landscape	1992.25

Figure 5-71 *The Group By feature doesn't quite yield what you want.*

2. Edit the formula in the Formula Bar so that the fourth and fifth arguments of the Table.Group function become:
```
,null,Comparer.FromCulture("en-US",true)
```

As shown in Figure 5-72, the report to show costs by supplier is complete. The French character œ was equated to the English characters oe, and the Norwegian character Æ was equated to the English characters Ae. Notice that null was used in the fourth argument, groupKind. The null was necessary in order to skip the argument. If you skipped the argument and left it empty, you would receive an error. Null means that you accept the default, which in this case is GroupKind.Global, or 1. (Note that you could type fewer characters if you used 1 rather than null.)

```
X   ✓   fx    = Table.Group(AddDataTypes, {"Supplier"},
                    {{"TotalCosts", each List.Sum([Costs]), type nullable number}},
                    null,Comparer.FromCulture("en-US",true))
```

	A^BC Supplier	1.2 TotalCosts
1	Cœur Work Landscape	4354.61
2	Aerial Surveyor	5138.94
3	Æsthetic Landscape	1992.25

Figure 5-72 *The Comparer.FromCulture function gets you the report you want.*

Comparer Function Example: Creating a Case-Insensitive Group By Report

Next, let's look at how to create a case-insensitive group by report. Figure 5-73 shows a sales table with inconsistent case in the SalesRep column. To create a report that shows total sales by sales rep and ignores case, follow these steps:

1. Select the InconsistentCaseQ query in the Chapter05 group, select the last query step, AddDataTypes, and group by the SalesRep column to get total sales. Figure 5-74 shows the result.

	A^BC SalesRep	1²3 Sales
1	Sioux Rad	45
2	chantel Mims	98
3	Juniper Snap	59
4	sioux rad	39
5	Chantel mims	63

Figure 5-73 *The goal is to group by and ignore case in the SalesRep column.*

```
X   ✓   fx    = Table.Group(AddDataTypes, {"SalesRep"}, {{"Total Sales", each List.Sum(      ⌃
                    [Sales]), type number}},1,Comparer.OrdinalIgnoreCase)
```

	A^BC SalesRep	1.2 Total Sales
1	Sioux Rad	128
2	chantel Mims	223
3	Juniper Snap	132

Figure 5-74 *Comparer.OrdinalIgnoreCase allows you to group by and ignore case in the SalesRep column.*

2. Edit the formula in the Formula Bar so that the fourth and fifth arguments of the Table.Group function become:
    ```
    ,1,Comparer.OrdinalIgnoreCase
    ```

3. In Figure 5-74, notice that Comparer.OrdinalIgnoreCase takes the first occurrence of each case-insensitive item it encounters, and therefore, in the second row of the report, the sales rep's first name starts with a lowercase letter. If the case is not important in the final report, this may be exactly what you want. However, if you want the first letter in each name to be capitalized, you could transform the SalesRep column to proper case before you perform the grouping (by right-clicking the column header, hovering over Transform, and selecting Capitalize Each Word).

    Transforming to proper case and then grouping takes two query steps and is fast and easy to do. However, you can accomplish this this task in a single step. To transform to proper case and then group by using a single-step formula, select the CaseInsentiveGrouping query step, add a new step, and type the formula shown in Figure 5-75. Name the step ProperCaseGrouping. As shown in Figure 5-75, all the sales reps' names are now in proper case.

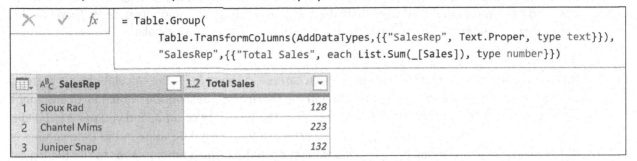

Figure 5-75 *This method transforms the names to proper case before grouping.*

Here are the arguments for the Table.TransformColumns function:

```
Table.TransformColumns(
    table as table,
    transformOperations as list,
    optional defaultTransformation as nullable function,
    optional missingField as nullable number) as table
```

The **table** argument contains the table to transform. The **transformOperations** argument contains one or more lists within a list, with each sublist containing the name of the column to transform, the function to make the transformation, and the data type for the column. In Figure 5-75, the transformOperations argument contains the **Text.Proper** function, which converts text to proper case. The **defaultTransformation** argument allows you to specify a transforming function for all columns not listed in transformOperations. If a column listed in transformOperations doesn't exist, the **missingField** argument allows you to specify an alternative to an error, such as MissingField.UseNull or MissingField.Ignore.

Comparer Function Example: Creating a Grouped Report Based on a Date Column with Empty Cells

Next, let's look at how to create a grouped transactional sales report based on a sales transaction table that is not set up for grouping.

The left side of Figure 5-76 shows a sales transaction dataset without a key column (a column that uniquely identifies the groups to be summarized) and without an invoice column to identify unique transactions. Grouping without a key column is difficult. However, it is not uncommon to see sales transactions, scientific data, or banking records that do not have a key column but that do contain a date column with null values like the one we have here. The right side of Figure 5-76 shows a grouped report that lists unique transactions.

Date	Description	Amount	→	Date	Description	Total Sales
2/14/2024	2 gallon paint	35		2/14/2024	2 gallon paint, Brushes	50
	Brushes	15		2/14/2024	Drop cloth, 10 gallon paint, HVLP hose, Brushes	164
2/14/2024	Drop cloth	5		2/15/2024	4 gallon paint, Brushes	58
	10 gallon paint	102		2/15/2024	Lacquer 4 gallon, Drop Cloth, Paint Sticks	76
	HVLP hose	35		2/16/2024	6 gallon paint, Buckets	83
	Brushes	22				
2/15/2024	4 gallon paint	43				
	Brushes	15				
2/15/2024	Lacquer 4 gallon	65				
	Drop Cloth	10				
	Paint Sticks	1				
2/16/2024	6 gallon paint	68				
	Buckets	15				

Figure 5-76 *The table on the right lacks a key column to identify unique transactions.*

To use the fourth and fifth arguments of the Table.Group function to create this report, follow these steps:

1. Select the fPaintStoreQ query in the Chapter05 group, select the last query step, AddDataTypes, invoke the Group By feature on the Date column, and add a new column named Descriptions that shows all rows and a column named Total Sales that adds the amounts from the Amounts column. Then edit the aggregate calculation for the Description column so that it matches this formula:

```
{"Description", each Text.Combine(_[Description],", "), type text}
```

2. Name the query step GroupByTotalSales. As you can see in Figure 5-77, the calculations are correct, but the grouping is not correct. You need to add the GroupKind.Local option in the fourth argument to allow duplicate dates like 2/14/2024 to appear in the final date column, and you need to build a custom function in the comparer argument to establish that each date value in the Date column is the beginning of a new grouping. The custom function in the fifth argument needs to run the logical test "is the value in the Date column not a null value?" With that logical test, each date will be the beginning of a new grouping.

```
= Table.Group(AddDataTypes, {"Date"},
        {{"Description", each Text.Combine(_[Description],", "), type text},
         {"Total Sales", each List.Sum([Amount]), type number}})
```

Date	Description	Total Sales
1	2/14/2024	2 gallon paint, Drop cloth	40
2	null	Brushes, 10 gallon paint, HVLP hose, Brushes, Br...	215
3	2/15/2024	4 gallon paint, Lacquer 4 gallon	108
4	2/16/2024	6 gallon paint	68

Figure 5-77 *The aggregate calculations are correct, but the grouping is not.*

3. To complete the formula, in the fourth argument of the groupKind argument, add a zero to perform the local grouping and then, in the fifth argument, create this formula:

```
(InitialValue, ArrayToIterate) => Number.From(ArrayToIterate[Date] <>
null)
```

Figure 5-78 shows the completed formula and report based on a dataset that did not have a proper key for grouping. In just a single query step, you performed a complex grouping task with ease. Table.Group and all of its arguments are great!

```
Local                   = Table.Group(AddDataTypes, {"Date"},
grouping                        {{"Description", each Text.Combine(_[Description],", "), type text},
                                 {"Total Sales", each List.Sum([Amount]), type number}},
                                 0,
Function                        (InitialValue, ArrayToIterate) => Number.From(ArrayToIterate[Date] <> null) )
```

Date	Description	Total Sales
1	2/14/2024	2 gallon paint, Brushes	50
2	2/14/2024	Drop cloth, 10 gallon paint, HVLP hose, Brushes	164
3	2/15/2024	4 gallon paint, Brushes	58
4	2/15/2024	Lacquer 4 gallon, Drop Cloth, Paint Sticks	76
5	2/16/2024	6 gallon paint, Buckets	83

Figure 5-78 *A complex grouping task completed in a single query step.*

Comparer Function Example: Grouping Data from a Single-Column Table

Finally, let's look at how to use the Table.Group function to group data that comes from a single-column table.

The dataset shown in Figure 5-79 is not properly structured for easy analysis. It is not uncommon to get data in this form.

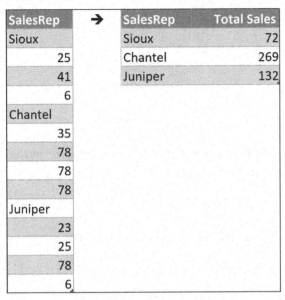

Figure 5-79 *The goal is to create a sales report by grouping data that is not in proper table format.*

If your goal is to group by SalesRep name, there are multiple ways to solve this problem. For example, you can use this five-step let expression to convert the data in Figure 5-79 into a sales report grouped by sales rep:

```
let
    Source = Excel.CurrentWorkbook(){[Name="GroupBadData"]}[Content],
    NewColumn = Table.AddColumn(Source, "Sales Reps",
        each if [SalesRep] is text then [SalesRep] else null),
    FillNamesDown = Table.FillDown(NewColumn,{"Sales Reps"}),
    FilteredOutText = Table.SelectRows(FillNamesDown, each not
    ([SalesRep] is text)),
    TotalSalesGroupBy = Table.Group(FilteredOutText, {"Sales Reps"},
        {{"Total Sales", each List.Sum([SalesRep]), type number}})
in
TotalSalesGroupBy
```

You can see this five-step method in the GroupBadDataFiveStep query in the Chapter05 group.

However, if you use the fifth argument in the Table.Group function, you can create a two-step query to accomplish the same goal By following these steps:

1. Select the GroupBadDataQ query in the Chapter05 group, select the first query step, Source, invoke the Group By feature on the SalesRep column (by using the button in the Home tab or the Transform tab), and add a new column named Total Sales that shows all rows. Name the query step GroupByTotalSales.

    As shown in Figure 5-80, the default global grouping worked on duplicate values; for example, there were two 25 values. But what you would really like to do is to group by the text values in the SalesRep column and gather up all the numbers below each text item. To accomplish this, you can build a comparer function that will run a logical test to see if items in the SalesRep column are text. When you do this, you will get three true values, one for each text item. This will not work for a global grouping because all three true values would be consolidated into one grouping. However, if you use a local grouping in the fourth argument, then each of the true values will be treated as a separate grouping—which is just what you want.

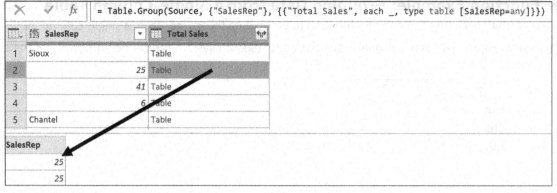

Figure 5-80 *GroupKind.Global creates a unique list and aggregates but is not what you want here.*

2.   To edit the formula, in the fourth argument of the groupKind argument, add a zero to perform the local grouping and then, in the fifth argument, create this formula (see Figure 5-81):

```
(InitialValue, ArrayToIterate) =>
    Number.From(ArrayToIterate[SalesRep] is text)
```

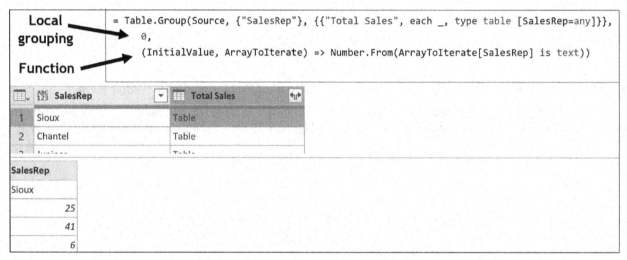

Figure 5-81 *Using GroupKind.Local and a function to identify text groupings is the next step.*

3.   As shown in Figure 5-82, to extract the grouped values as a list, edit the Total Sales aggregate list so that it becomes:

```
{"Total Sales", each _[SalesRep]}
```

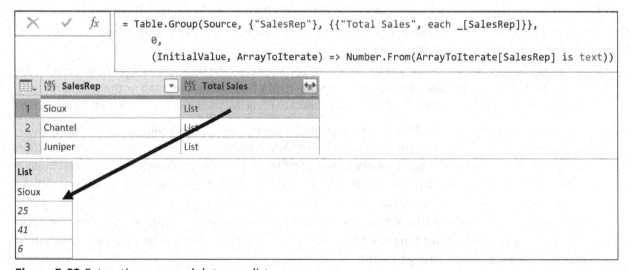

Figure 5-82 *Extracting grouped data as a list.*

4. As shown in Figure 5-83, to remove the first row from the list in each row, edit the Total Sales aggregate list so that it becomes:

```
{"Total Sales", each List.Skip(_[SalesRep])}
```

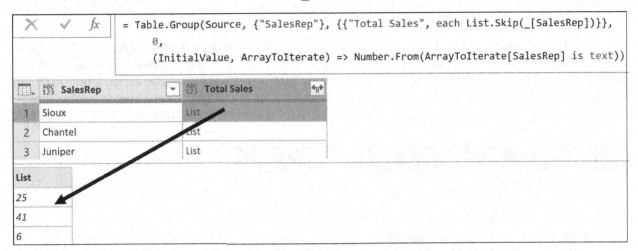

Figure 5-83 *Removing the first row from the list so that just numbers remain in the list.*

5. As shown in Figure 5-84, to add the list of numbers in each row, edit the Total Sales aggregate list so that it becomes:

```
{"Total Sales", each List.Sum(List.Skip(_[SalesRep]))}
```

Figure 5-84 shows the final report created from a column of sales rep names and sales data.

```
    fx    = Table.Group(Source, {"SalesRep"}, {{"Total Sales", each List.Sum(List.Skip(_[SalesRep]))}},
              0,
              (InitialValue, ArrayToIterate) => Number.From(ArrayToIterate[SalesRep] is text))
```

SalesRep	Total Sales
1 Sioux	72
2 Chantel	269
3 Juniper	132

Figure 5-84 *Including the Source step, the grouping task was accomplished in two steps.*

Other List Functions and Table.Sort, Too

There are some other functions that use comparer functions, including List.Sort, Table.Sort, List.Distinct, and List.Min and List.Max.

The List.Sort Function

List.Sort sorts the items in a list. Here are the arguments for this function:

```
List.Sort(
    list as list,
    optional comparisonCriteria as any) as list
```

The **list** argument contains the list of values to be sorted. The **comparisonCriteria** argument allows you to test equality and determine ordering for the sorting operation with functions from the table shown back in Figure 5-60 and with the options shown in Figure 5-85. In addition, there is a sort order for M code values. In ascending order, the sort order is null, time, date, datetime, datetimezone, duration, number, logical (false then true), text (Unicode numbers), binary (small to big). The M code values list, record, table, type, and function are not sorted unless you build a custom comparer function.

Consider these four List.Sort examples (which are available in the SortExamples query in the Chapter05 group):

```
List.Sort({null,43,100}) = {null,43,100}
List.Sort({null,43,100},1) = {100,43,null}
List.Sort({null,43,100},Order.Descending) = {100,43,null}
```

```
List.Sort({43,#date(2024,1,1),#date(2024,1,2),#time(09,10,10),
    #datetime(2024,1,1,09,10,10),true,false,"Terrific",
    #duration(2,2,2,2)}) =
{9:10:10 AM, 1/1/2024, 1/2/2024, 1/1/2024 9:10:10 AM, 2.02:02:02, 43, FALSE,
TRUE, Terrific}
```

Notice that in the fourth example, the datetime 1/1/2024 9:10:10 AM is sorted after 1/2/2024. In an Excel worksheet, 1/2/2024 would be sorted after 1/1/2024 9:10:10 AM because the underlying serial number is bigger. In a list or in a list that is converted to a table, 1/1/2024 9:10:10 AM would be sorted after 1/2/2024. However, if you tried to import mixed date and datetime values into Power Query, the data type feature would convert all the values to datetime, and then 1/2/2024 would be sorted after 1/1/2024 9:10:10 AM, as in the worksheet.

Option	Value	Description
Order.Ascending	0	Ascending, A-Z
Order.Descending	1	Descending, Z-A

Figure 5-85 *Options for the comparisonCriteria argument in the List.Sort function.*

The comparisonCriteria argument also allows you to enter a list with three arguments, as shown here:

```
{Transformer as function, Order as number, Comparer as function}
```

Here is an example of the use of this list in the Sort.List function to sort case-insensitive by last name:

```
= List.Sort(Table[First Last Name], {each Text.AfterDelimiter(_," "), 0, Com-
parer.OrdinalIgnoreCase})
```

Figure 5-86 shows a single-column table that contains a column with first and last names. If the goal is to sort by last name and ignore case, you can use the comparisonCriteria argument in List.Sort and enter a list with these three component parts:

```
{Transformer as function, Order as number, Comparer as function}
```

	ABC FirstLast
1	Sioux Rad
2	chantel Mims
3	Juniper Snap
4	Moham Fitz

Figure 5-86 *Data that needs to be sorted by last name, ignoring case.*

To try this example, follow these steps:

1. Select the LastNameSortQ query in the Chapter05 group, select the last query step, AddDataTypes, create a new query step, and type this formula:

   ```
   = List.Sort(AddDataTypes[FirstLast],
       {each Text.AfterDelimiter(_," ")})
   ```

2. Name the query step SortListByLastNameIgnoreCase.

3. As shown in Figure 5-87, the Text.AfterDelimiter function allows you to transform the text being sorted before the sort occurs. Notice that the last name mims starts with a lowercase letter and is therefore sorted to the bottom. You can fix this by adding the second and third components of the list, as shown in Figure 5-88:

   ```
   {each Text.AfterDelimiter(_," "),0,Comparer.OrdinalIgnoreCase}
   ```

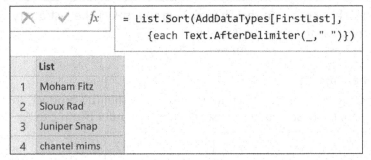

Figure 5-87 *Sorting the list by last name (with lowercase appearing at the end).*

Figure 5-88 shows the result of sorting the list by last name without considering case.

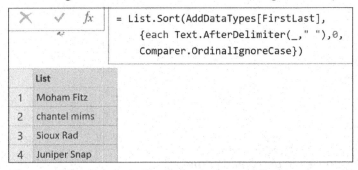

Figure 5-88 *Sorting the list by last name while ignoring case.*

The Table.Sort Function

The Table.Sort function can sort a table by one or more columns. The arguments for this function are shown here:

```
Table.Sort(
    table as table,
    comparisonCriteria as any) as table
```

However, the Table.Sort function does not allow the comparison functions shown back in Figure 5-60. The list that is allowed in the second argument has two components:

```
{Transformer as function or column name as any, Order as number}
```

In addition, because a table can have more than one column, you can sort by one or more columns. When you are sorting by more than one column, you use a list within a list in the second argument, as shown here:

```
{{function or column name, order},{function or column name, order}…}
```

The order of the columns entered in the list will determine the hierarchy of the sort order. For example, {{"Supplier", 1},{"Product",1}} would sort by supplier and then by product—that is, it would sort by product within supplier. To see Table.Sort in action, follow these steps:

1. To sort a column by last name, select the LastNameSortQ query, select the last step, SortListByLastNameIgnoreCase, and create the formula shown here:

    ```
    = Table.Sort(AddDataTypes,
        {each Text.AfterDelimiter([FirstLast], " "),1})
    ```

    Figure 5-89 shows the sorted table.

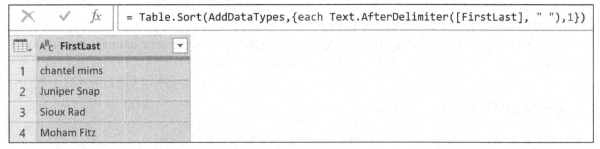

Figure 5-89 *The table column is sorted by last name.*

2. To sort by two columns, select the SortTableQ query in the Chapter05 group, select the last query step, AddDataTypes, create a new query step, and type this formula:

```
= Table.Sort(AddDataTypes,{{"Supplier",1},{"Product",1}})
```

3. Name the query step SortBySupplierThenProduct.

Figure 5-90 shows that the table is sorted first by supplier, in descending order, and then by product, in descending order, so that for each supplier, products are sorted in reverse alphabetical order (from Z to A).

	A^B_C Supplier	A^B_C Product	1^2_3 Sales
	= Table.Sort(AddDataTypes,{{"Supplier",1},{"Product",1}})		
1	Gel Booms	Sunset	72
2	Gel Booms	Quad	132
3	Gel Booms	Carlota	24
4	Gel Booms	Carlota	120
5	Colorado Booms	Yanaki	144
6	Colorado Booms	Aspen	12
7	Colorado Booms	Aspen	24

Figure 5-90 *The table is sorted by product within supplier, in descending order.*

The List.Distinct Function

The List.Distinct function can extract a unique list of values from a list. The arguments for this functions are shown below:

```
List.Distinct(
     list as list,
     optional equationCriteria as any) as list
```

The **list** argument contains the list of values from which duplicates are to be removed. The **equationCriteria** argument allows you to test equality and inclusion with the functions, as shown back in Figure 5-60. To see how it works, follow these steps:

1. To extract a unique list from a list of values, select the InconsistentCaseQ query, select the last step, ProperCaseGrouping, add a new query step, and create the formula shown here:

```
=List.Distinct(AddDataTypes[SalesRep],
     Comparer.OrdinalIgnoreCase)
```

2. Name the query step CaseInsentitiveDistinctList. Figure 5-91 shows the resulting distinct list.

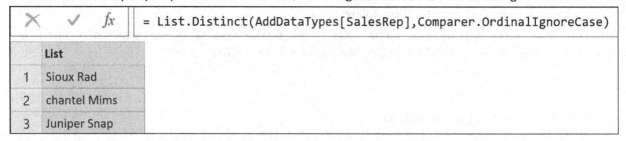

	List
	= List.Distinct(AddDataTypes[SalesRep],Comparer.OrdinalIgnoreCase)
1	Sioux Rad
2	chantel Mims
3	Juniper Snap

Figure 5-91 *This formula extracts a unique list and ignores case.*

3. To create a formula to convert the text to proper case first and then extract a unique list, add a new query step, name it ProperCaseDistinctList, and create this formula:

```
= List.Distinct(List.Transform(AddDataTypes[SalesRep],Text.Proper))
```

The result is shown in Figure 5-92.

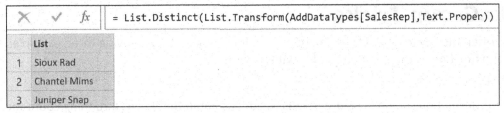

```
= List.Distinct(List.Transform(AddDataTypes[SalesRep],Text.Proper))
```

	List
1	Sioux Rad
2	Chantel Mims
3	Juniper Snap

Figure 5-92 *This formula converts to proper case and then extracts a unique list.*

The List.Min and List.Max Functions

The **List.Min** and **List.Max** functions can extract the minimum and maximum values from an alphanumeric list of values that contains values such as numbers, date, times, and even text values. The two functions have identical arguments. Although I show List.Min's functions here, List.Max's look just like this:

```
List.Min(
    list as list,
    optional default as any,
    optional comparisonCriteria as any,
    optional includeNulls as nullable logical) as any
```

The **list** argument contains the list of alphanumeric values from which the minimum value or maximum value should be extracted. The **default** argument contains the value to return if the list is empty. The **comparison-Criteria** argument may be specified to determine how to compare the items in the list, as shown in Figure 5-60. The **includeNulls** argument allows you to include (true) or exclude (false) null values. By default, the functions exclude null values. The Unicode numbering system is used to compare values.

Here is a large list of List.Min and List.Max examples (which you can find in the MinExamples query in the Chapter05 group):

```
List.Min({3,5}) = 3
List.Max({3,5}) = 5
List.Min({3,5,"a"}) = 3
List.Max({5000,"a"}) = a
List.Min({"A","a"}) = A
List.Max({"A","a"}) = a
List.Min({},"EmptyList") = Empty List
List.Max({},"EmptyList") = Empty List
List.Min({"a","A","b"},null,Comparer.OrdinalIgnoreCase) = a
List.Max({"A","a","B"},null,Comparer.OrdinalIgnoreCase) = B
List.Min({null,-2,5}) = -2
List.Max({null,-2,5}) = 5
List.Min({null,-2,5},null,null,true) = null
List.Max({null,-2,5},null,null,true) = 5
List.Min({null,-2,5},null,null,false) = -2
List.Max({null,-2,5},null,null,false) = 5
List.Min({true,false}) = false
List.Max({true,false}) = true
List.Min({#date(2023,1,1),#date(2022,1,1)}) = 1/1/2022
List.Max({#date(2023,1,1),#date(2022,1,1)}) = 1/1/2023
List.Min({#time(9,10,10),#time(10,10,10)}) = 9:10:10 AM
List.Max({#time(9,10,10),#time(10,10,10)}) = 10:10:10 AM
List.Min({#time(9,10,10),#date(2023,1,1),43,true,"a"}) = 9:10:10 AM
List.Max({#time(9,10,10),#date(2023,1,1),43,true,"a"}) = a
List.Min({[Product = "Quad", Sale = 100], [Product = "Sunset", Sale
    = 1000]}, null, (Amount) => Amount[Sale]) =
        [Product = "Aspen", Sale = 100]
List.Max({[Product = "Quad", Sale = 100], [Product = "Sunset", Sale
    = 1000]}, null, (Amount) => Amount[Sale]) =
        [Product = "Sunset", Sale = 1000]
```

Three Table.Group Tricks

The group by action is often the key to data transformations. The following sections provide three examples of using the Table.Group function as the key element for data analysis.

Running Count

The goal of the data transformation shown in Figure 5-93 is to add a column that keeps a running count for each product.

TransactionNo	Product	Sales		TransactionNo	Product	Sales	Running Count
203	Quad	305	→	203	Quad	305	1
204	Carlota	1021		204	Carlota	1021	1
205	Quad	854		205	Quad	854	2
206	Yanaki	560		206	Yanaki	560	1
207	Quad	1039		207	Quad	1039	3
208	Carlota	888		208	Carlota	888	2
209	Aspen	1263		209	Aspen	1263	1
210	Yanaki	139		210	Yanaki	139	2
211	Quad	1183		211	Quad	1183	4

Figure 5-93 *The goal is to get a running count for each product.*

Figure 5-94 shows the let expression that makes this transformation. The key to this transformation is the GroupAddTableIndex step, which groups together tables of related product records and then uses the Table. AddIndexColumn function to add an index to each subtable. The first argument in the **Table.AddIndexColumn** function contains the underscore syntax for the table of grouped records, the second argument contains the name of the new column, the third argument designates the starting index number, and the fourth argument designates the increment for the index count.

The CombineTables step combines the tables, and the SortBack step sorts the transaction numbers back to the original order. You can try this example in the RunningCount query in the Chapter05 group.

RunningCount

```
let
    Source = Excel.CurrentWorkbook(){[Name="TwoGroupByTricks"]}[Content],
    AddDataTypes = Table.TransformColumnTypes(Source,
        {{"TransactionNo", Int64.Type}, {"Product", type text}, {"Sales", Int64.Type}}),

    GroupAddTableIndex = Table.Group(AddDataTypes, {"Product"},
        {{"Count", each Table.AddIndexColumn(_,"Running Count",1,1)}}),

    CombineTables = Table.Combine(GroupAddTableIndex[Count]),
    SortBack = Table.Sort(CombineTables,"TransactionNo")
in
    SortBack
```

Underscore is table of grouped records

Table.AddIndexColumn adds running count for each sub table

Figure 5-94 *Creating an individual index column for each grouped table of records.*

Adding a Blank Row After Each Group

The goal of the data transformation shown in Figure 5-95 is to add a blank row after each set of grouped records. It is usually a bad idea to have blank rows in a table because blank rows make a table hard to use with data analysis tools. However, I show this example because it has been a common request over my decades of consulting. People really like the visual effect of a blank row to separate related records.

TransactionNo	Product	Sales
203	Quad	305
204	Carlota	1021
205	Quad	854
206	Yanaki	560
207	Quad	1039
208	Carlota	888
209	Aspen	1263
210	Yanaki	139
211	Quad	1183

→

TransactionNo	Product	Sales
203	Quad	305
205	Quad	854
207	Quad	1039
211	Quad	1183
204	Carlota	1021
208	Carlota	888
206	Yanaki	560
210	Yanaki	139
209	Aspen	1263

Figure 5-95 *Even though blank table rows cause problems, many people want them.*

Figure 5-96 shows the let expression that makes this transformation. The key to this transformation is the GroupAddNullRow step. This step groups tables of related product records together and then uses the intrinsic table function to add a blank row to the bottom of each grouped record table.

BlankRows

```
let
    Source = Excel.CurrentWorkbook(){[Name="TwoGroupByTricks"]}[Content],
    AddDataTypes = Table.TransformColumnTypes(Source,
        {{"TransactionNo", Int64.Type}, {"Product", type text}, {"Sales", Int64.Type}}),

    GroupAddNullRow = Table.Group(AddDataTypes, {"Product"},
        {{"Count", each _&#table(type table [Product],{{null}})}}),

    CombineTables = Table.Combine(GroupAddNullRow[Count])
in
    CombineTables
```

Underscore is table of
grouped records

Add intrinsic table with a
Product column and one
null to add full null row to

Figure 5-96 *Adding a blank row to the bottom of each grouped table of records.*

The function creates only a single column, Product, and the single record in the Product column contains null. When this one-column, one-row table is appended to the bottom of the grouped table, the Product column from the intrinsic table is matched with the Product column from the grouped record table, and a single null is added to the bottom of the Product column in the new appended table. Further, because the TransactionNo and Sales columns are missing from the intrinsic table, nulls are automatically added below the TransactionNo and Sales columns. (I originally learned this trick from Bill Szysz.)

The last step combines the tables and yields the desired result. You can try this example in the BlankRows query in the Chapter05 group.

Finding the Frequency for Class Combination Failed Grades

The goal of the data transformation shown in Figure 5-97 is to take a large sample of student grades and create a report that shows the frequency with which certain combinations of classes result in failed grades for all the classes in the combination. Advisors can use this type of report to advise students against taking those problematic combinations of classes. As you can see on the right in Figure 5-97, it looks like students taking math classes with English Composition 1 have the highest frequency of failure.

SID	Quarter	Class	Grade
AD43-9431	1999-Q2	Calculus	1.9
AD43-13653	2000-Q3	Origin Of Landforms	3.5
AD43-22906	2001-Q4	Essay Writing	1.6
AD43-7053	2003-Q3	Academy Programs	3.2
AD43-4695	2004-Q2	College Success Seminar	1.8
AD43-21676	2005-Q2	Intro To Psychology	3.4
AD43-20542	2005-Q3	Principles Of Marketing	3
AD43-12576	2006-Q2	Essentials Of Economics	0.2
AD43-22954	2006-Q2	Explore Comp Sci/W C++	1
AD43-1477	2007-Q3	Precalculus II	1
AD43-18255	2007-Q3	Intro to Sociology	3.1
AD43-11575	2008-Q1	Total Fitness	1.3
AD43-26158	2008-Q3	Esl 4:High Intermediate	3.9
AD43-21725	2008-Q4	Film Classics	3.8
AD43-2424	2008-Q4	Standard First Aid/CPR	1.8
AD43-26017	2009-Q2	Essentials Of Economics	0.5

Combination of Classes With Failed Grades	Frequency
College Algebra, English Composition I	6
Calculus I, English Composition I	4
College Algebra, Introduction To Stats	3
English Composition I, Introduction To Stats	3
English Composition I, Introduction To Stats, Spanish I	1
General Biology W/Lab, Introduction To Comm	1
Astronomy, Western Civilization I	1
English Composition I, General Psychology	1
English Composition I, Essentials Of Interm Alg	1
English Composition I, Principles of Accounting II	1

Figure 5-97 *What combinations of classes yield failed grades?*

Figure 5-98 shows the let expression and includes notes about what each step does. You can try this example in the StudentGradeDataQ query in the Chapter05 group.

StudentGradeDataQ

```
let
    Source = Excel.CurrentWorkbook(){[Name="StudentGradeData"]}[Content],
    AddDataTypes = Table.TransformColumnTypes(Source,{{"SID", type text},
        {"Quarter", type text}, {"Class", type text}, {"Grade", type number}}),
    RemoveFailedGrades = Table.SelectRows(AddDataTypes, each [Grade] < 0.7),       ← Filter out passing grades
    GroupByUniqueIDandQuarter = Table.Group(RemoveFailedGrades, {"SID", "Quarter"},   ← Group by ID and Quarter
        {{"Count", each Table.RowCount(_), Int64.Type},                            ← Count failed class
        {"Combination of Classes With Failed Grades", each Text.Combine(List.Sort(_[Class]),", ")}}),   ← Join class names

    FilteredOut1FailedClass = Table.SelectRows(GroupByUniqueIDandQuarter, each [Count] > 1),   ← Filter out just 1 failed class

    GroupByFailedClasses = Table.Group(FilteredOut1FailedClass, {"Combination of Classes With Failed Grades"},
        {{"Frequency", each Table.RowCount(_), Int64.Type}}),     ← Group by 2 or more failed classes and count

    SortFrequencyBigToSmall = Table.Sort(GroupByFailedClasses,{"Frequency",1})
in
    SortFrequencyBigToSmall
```

Figure 5-98 *Two group by query steps are the key to this query.*

Summary

In this chapter we have looked at common data transformation tasks, such as unpivoting, appending, joining, and grouping by. You have learned about using the Table.UnpivotOtherColumns function to unpivot cross-tabulated tables into proper tables. You have seen how to append tables from a column with the expand button and with the Table.Combine function. You have learned that the Table.NestedJoin function can perform six join operations: left outer, right outer, left anti, right anti, inner, and full outer. You have seen the power of using the Table.Group function for simple group by tasks with the user interface, complex group by tasks that involve hacking the user interface, and unusual group by tasks that use the fourth and fifth arguments of the Table.Group function. You have learned about using the Number.Round function to perform different types of rounding. You have also learned about using the comparer functions to include, order, sort, and group data, and you have seen that these functions can be used in the arguments of other functions, such as Table.Group, List.Sort, Table.Sort, List.Distinct, List.Min, and List.Max.

In Chapter 6, you will learn about data connector functions and how they allow you to import or connect to data from many different sources.

Chapter 6: Data Connectors

A data connector is an M code function that allows you to connect to a data source like an Excel file or an SQL Server database. One of the most amazing things about Power Query is that it has more than 110 data connectors (see https://learn.microsoft.com/en-us/power-query/connectors/).

Most of the time you do not need to write M code to connect to data because the user interface does a good job of writing it for you. However, there are a few data connector functions that I have found worth studying because they are useful in conjunction with the From Folder feature (and the Folder.Files and Folder.Contents functions), which you will learn about in Chapter 7.

In this chapter, you will see how to use data connector functions to import files in various formats, learn about on-premises file paths and how to avoid them by using dynamic file paths in Excel and Dataflows in the online Power BI service, and learn how to use the Local date feature to import data with dates from different countries. Finally, you will see how to connect to online data from Dataflows, the Web, an SQL Server database, and Power BI Workspaces.

CSV Files vs. Text Files

Since the beginning of databases over 50 years ago, files such as comma-separated values (CSV) files and text files have been used for moving data from one system to another system. A CSV file, which has the filename extension .csv, contains data that uses a comma as a delimiter. Figure 6-1 shows a CSV file with column names in the first row, separated by commas, and records of data in subsequent rows, also separated by commas.

```
Date,Sales,Product¶
1/23/25,1020.35,Quad¶
8/30/25,2305.75,Carlota¶
3/5/24,2054.23,Carlota¶
6/6/25,1639.34,Carlota¶
5/6/24,936.74,Aspen¶
8/31/25,856.93,Quad¶
```

Figure 6-1 *Comma-separated values in a CSV file.*

A text file, which has the extension .txt, contains data that uses a tab as a delimiter. Figure 6-2 shows a text file with column names in the first row, separated by tabs, and records of data in subsequent rows, also separated by tabs.

```
Date → Sales→Product¶
1/23/25   →   1020.35   →   Quad¶
8/30/25   →   2305.75   →   Carlota¶
3/5/24    →   2054.23   →   Carlota¶
6/6/25    →   1639.34   →   Carlota¶
5/6/24    →   936.74    →   Aspen¶
8/31/25   →   856.93    →   Quad¶
```

Figure 6-2 *Tab-separated values in a text file.*

Note: If you open a CSV file in Excel, even though it looks like an Excel file, it is still just a CSV file. For either a CSV file or a text file, if you want to see all the delimiters and hard returns, you can open the file in Word and turn on the nonprinting characters using the Show/Hide button.

Importing CSV Files

The **Csv.Document** function converts a text file that contains a specified delimiter into a table. By default, the function assumes a comma delimiter, but you can specify any delimiter you like, such as a tab character. The Csv.Document function extracts the data from the text file and converts it to a table.

The arguments for the Csv.Document function are shown here:

```
Csv.Document(
    source as any,
    optional columns as any,
```

```
optional delimiter as any,
optional extraValues as nullable number,
optional encoding as nullable number) as table
```

The **source** argument can accept CSV files and other text files with a specified delimiter.

The **columns** argument allows you to specify which columns to import and can accept null (all columns), the number of columns, a list of column names, a table type, or a record with up to five parameters. By default, all columns are imported. The columns argument can be helpful if you want to specify not all columns but just certain ones; you might do this, for example, to avoid needing to create later query steps to remove columns. If you enter 2 as the value for this argument and there are four columns, the two columns from the left are imported. You can also include a list of the names of columns to import; this way, you can pick and choose which columns you want to import, regardless of the order of the columns. If the number of columns in the source CSV file might change, you can omit the columns argument or you can use a null value to skip it; in either case, Csv.Document infers the number of columns each time the file is refreshed. We will look at the record and table options for the columns argument later.

The **delimiter** argument can accept almost any set of characters, but most CSV and text files use a comma or a tab character as the delimiter. In the delimiter argument, you can enter a single delimiter, a list of delimiters, or a list of fixed widths. Special delimiter characters require specific M code. For example:

- The delimiter for a carriage return is "#(cr)".
- The delimiter for a linefeed is "#(lf)".
- The delimiter for a tab is "#(tab)"
- The delimiter for consecutive white spaces is "".

The **extraValues** argument works with the columns argument to determine what happens to columns that are skipped. Here are the options that you can enter for this argument:

- **ExtraValues.List, or 0:** If the splitter function returns more columns than the table expects, those columns should be collected into a list.
- **ExtraValues.Error, or 1:** If the splitter function returns more columns than the table expects, an error should be raised. This is the default.
- **ExtraValues.Ignore, or 2:** If the splitter function returns more columns than the table expects, those columns should be ignored. If you remove columns by using the columns arguments, you probably want to use ExtraValues.Ignore, or the equivalent 2, so that you don't get an error.

The **encoding** argument specifies the text encoding type. For example, when you use Save As to save a CSV file, you can see the encodings for some file types in the Save As Type textbox. For example, the option CSV UTF-8 (Comma delimited) (*csv) indicates that the encoding is UTF-8. Here is a list of some of the many encodings:

- 65000, UTF-7, Unicode (UTF-7)
- 65001, UTF-8, Unicode (UTF-8). (This is the default.)
- 10001, X-Mac-Japanese, Japanese (Mac)
- 1252, Windows-1252, ANSI Latin 1; Western European (Windows)
- 865, IBM865, OEM Nordic; Nordic (DOS)

You can find a full list of encodings at https://learn.microsoft.com/en-us/windows/win32/intl/code-page-identifiers?redirectedfrom=MSDN.

As shown in Figure 6-3, you can provide a record in the columns argument that defines the five parameters Delimiter, Columns, Encoding, QuoteStyle, and CsvStyle. You can provide one to five parameters in a record; Figure 6-3 shows four of these parameters. If you use the user interface to import text files, the record in the columns argument is automatically generated.

```
X  ✓  fx     = Csv.Document(File.Contents("E:\MCodeExcelisfunBook\FruitSales.csv"),
                   [Delimiter=",", Columns=4, Encoding=65001, QuoteStyle=QuoteStyle.None])
```

ABC Column1	ABC Column2	ABC Column3	ABC Column4
1 Date	Fruit	Sales	Customer
2 1/2/2025	Apple	500	Jun
3 1/3/2025	Orange	600	Iggy
4 1/2/2025	Apple	450	Lim
5 1/4/2025	Orange	375	Ty

Figure 6-3 *You can specify a record with parameters in the columns argument.*

Let's look at each of the five parameters:

- **Delimiter:** You can set a tab delimiter in a record like this:
  ```
  Delimiter="#(tab)"
  ```

- **Columns:** You can set the number of columns to import like this:
  ```
  Columns=3
  ```

  If you anticipate that the number of columns might change, you can omit the Columns parameter to accommodate a varying number of columns.

- **Encoding:** You can set the text encoding type, like this:
  ```
  Encoding=65001
  ```

- **QuoteStyle:** You can specify how quoted line breaks are handled, using one of two options (see Figure 6-4):
  - **QuoteStyle.None, or 0:** Quoted line breaks are ignored. This is the default.
  - **QuoteStyle.Csv, or 1:** All line breaks are applied.

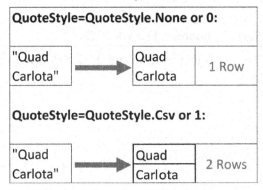

Figure 6-4 *The QuoteStyle argument defines how line breaks are interpreted.*

- **CsvStyle:** You can specify how quotes are handled with one of two options:
  - **CsvStyle.QuoteAfterDelimiter, or 0:** Quotes in a field are only significant immediately following the delimiter. This is the default. If you use this option to import a record with 43 and "Rad", for example, Figure 6-5 shows that the quotes around the word Rad are included in column 2.
  - **CsvStyle.QuoteAlways, or 1:** Quotes in a field are always significant, regardless of where they appear. If you use this option to import a record with 43 and "Rad", for example, Figure 6-6 shows that the quotes around the word Rad are not included in column 2.

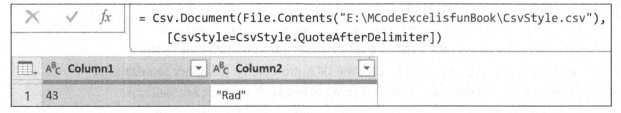

```
X  ✓  fx     = Csv.Document(File.Contents("E:\MCodeExcelisfunBook\CsvStyle.csv"),
                   [CsvStyle=CsvStyle.QuoteAfterDelimiter])
```

ABC Column1	ABC Column2
1 43	"Rad"

Figure 6-5 *The option CsvStyle.QuoteAfterDelimiter allows you to import quotation marks.*

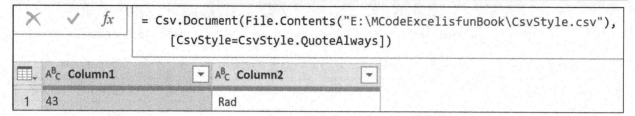

Figure 6-6 *CsvStyle.QuoteAlways allows you to ignore quotation marks.*

As shown in Figure 6-7, you can provide a table in the columns argument that defines the column names and data types for each column. However, I have not found a good use for this because although data types are defined at the top of each column, the data is still all text. In Figure 6-7, the sales numbers are aligned left and are text values. If you try to add the numbers, you will get an error.

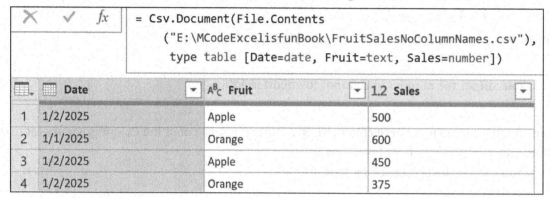

Figure 6-7 *A table in the columns argument of Csv.Document defines column names.*

Now that you have learned about the Csv.Document function, you're ready to try an example. In this case, you will import data from the file SalesData.csv, which is a file in the folder MCodeExcelisfunBook that you downloaded. To import a comma-separated sales file, follow these steps:

1. In the Power Query Editor, select the Chapter06 group and then, in the Home tab, go to the New Query group, click the New Source dropdown arrow, hover over the File option, and click Text/CSV.

2. In the Import Data dialog box, navigate to the SalesData.csv file, select the file, and then click Open. Figure 6-8 shows the SalesData.csv dialog box that appears.

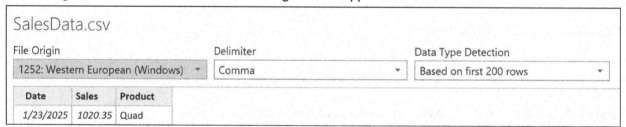

Figure 6-8 *Dialog box used to import CSV data through the user interface.*

3. In the SalesData.csv dialog box, select from the File Origin dropdown arrow to set the encoding parameter, select from the Delimiter dropdown arrow to set the delimiter parameter, and select one of these options from the Data Type Detection dropdown arrow:

    • Based on First 200 Rows (This option is usually sufficient.)

    • Based on Whole Data Set (This option might slow down the query when there is a lot of data.)

    • Do Not Detect Data Types

    The option selected does not appear in the resulting record in the columns argument of the Csv. Documents function, but it does help set data types in subsequent query steps.

4. When the parameters are correct, click the OK button. Name the query SalesDataCsv.

5. In Excel, load the query as a connection only. In Power BI, uncheck Enable Load.

Figure 6-9 shows the result of the user interface CSV file import. Three query steps are automatically created for you (unless you have data type detection turned off): Source, Promoted Headers, and Changed Type.

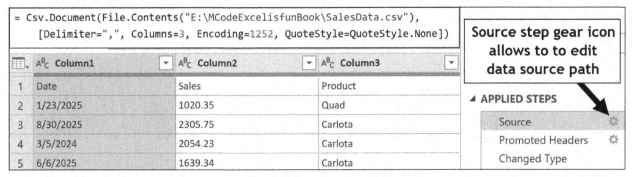

Figure 6-9 *A record with parameters is created in the columns argument.*

> **Note:** You can turn off automatic data type detection in the Power Query Editor by going to File, Options and Settings, Query Options, Data Load and then unchecking Detect Column Types and Headers for Unstructured Sources.

The first query step that is created for you, Source, uses the Csv.Document and File.Contents functions. The **File.Contents** function gets the contents of the file and is used inside many data connector functions, such as Csv.Document, Excel.Workbook, Json.Document, and Xml.Tables. Inside the File.Contents functions is an on-premises file path, which is a hard-coded file path that is unique to your computer.

The second and third steps, Promoted Headers and Changed Type, are automatically created when you select the option Based on First 200 Rows from the Data Type Detection dropdown arrow.

On-Premises File and Folder Paths

As shown in Figure 6-9, in the Source query step, in the first argument of the File.Contents function, the file path for the SalesData.csv file is hard-coded into the formula. When you hard-code a file path into a query, if you move that source data file to a different location, or if you e-mail the file that contains the query to a colleague, the connection to the source data is broken, and you receive the error "Data Source Not Found."

When you hard-code a file or folder path into a query, the path is called an **on-premises path**. As you can imagine, on-premises paths cause a lot of trouble if you are sharing files or moving files around. An online data source—such as an SQL Server database, Dataflow, or Power BI—does not have this problem because the data is stored online, in a location that does not move. Multiple credentialed people can have access to "a single source of truth," where there are no on-premises paths and no conflicts with multiple versions of the same file. Nevertheless, not all data is stored online, and on-premises paths are common.

The good news is that if you know where the source data file is, it is easy to redirect the query to the new location. There are at least three ways to change the on-premises path:

- In the Source step for almost any query, you can edit the on-premises path in the Formula Bar.
- As shown in Figure 6-9, you can click the gear icon in the Source query step to open the source data dialog box. Many data sources—such as CSV, Excel, SQL Server databases, websites, and more—allow you to use the gear icon in the Source query step to edit the connection details. As shown in Figure 6-10, the source data dialog box for the SalesDataCsv Source query step allows you to edit the parameters for the CSV file import.

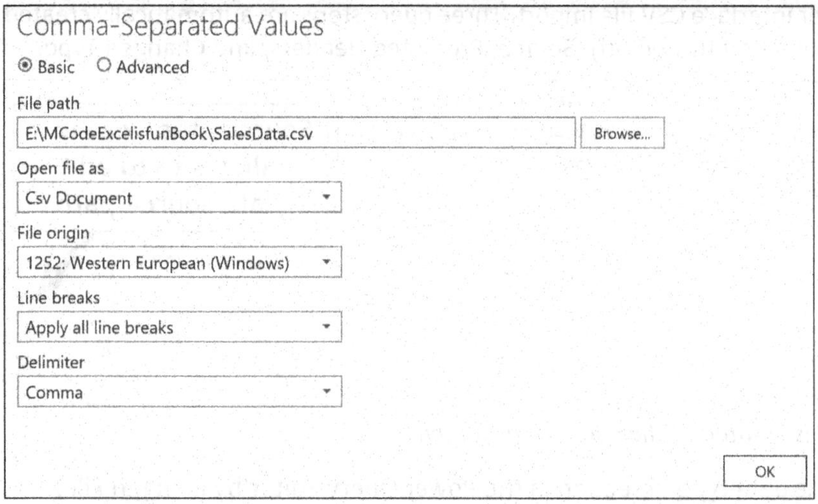

Comma-Separated Values

⦿ Basic   ○ Advanced

File path

| E:\MCodeExcelisfunBook\SalesData.csv | Browse... |

Open file as

Csv Document   ▼

File origin

1252: Western European (Windows)   ▼

Line breaks

Apply all line breaks   ▼

Delimiter

Comma   ▼

OK

Figure 6-10 *The source data dialog box for the Sales.csv file.*

- If you have used the same file or folder in multiple queries, it is most efficient to edit the path universally in the Data Source Settings dialog box. There are multiple ways to open this dialog box in Excel and Power BI:
  - **Excel Power Query Editor:** On the Home tab, go to the Data Sources group and click the Data Source Settings button.
  - **Power BI Desktop Power Query Editor:** On the Home tab, go to the Data Sources group, click the Transform Data dropdown, and then click Data Source Settings.
  - **Dataflow Power Query Editor:** On the Home tab, go to the Data Sources group and click the Manage Connections button.

Data Source Settings

Figures 6-11 and 6-12 show the Data Source Settings dialog box, which is the same in Excel and Power BI Desktop. In Dataflow, this dialog box is slightly different as it contains only online sources.

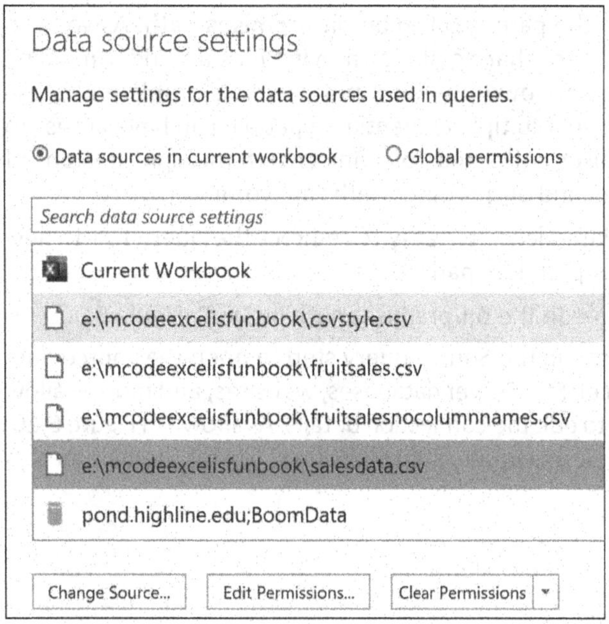

Data source settings

Manage settings for the data sources used in queries.

⦿ Data sources in current workbook   ○ Global permissions

Search data source settings

🗎	Current Workbook
🗋	e:\mcodeexcelisfunbook\csvstyle.csv
🗋	e:\mcodeexcelisfunbook\fruitsales.csv
🗋	e:\mcodeexcelisfunbook\fruitsalesnocolumnnames.csv
🗋	e:\mcodeexcelisfunbook\salesdata.csv
🗑	pond.highline.edu;BoomData

| Change Source... | Edit Permissions... | Clear Permissions ▼ |

Figure 6-11 *Data Source Settings dialog for sources in the current workbook (or Power BI file).*

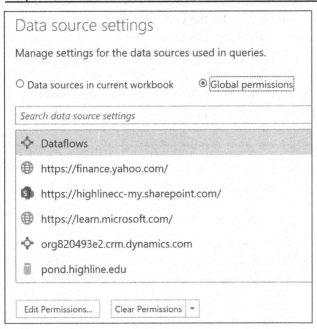

Figure 6-12 *Data Source Settings dialog global permissions.*

Figure 6-11 shows data sources in the current workbook (or Power BI file), and Figure 6-12 shows global data sources that have been used in other files. The Change Source button allows you to change the path for the selected on-premises file. Edit Permissions and Clear Permissions allow you to edit and clear credentials for online data sources or other sources that require credentials. When you use the same file in many queries, it is convenient to have one universal location to edit and change the file or folder path. In addition, if your credentials for an online source have changed, or if you want to clear a permission, these dialog boxes are convenient.

Dynamic Folder and File Locations in Excel

If you are working in Excel, there is a great method you can use to create dynamic, self-updating folder and file paths so that you don't have to use an on-premises folder or file path. However, for this method to work, when the source data file moves to a new location, the destination file (the file that imports the source data) must move to the same location. I use this method often when I provide Power Query solutions to students or clients who must save the files in a new location, and I describe it in this section. In Chapter 7 I will show you a similar method that involves a SharePoint online storage location, and later in this chapter, I will show you an example of how to use Dataflow to create a dynamic file path.

In this section, you will see how to use Excel to create a dynamic folder path that can be used to dynamically connect to a folder or files within that folder. To do this, you will use the CELL worksheet function, which can automatically determine the complete file or folder path for the workbook file where this function is used. For this example, you will use the destination file DynamicFolderPath.xlsx and the data source file SalesDataDynamic.csv, which are both in the folder named DynamicFolderPath. To create a dynamic folder path to DynamicFolderPath, follow these steps:

1. In the downloaded folder MCodeExcelisfunBook, open the folder named DynamicFolderPath and then, from within that folder, open the Excel file DynamicFolderPath.xlsx as the destination file.

2. Go to the FolderPath worksheet, click in cell B2, and create the formula shown in Figure 6-13. Be sure to anchor the formula by entering the cell reference B2 (yes, the same cell where the formula sits) into the reference argument in the CELL function.

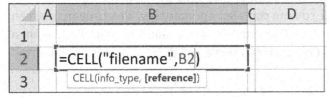

Figure 6-13 *The CELL worksheet function can return the file path for the workbook file.*

As shown in Figure 6-14, the CELL function returns the file path for the Excel file. The path on your computer will be different from what I show here (unless you have the downloaded folder on a drive named E). On my computer, the path is as follows: E drive, MCodeExcelisunBook folder, DynamicFolderPath folder, DynamicFolderPath.xlsx file, FolderPath worksheet. This path will update no matter where the file is moved. However, you do not need the full file path; all you need is the folder path before the worksheet and file reference. Notice that the file reference is in square brackets and that the folder path sits before the open square bracket, [.

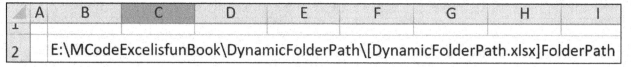

Figure 6-14 *The file path on my computer may be different than the file path on your computer.*

3. Edit the formula as shown in Figure 6-15 to extract the folder path before the open square bracket. The **TEXTBEFORE** worksheet function you use here extracts text from a text string before a delimiter (in this case, [). Figure 6-16 shows the resultant folder path: E:\MCodeExcelisfunBook\ DynamicFolderPath\.

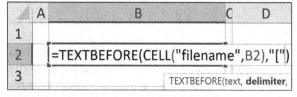

Figure 6-15 *This formula creates a dynamic folder path in the worksheet.*

4. As shown in Figure 6-16, with cell B2 selected, click in the Name Box, type FolderPath, and then press Enter. Excel creates a defined name that references cell B2 and that can be imported into Power Query.

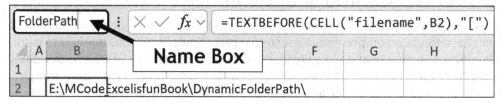

Figure 6-16 *Excel defined names can be imported into Power Query.*

Next, you need to import the defined name into the Power Query Editor. To import objects such as Excel tables, defined names, or array objects from within the current workbook into the Power Query Editor, you can use the Excel.CurrentWorkbook M code function. This argumentless function delivers a table of objects and unique names for each object. Once you import the table of objects, you can use a key match two-way lookup (which you learned about in Chapter 4) to extract the defined name.

5. To import the defined name, open the Power Query Editor by using the keyboard shortcut Alt+F12.
6. Select the Chapter06 group and create a blank query. Name the query DynamicFolderPath.
7. In the Formula Bar type this formula:

```
= Excel.CurrentWorkbook()
```

As shown in Figure 6-17, the Excel.CurrentWorkbook function creates a table with a Content column that contains all the workbook objects and a Name column that contains a unique name for each object. As you learned in Chapter 4, the Name column contains a primary key, which means you can use a key match lookup. In Figure 6-17, row 2 of the Content column contains the FolderPath defined name as a table with a single column named Column1. (All single-cell defined names are imported with the default name Column1.)

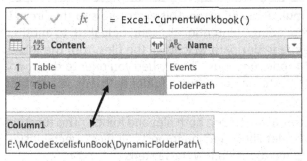

Figure 6-17 *Excel.CurrentWorkbook() imports all objects from the current workbook.*

8.   To look up the defined name, create the formula shown in Figure 6-18 and notice that the formula returns a row (a record) from the table that the Excel.CurrentWorkbook function created.

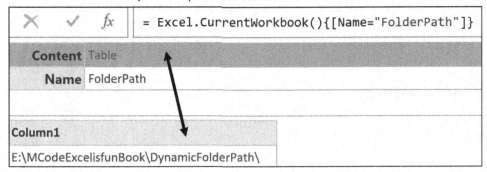

Figure 6-18 *A key match lookup to extract the FolderPath row.*

9.   To extract the table from the Content column, create the two-way lookup formula shown in Figure 6-19. When you import a defined name, because it is not an Excel table with field names in the first row, Power Query creates a table with the default field name Column1. In this, because the define name was for a single cell, the content of that single cell was imported and delivered in a one-column, one-row table. The defined name is for the cell that contained the content E:\MCodeExcelisfunBook\DynamicFolderPath\.

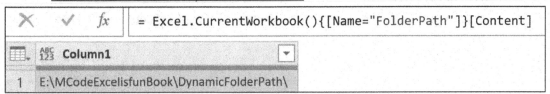

Figure 6-19 *A two-way lookup to extract the defined name table.*

10.   To extract the dynamic folder path using a two-way lookup, create the formula shown in Figure 6-20. Notice that because there will always be only one row in a single-cell defined name, you can use a row match lookup and hard-code the 0 into the formula.

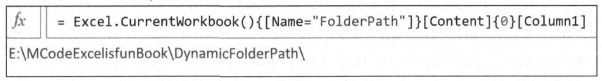

Figure 6-20 *A two-way lookup to retrieve the dynamic folder path.*

> **Note:** When you create a dynamic folder path with manually created M code, you see the following message in the Data Source Settings dialog box: "Some data sources may not be listed because of hand-authored queries." Luckily, you will not need to use that dialog box to change the path anyway!

Folder.Contents vs. Folder.Files

As shown in Figure 6-20, the DynamicFolderPath query delivers the dynamic folder path. At this point, you might want to be able to load the query and use this folder path directly in other queries. However, if you use a direct folder path in another query, you will get a **Formula.Firewall error**. This error refers to the firewall that exists in M code to prevent data from one source from being unintentionally sent, or leaked, to another source. The way you will get around this error is to use the folder path to load all the files from the folder into a table by using the Folder.Contents or Folder.Files M code functions. Then, when you refer to the query in other queries, because it is not a direct reference to the external data source folder path, you will not get the error.

The **Folder.Contents** function imports all content directly inside the folder: both files and folders. This function does not retrieve any files from within subfolders. The **Folder.Files** function imports all files directly inside the folder and from within all subfolders. To try out these functions, follow these steps:

1. Create the formula shown in Figure 6-21. This formula returns a table with Content, Name, Extension, and other columns. Notice that the Extension column shows only some rows with extensions. The rows without extensions are the rows with folders.

```
= Folder.Contents(
    Excel.CurrentWorkbook(){[Name="FolderPath"]}[Content]{0}[Column1]
)
```

	Content	Name	Extension	Date acc
1	Binary	DynamicFolderPath.xlsx	.xlsx	3/8
2	Table	OtherFiles		3/8
3	Binary	SalesDataDynamic.csv	.csv	3/8
4	Binary	~$DynamicFolderPath.xlsx	.xlsx	3/8

Figure 6-21 *Folder.Contents imports files and folders.*

2. Edit the formula so it looks like the one shown in Figure 6-22. Notice that all rows in the Extension column contain extensions. This is because the function imported all files directly inside the folder and from within all subfolders.

```
= Folder.Files(
    Excel.CurrentWorkbook(){[Name="FolderPath"]}[Content]{0}[Column1]
)
```

	Content	Name	Extension	Date acc
1	Binary	DynamicFolderPath.xlsx	.xlsx	3/8
2	Binary	SalesDataDynamic.csv	.csv	3/8
3	Binary	~$DynamicFolderPath.xlsx	.xlsx	3/8
4	Binary	OtherData.csv	.csv	3/8
5	Binary	OtherData.txt	.txt	3/8
6	Binary	OtherData.xlsx	.xlsx	3/8

Figure 6-22 *Folder.Files imports all files from the folder and all subfolders.*

3. In Excel, load the query as a connection only. In Power BI, uncheck Enable Load.

> **Note:** When you use Folder.Files, if you have files with the same name in the top folder and in subfolders, you have duplicate filenames in the Name column, which will prevent you from using a key match lookup. However, sometimes when you are appending tables, it is not an issue to have duplicate filenames.

Now that you have a dynamic connection to a folder and have brought all the files from that folder into a table, you can reference this query to get any one of the files, and the connection will be dynamic. In addition, you can use the DynamicFolderPath query as often as you like.

4. Next, you need to dynamically connect to the file named SalesDataDynamic.csv, which contains more than 100,000 rows of sales data. To start, reference the DynamicFolderPath query and create a dynamic file path by going to the Queries pane, right-clicking the DynamicFolderPath query, and selecting Reference. Name the new query DynamicCsvPath. Figure 6-23 shows the result.

Queries [2]	Content	Name	Extension
DynamicFolderPa...			
DynamicCsvPath			

= DynamicFolderPath

#	Content	Name	Extension
1	Binary	DynamicFolderPath.xlsx	.xlsx
2	Binary	SalesDataDynamic.csv	.csv
3	Binary	~$DynamicFolderPath.xlsx	.xlsx
4	Binary	OtherData.csv	.csv
5	Binary	OtherData.txt	.txt
6	Binary	OtherData.xlsx	.xlsx

Figure 6-23 *The formula to reference a query is simply the name of the referenced query.*

Note: There is a difference between referencing a query and duplicating a query. **Referencing** a query involves creating a new query by referencing an existing query. When the referenced query changes, the new query changes also. **Duplicating** a query involves creating a new query by copying the underlying code from another query. When the copied query changes, the new query does not change.

5. To perform a two-way lookup to retrieve the data source file named SalesDataDynamic.csv, edit the Source step formula so it becomes:

```
= DynamicFolderPath{[Name="SalesDataDynamic.csv"]}[Content]
```

6. In Excel, load the query as a connection only. In Power BI, uncheck Enable Load.

When you finish the formula and press Enter, three extra steps are added because Power Query understands that this is a CSV file. Figure 6-24 shows the resulting table and the four query steps.

#	Date	Sales	Product
1	1/23/2025	108.21	Quad
2	8/30/2025	3955.29	Carlota
3	3/5/2024	1073.91	Carlota
4	6/6/2025	1682.13	Carlota
5	5/6/2024	2070.03	Aspen
6	8/31/2025	3627.82	Quad
7	7/19/2025	3488.95	Carlota
8	7/18/2025	1298.81	Yanaki
9	5/16/2024	4354.02	Carlota

PROPERTIES
Name
DynamicCsvPath
All Properties

APPLIED STEPS
Source
Imported CSV
Promoted Headers
× Changed Type

Figure 6-24 *Power Query knows this is a CSV file and adds three useful query steps.*

Figures 6-25 to 6-28 illustrate the query steps. Figure 6-25 shows that the lookup formula extracts the CSV file from the DynamicFolderPath table. Figure 6-26 shows that the first automatic step uses the Csv.Document function with a record in the second argument to define the parameters of the conversion from a file to a table. Figure 6-27 shows the use of the Table.PromoteHeaders function to promote the first row text to column headers, and Figure 6-28 shows the use of the Table.TransformColumnTypes function to add a data type to each column.

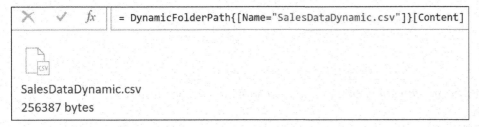

```
= DynamicFolderPath{[Name="SalesDataDynamic.csv"]}[Content]
```

SalesDataDynamic.csv
256387 bytes

Figure 6-25 *In the first query step, the two-way lookup formula returns the CSV file.*

```
= Csv.Document(Source,
    [Delimiter=",", Columns=3, Encoding=1252, QuoteStyle=QuoteStyle.None])
```

Column1	Column2	Column3
1 Date	Sales	Product
2 1/23/2025	108.21	Quad

Figure 6-26 *In the second query step, the Csv.Document function retrieves the table.*

```
= Table.PromoteHeaders(ImportedCSV, [PromoteAllScalars=true])
```

Date	Sales	Product
1 1/23/2025	108.21	Quad

Figure 6-27 *In the third query step, the Table.PromoteHeaders function promotes headers.*

```
= Table.TransformColumnTypes(PromoteHeaders,
    {{"Date", type date}, {"Sales", type number}, {"Product", type text}})
```

Date	1.2 Sales	Product
1	1/23/2025	108.21 Quad

Figure 6-28 *In the fourth query step, the Table.TransformColumnTypes function adds data types.*

To test whether the dynamic folder path works, I moved the folder named DynamicFolderPath—which contains both the destination file, DynamicFolderPath.xlsx, and data source file, SalesDataDynamic.csv—to a different computer. As you can see in Figure 6-29, when I open the destination file, the formula delivering the dynamic folder path reflects the new file path. Figure 6-30 shows that the DynamicCsvPath query updates to the new file path. Figure 6-31 shows the error you get if you use an on-premises file path and then move the destination file to a new location. You should try this experiment on your own computers to see what results you get.

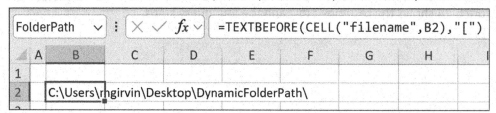

FolderPath   =TEXTBEFORE(CELL("filename",B2),"[")

	A	B	C	D	E	F	G	H	
1									
2		C:\Users\rhgirvin\Desktop\DynamicFolderPath\							

Figure 6-29 *When the destination file is moved, the worksheet folder path updates.*

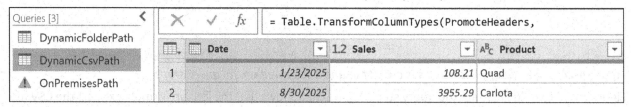

Queries [3]
- DynamicFolderPath
- **DynamicCsvPath**
- ⚠ OnPremisesPath

```
= Table.TransformColumnTypes(PromoteHeaders,
```

Date	1.2 Sales	Product
1	1/23/2025	108.21 Quad
2	8/30/2025	3955.29 Carlota

Figure 6-30 *The dynamic folder path query to import the CSV file works perfectly.*

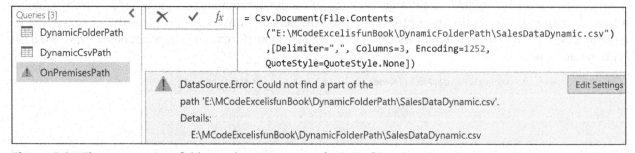

Queries [3]
- DynamicFolderPath
- DynamicCsvPath
- ⚠ **OnPremisesPath**

```
= Csv.Document(File.Contents
    ("E:\MCodeExcelisfunBook\DynamicFolderPath\SalesDataDynamic.csv")
    ,[Delimiter=",", Columns=3, Encoding=1252,
    QuoteStyle=QuoteStyle.None])
```

⚠ DataSource.Error: Could not find a part of the   [Edit Settings]
path 'E:\MCodeExcelisfunBook\DynamicFolderPath\SalesDataDynamic.csv'.
Details:
    E:\MCodeExcelisfunBook\DynamicFolderPath\SalesDataDynamic.csv

Figure 6-31 *The on-premises folder path query cannot find the file related to the path.*

> **Note:** You have just learned how to create a dynamic folder path in Excel that allows you to create dynamic file paths. In Chapter 7, which covers the From Folder feature, you will see how to use the same method for a folder with many files that you need to import.

Dataflow as a Dynamic Data Source

Dataflow is available in Microsoft online services like Power BI, Power Apps, and Dynamics 365 Customer Insights. Dataflow is simultaneously the online version of Power Query and an online data source that can be accessed by apps like Excel and Power BI, without the use of on-premises file paths. However, the services that contain Dataflow are enterprise-level services. Individuals cannot purchase these services, so not all people have access to Dataflow. However, many people work for entities that have these enterprise packages.

To use Dataflow as a data source (or to use online Power Query), you must create workspaces in the Power BI service and assign people to each workspace. The people who are assigned to a workspace are the ones who can create data sources, consume data sources from within apps like Excel and Power BI, and do other data-related tasks.

This section of the chapter does not include step-by-step instructions for you to follow. Instead, this section just shows an example using Highline College's enterprise Power BI service and the HighlineProject12 workspace that I created. It illustrates how to upload a CSV file to Dataflow and then access it in apps like Excel and Power BI from any location. This section does not provide a lesson on M code; it only shows the use of the user interface to create the Dataflow data source. You can use what you learn in this example as an alternative to using a dynamic file path in Excel.

Figures 6-32 through 6-42 show how I upload a file from my computer to Dataflow and then access the file in apps on different devices.

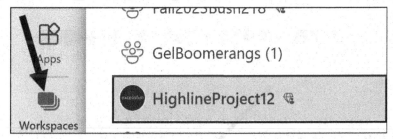

Figure 6-32 *Log in to Power BI and then select a workspace.*

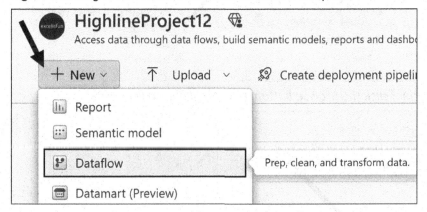

Figure 6-33 *From the New dropdown, select Dataflow.*

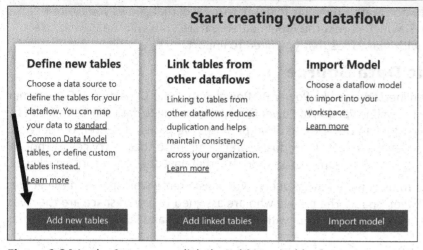

Figure 6-34 *In the Start area, click the Add New Tables button.*

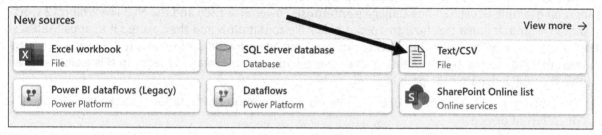

Figure 6-35 *Select the Text/CSV data connector.*

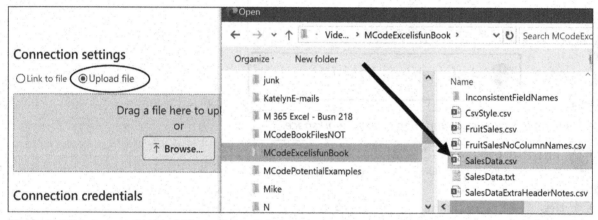

Figure 6-36 *Select the Upload File option, click the Browse button, select a file, and click Next.*

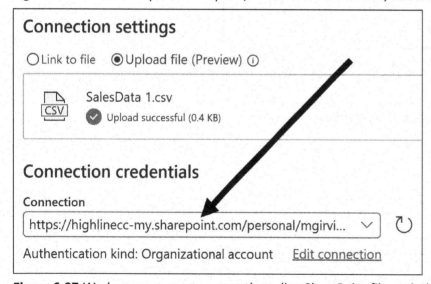

Figure 6-37 *Workspace users can access the online SharePoint file path that is created.*

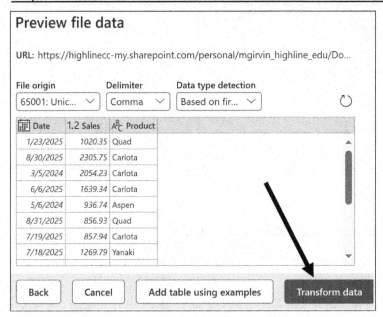

Figure 6-38 *Bring the data into the Power Query Editor.*

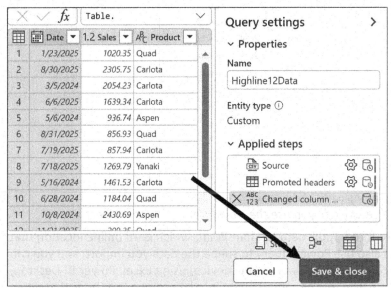

Figure 6-39 *After you have cleaned and transformed the data, click Save & Close.*

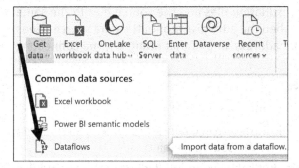

Figure 6-40 *In Power BI Desktop, the Dataflows connector is available on any device.*

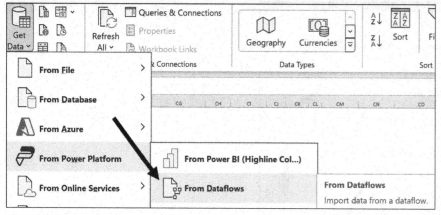

Figure 6-41 *In Excel, the From Dataflows connector is available on any device.*

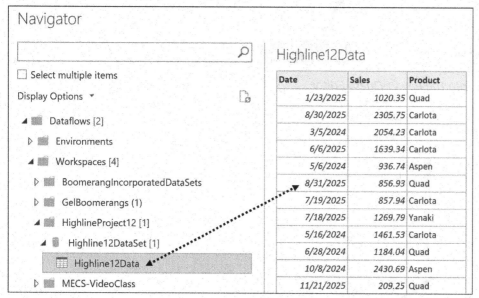

Figure 6-42 *When using Dataflow as a source of data, you use the Navigator dialog to connect to data.*

The beauty of Dataflow is that you can use it to import data to SharePoint, which is an online location that never uses on-premises file paths. You can also use Power Query to shape the data you import, and you can save the data to a workspace and then later access the data on any device, using Excel, Power BI Desktop, Power BI service, Power Apps, or other tools. The real benefit of an online data source like this is that when you move the destination file to a location where you have access to the workspace, the file path works perfectly. You don't have to worry about moving both the destination files and the source files to the same location, as you do in Excel with a dynamic file path. Finally, when the administrator of the data source needs to change the data, they save the new data to the SharePoint address, and at that point, anyone connecting to the data gets the updated data.

Dealing with On-Premises File Paths

When dealing with on-premises file paths, keep in mind these important points:

- In Excel and Power BI Desktop, if the source data file is moved, you can use the query's Source step or the Data Source Settings dialog box to edit and correct the source file path.

- In Excel, you can build a dynamic source data file path. But keep in mind that when you copy or move the source file to a new location, you must also copy or move the destination file to the same new location.

- If you have access to the Power BI service or other Microsoft services, you can use Dataflow to upload files to SharePoint, clean and transform the data, and later connect to the Dataflow online data source from apps like Excel and Power BI Desktop on various devices or online services.

Importing Text Files with the Csv.Document Function

Importing a tab-delimited text file is no different from importing a CSV file except that the delimiter is a tab, so we don't really need a section on text files. However, this section shows how to create a blank query and type out the formula to import a text file. It will give you good practice for Chapter 7, where you will need to manually type out formulas like this in more complex data imports.

For a text file that is on a computer, normally I would use a dynamic file path technique, as described earlier in this chapter. But because you may be using one of several apps while learning M code, I use on-premises paths in this section. For a single formula to import a text file, you need to use these three functions:

- **File.Contents:** To retrieve the contents of the file
- **Csv.Document:** To convert the contents of the file to a table
- **Table.PromoteHeaders:** To promote the first row in the table to column headers

To follow along, complete these steps:

1. In Windows Explorer, find the file SalesData.txt file and copy the folder path from the address bar (or just remember the path and type it in the next step).

2. In the Power Query Editor, select the Chapter06 group, create a bank query, and type the formula shown in Figure 6-43. Be sure to use your on-premises file path. The step will automatically be named Source. Name the query SalesDataTxt.

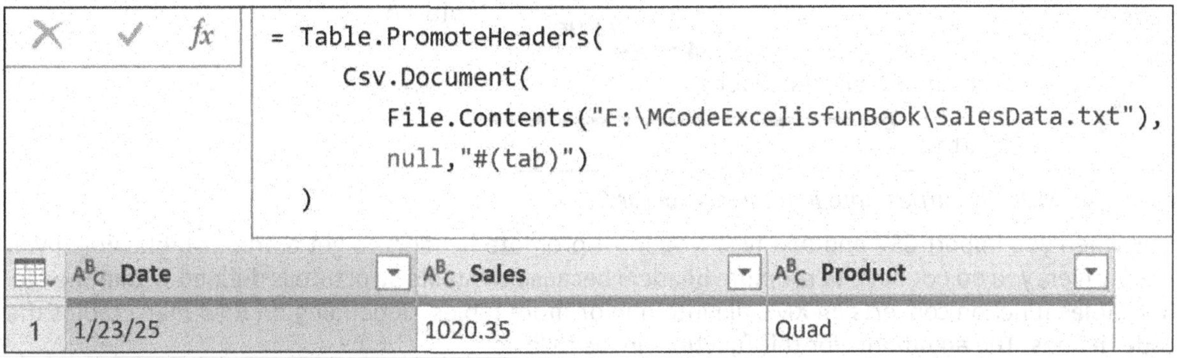

✕ ✓ _fx_	= Table.PromoteHeaders(
	Csv.Document(
	File.Contents("E:\MCodeExcelisfunBook\SalesData.txt"),
	null,"#(tab)")
	)

⊞ Aᴮ_C Date	▼	Aᴮ_C Sales	▼	Aᴮ_C Product	▼
1 1/23/25		1020.35		Quad	

Figure 6-43 *The tab delimiter is specified in the third argument of the Csv.Document function.*

3. Add a new step and type the formula shown in Figure 6-44. Add a data type to each column. Name the step SourceRecord.

4. In Excel, load the query as a connection only. In Power BI, uncheck Enable Load.

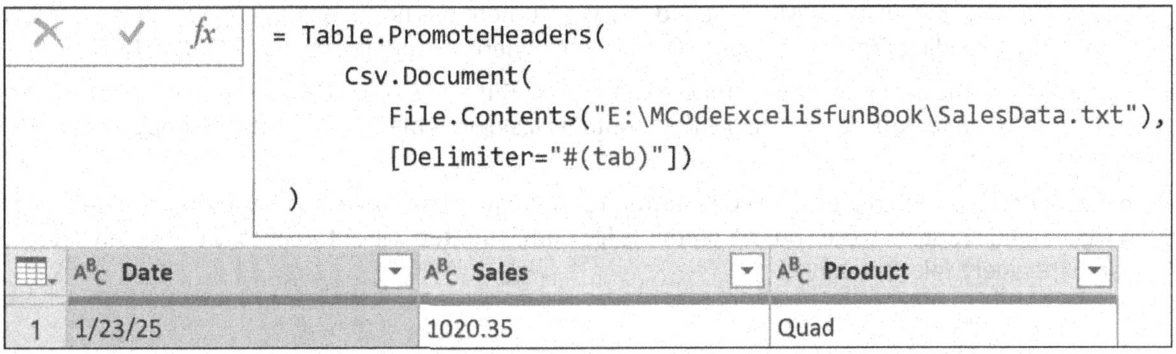

✕ ✓ _fx_	= Table.PromoteHeaders(
	Csv.Document(
	File.Contents("E:\MCodeExcelisfunBook\SalesData.txt"),
	[Delimiter="#(tab)"])
	)

⊞ Aᴮ_C Date	▼	Aᴮ_C Sales	▼	Aᴮ_C Product	▼
1 1/23/25		1020.35		Quad	

Figure 6-44 *A record in the second argument of the Csv.Document function specifies the delimiter.*

The two formulas that you just created accomplish the same goal in slightly different ways:

- For the first formula, you use three arguments in the Csv.Document function. In the first argument, you use the File.Contents function to retrieve the contents of the file. In the second argument, you type null to avoid hard-coding the number of columns into the formula. When you do this, if the number of columns changes, Csv.Document can accommodate the change without an error. In the third argument, you use the special character for a tab: "#(tab)". You omit the fourth argument because it is unnecessary when null is entered into the second argument. Finally, you omit the fifth argument and assume the default encoding 65001 UTF-8, which works for most standard CSV and text files.

- For the second formula, you use only two arguments in the Csv.Document function. The first argument is identical to the first argument in the first formula. However, in the second argument, you use a record with only one of the five possible parameters. You use the Delimiter parameter to indicate that you have a tab delimiter, and by leaving out the columns and encoding parameters, you assume that you want to accommodate any changes in number of columns and that the encoding is 65001 UTF-8.

Finally, both formulas use the Table.PromoteHeaders function. Both formulas achieve the same goal, and which one you use is up to preference.

The Xml.Tables Function

Extensible Markup Language (XML) files have the extension .xml . An XML file carries data in XML containers to create a table structure, as shown in Figure 6-45. The file contains records, the records contain column names, and the column names contain values.

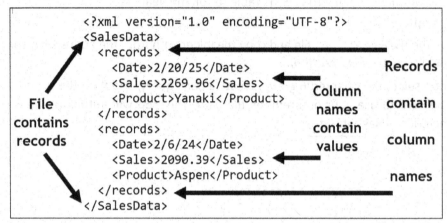

Figure 6-45 *An XML file carries data in a table structure.*

Whereas when you import CSV and text files, you must promote headers to get a proper table, when you import XML files, you do not have to promote headers because the table structure is defined within the file. The **Xml.Tables** function converts an XML file into one or more tables, depending on how many tables the XML code defines. The arguments for this function are as follows:

```
Xml.Tables(
    contents as any,
    optional options as nullable record,
    optional encoding as nullable number) as table
```

The **contents** argument contains the XML file, the **options** argument has not been defined (yes, it is a useless argument), and the **encoding** argument is for text encoding, where the default is code 65001 UTF-8.

Usually, you would use the user interface to import an XML file. But for M code practice, in this section you're going to write a formula to import an XML file that contains a single table of sales data. To import this XML file, follow these steps:

1. In the Power Query Editor, select the Chapter06 group, create a bank query, and type the formula shown in Figure 6-46. Be sure to use your on-premises file path. The step will automatically be named Source. Name the query SalesDataXml.

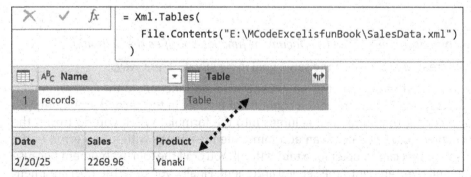

Figure 6-46 *Using Xml.Tables and File.Contents to return a table with a single record.*

The Xml.Tables function returns a table with the column names Name (name of table) and Table (table of data). Because this file has only one table, the returned table has only one record. Unlike the Excel.CurrentWorkbook function, the Xml.Tables function does not define a primary key on the Name column. If you drill down to extract the table or if you use the user interface to import the file, you are using a row index lookup, which is fine. However, when you use Xml.Tables, the Name column does not contain duplicates because the XML code does not allow tables with the same name. Therefore, it is fine to use a key match lookup to extract the table from the Xml.Tables-generated table. Because you have only one table in this case, you can use a row index lookup.

2. Complete the formula using a row index lookup, as shown in Figure 6-47. Add a data type to each column.

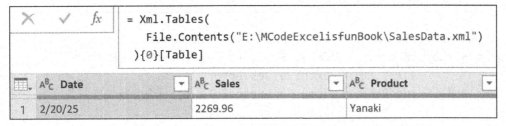

Figure 6-47 *Using a row index lookup to extract the table of XML data.*

3. In Excel, load the query as a connection only. In Power BI, uncheck Enable Load.

The Json.Document Function

Now that we have looked at XML files, which carry data in a table structure, we are ready to look at the JavaScript Object Notation (JSON) file format, which carries data in a record structure.

JSON files use the extension .json. As shown in Figure 6-48, JSON files carry data in a record structure, without any column name structure. This means that when you import JSON records, you have to add some extra M code to convert the records to a table. The **Json.Document** function returns the content of a JSON file and has these arguments:

```
Json.Document(
    jsonText as any,
    optional encoding as nullable number) as any
```

The **contents** argument contains the JSON file, and the **encoding** argument is for text encoding, where the default is code 65001 UTF-8.

```
[
  {
    "Date": "2/20/25",        One
    "Sales": 2269.96,         record
    "Product": "Yanaki"
  },
  {
    "Date": "2/6/24",
    "Sales": 2090.39,
    "Product": "Aspen"
  },
]
```

Figure 6-48 *A JSON file carries data in a record structure.*

If you use the user interface to import a JSON file, you get a different set of M code steps in Excel than in Power BI. In Excel, when you use the user interface, the records from the JSON file are imported, but it is up to you to write the code to convert the records to a table. In Power BI, when you use the user interface, four query steps are created, and the result is a finished table.

Before you type your own M code, I want to show you the user interface method in Power BI. Follow these steps:

1. In the Power Query Editor in Power BI, select the Chapter06 group and then, on the Home tab, go to the Data group, click the Get Data dropdown, click More, click JSON, and click Connect.

2. In the Open dialog box, select the file named SalesData.json and click Open. Name the query SalesDataJson. For loading, be sure to uncheck Enable Load.

Figure 6-49 shows the four steps that were automatically created in the Advanced Editor (but note that I renamed the last three query steps here so the names don't include spaces):

- As shown in Figure 6-49, the Source step uses a combination of the File.Contents and Json.Document functions to return a list of records. (Figure 6-50 shows this list of records.)

- The ConvertToTable step uses the Table.FromList function to create a table from a list.

- The ExpandColumn1 step uses the Table.ExpandRecordColumn function to expand the default column, Column1, and name the three columns based on the column names in the JSON file.

- The AddDataTypes step adds data types to the three columns.

```
let
    Source = Json.Document(File.Contents("E:\MCodeExcelisfunBook\SalesData.json")),
    ConvertedToTable = Table.FromList(Source, Splitter.SplitByNothing(),
                       null, null, ExtraValues.Error),
    ExpandColumn1 = Table.ExpandRecordColumn(ConvertedToTable, "Column1",
                       {"Date", "Sales", "Product"},
                       {"Date", "Sales", "Product"}),
    AddDataTypes = Table.TransformColumnTypes(ExpandColumn1,
                       {{"Date", type date},
                       {"Sales", type number},
                       {"Product", type text}})
in
    AddDataTypes
```

Figure 6-49 *The user interface creates four steps to convert a JSON file to a table.*

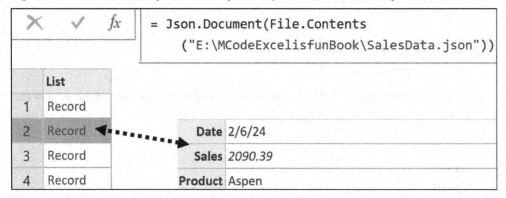

Figure 6-50 *The File.Contents and Json.Document functions return lists of records.*

Notice that the automatic process we just looked at uses four query steps. As an alternative, you can replace those four steps with one or two steps by using the Table.FromRecords function. The **Table.FromRecords** function converts a list of records into a table. The arguments for this function are listed here:

```
Table.FromRecords(
    records as list,
    optional columns as any,
    optional missingField as nullable number) as table
```

The **records** argument contains the list of records. The **columns** argument allows you to define data types using the same record syntax that you learned for the #table intrinsic function:

```
type table [ColumnName1 = DataType1, ColumnName2 = DataType2 …]
```

However, I have found that defining data types this way for numbers and text works great, but defining data types for dates does not seem to work. The **missingField** argument allows you to define what happens if a column is missing, using functions like Missing.FieldError or MissingField.UseNull. If you use MissingField.

UseNull, the data types must be nullable data types. To try using the Table.FromRecords function, follow these steps:

1. In the Power Query Editor, select the Chapter06 group, start a blank query, and then create the formula shown in Figure 6-50. Be sure to use your on-premises file path. Name the query SalesDataJson. The formula returns a list of records.

2. To convert the list of records to a table, edit the formula so it looks like the one in Figure 6-51. (In this case, you do not use the second argument to define data types because you have a date column.)

3. Add a data type to each column, and for loading, use Create Connection Only.

4. To convert the list of records to a table, edit the formula so it looks like the one in Figure 6-51. (In this case, you do not use the second argument to define data types because you have a date column.)

```
= Table.FromRecords(
    Json.Document(File.Contents("E:\MCodeExcelisfunBook\SalesData.json"))
)
```

	Date	Sales	Product
1	2/20/25	2269.96	Yanaki

Figure 6-51 *The Table.FromRecords function does exactly what the function name describes.*

5. Add a data type to each column, and for loading, use Create Connection Only.

For JSON files, should you use the user interface method or the Table.FromRecords alternative? The interface method is quick and easy, especially in Power BI. But in Excel, because the user interface only imports records, and you must build code to convert the records to a table, I always use the Table.FromRecords method. I timed the two methods using 250,000 rows of data and found that the Table.FromRecords method processed a few seconds faster.

Excel Files and the Excel.Workbook Function

So far in this chapter, we have studied CSV, text, XML, and JSON files as data sources, each of which contains a single table. Now we will look at how to import data from an Excel file, which can have many different tables and objects inside it.

When you want to import data from an Excel file, you can use the **Excel.Workbook** function, which extracts all the objects from a specified external Excel workbook file and delivers a table of objects and attributes of those objects to the Power Query Editor. From that table, you can then choose which objects to import. Here's the funny thing, though: The Microsoft help website says that this function returns the contents of the Excel workbook. Contents? What does that mean? The Excel.Workbook function can import the following objects (or contents):

- Excel tables
- User-created defined names (LAMBDA and formula names are not imported.)
- Worksheets with all sheet contents
- Automatically created defined names when you use these features:
    - Print range
    - Advanced filter criteria and/or extract ranges
    - The auto filter feature

Note: If you import worksheets with tables (not Excel tables) that contain other data, the Excel.Workbook function will import the tables, the other data, and all the empty cells in between.

The arguments for the Excel.Workbook function are shown here:

```
Excel.Workbook(
    workbook as binary,
    optional useHeaders as any,
    optional delayTypes as nullable logical) as table
```

The **workbook** argument requires an Excel file as a binary value. The **useHeaders** argument allows you to promote headers (true) or not promote headers (false, which is the default). This argument is helpful when you are importing worksheets with tables that are not defined as Excel tables. The **delayTypes** argument allows you to delay applying data types (true) or not delay applying data types—that is, let the function apply the data types (false, which is the default). There are two problems with the delayTypes argument. First, it does not always apply the correct data types. (I have seen it misinterpret an integer as a decimal number.) Second, if you use this function to define data types, the query may run more slowly than if you define data types in a separate step. Because using false in the delayTypes argument is convenient, I often do so when the datasets are small and contain no integer data.

Now that we have looked at the details of the Excel.Workbook function, let's go through an example using the ExcelSalesData.xlsx file. As shown in Figure 6-52, the worksheet Samantha contains an Excel table of compressor sales data. The worksheets Mo, Chantel, and Timmy also contain Excel tables with compressor sales data. As shown in Figure 6-53, the worksheet Stuff has the following seven objects: two range-defined names (Cell and Date), a print area, an Excel table, two Advanced Filter–defined names (Criteria and Extract), and a Filter feature–defined name.

> **Note:** Understanding all the objects in a workbook helps you avoid getting unexpected results.

	A	B	C	D
1	Date	Sales	Product	
2	2/26/2024	769.56	Compressor Kit 2	
3	10/23/2023	1687.87	Compressor Kit 5	
4	9/18/2023	514.09	Compressor Kit 4	
5	3/11/2023	810.1	Compressor Kit 2	
6	4/15/2024	943.04	Compressor Kit 4	

Samantha | Mo | Chantel | Timmy | Stuff

Figure 6-52 *The Samantha, Mo, Chantel, and Timmy sheets hold compressor sales data.*

	A	B	C	D	E	F	G	H	I	J	K	L	M	N	O	P	Q	R	S
1													Advanced Filter						
2		Range Defined Names:			Print_Area:			Excel Table:					Criteria:	Extract:			Filtered Range:		
3																			
4		Calls	Date		Calls	Date		Product	Units	Price	Cost		Calls	Calls	Date		Calls	Date	
5		192	2/22/23		192	2/22/23		Quad	15	14	7		>170	192	2/22/23		192	2/22/23	
6		203	2/23/23		203	2/23/23		Carlota	14	9	4.5			203	2/23/23		203	2/23/23	
7		189	2/24/23		189	2/24/23		Quad	10	13	6.5			189	2/24/23		189	2/24/23	

Figure 6-53 *There are many different objects in the ExcelSalesData.xlsx file.*

The goal for this example is to import only the four Excel tables with compressor sales and append all four Excel tables into a single table. To try it, follow these steps:

1. In the Power Query Editor, select the Chapter06 group, start a blank query, and name the query CompressorSalesExcel.

2. Create the following formula:
   ```
   = Excel.Workbook(
         File.Contents("Your On-Premises-File-Path"),
         null, true)
   ```

   The result of this formula is shown in Figure 6-54, where you can see that the Excel.Workbook function delivered a table with five columns and 16 rows, with the objects and the attributes for those objects. The Name column contains the name of each object. The Data column contains the objects as table values. The Item column contains the reference for each object. The name in the Name column and the reference in the Item column are identical except for the automatically generated defined names. For example, in row 12, the name is _xlnm.Criteria, and the item is Stuff!_xlnm.Criteria. The difference comes from the fact that the Item column shows the actual formula from the Refers To text box in the Name Manager, whereas the Name column shows only the defined name. The Kind column tells you the type of object, such as Sheet for worksheet, Table for Excel table, and DefinedName for defined name. This column can be helpful for filtering out the objects that you do not want. The Hidden column tells you if the object is hidden. The filtered range defined name is always hidden in the source Excel file. The primary key of the returned table is the combination of the Item and Kind columns.

```
= Excel.Workbook(File.Contents("E:\MCodeExcelisfunBook\ExcelSalesData.xlsx"),null,true)
```

	ABC Name	Data	ABC Item	ABC Kind	Hidden
1	Samantha	Table	Samantha	Sheet	FALSE
2	Mo	Table	Mo	Sheet	FALSE
3	Chantel	Table	Chantel	Sheet	FALSE
4	Timmy	Table	Timmy	Sheet	FALSE
5	Stuff	Table	Stuff	Sheet	FALSE
6	T_Samantha	Table	T_Samantha	Table	FALSE
7	T_Mo	Table	T_Mo	Table	FALSE
8	T_Chantel	Table	T_Chantel	Table	FALSE
9	T_Timmy	Table	T_Timmy	Table	FALSE
10	fProduct	Table	fProduct	Table	FALSE
11	_xlnm._FilterDatabase	Table	Stuff!_xlnm._FilterDatabase	DefinedName	TRUE
12	_xlnm.Criteria	Table	Stuff!_xlnm.Criteria	DefinedName	FALSE
13	_xlnm.Extract	Table	Stuff!_xlnm.Extract	DefinedName	FALSE
14	Calls	Table	Calls	DefinedName	FALSE
15	Date	Table	Date	DefinedName	FALSE
16	_xlnm.Print_Area	Table	Stuff!_xlnm.Print_Area	DefinedName	FALSE

Figure 6-54 *The Excel.Workbook function returns 16 objects from the ExcelSalesData.xlsx file.*

Because the goal here is to append just the four tables with compressor sales data, you must look through the table of objects and determine a pattern within the attributes that you can use to filter and get necessary files. If you look through the Kind column, you might consider filtering to show just tables. However, this would yield the CallTable from the Stuff worksheet, which you do not want. If you look through the Name column, you can identify a pattern you can use to get the tables that you want: Each name begins with T_.

Note: If you plan to have multiple Excel tables in an Excel file that you want to combine or append later, it is best to not have other types of objects (besides worksheets) in the workbook file. In addition, if you do have other types of objects, you should use a consistent naming pattern so that it is easy to filter and get the tables you want.

3. To filter to get the compressor sales tables, click the filter dropdown at the top of the Name column, hover over Text Filters, in the menu that appears click Begins With, in the text box enter the text T_, and click OK. Name the step FilterToGetT_. Figure 6-55 shows the result.

```
fx = Table.SelectRows(Source, each Text.StartsWith([Name], "T_"))
```

	ABC Name	Data	ABC Item	ABC Kind
1	T_Samantha	Table	T_Samantha	Table
2	T_Mo	Table	T_Mo	Table
3	T_Chantel	Table	T_Chantel	Table
4	T_Timmy	Table	T_Timmy	Table

Figure 6-55 *The pattern to get the correct tables is T_.*

4. In the next query step, where you will append tables, determine whether you want the name attribute to be a new column in the resulting table. In this case, you don't; you just want the columns

from each Excel table: Date, Sales, and Product. However, in Chapter 7, you will see how easy it is to incorporate attributes such as name into the resulting table.

5. Add a new query step and create the column lookup formula shown in Figure 6-56. Name the step AppendTables. The result is a list of tables.

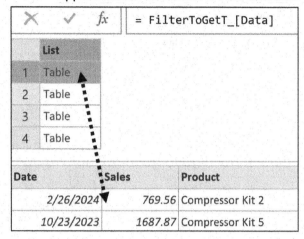

Figure 6-56 *Column lookup formula to get a list of Excel tables with compressor data.*

6. To append the tables from the list into one table, edit the formula and use the Table.Combine function (which you first saw in Chapter 2) as shown in Figure 6-57.

```
fx    = Table.Combine(FilterToGetT_[Data])
```

	ABC123 Date	ABC123 Sales	ABC123 Product
1	2/26/2024	769.56	Compressor Kit 2
2	10/23/2023	1687.87	Compressor Kit 5
3	9/18/2023	514.09	Compressor Kit 4
4	3/11/2023	810.1	Compressor Kit 2

Figure 6-57 *Table.Combine appends tables from a list.*

7. Notice in Figure 6-57 that there are no data types. Normally, you add a new step to add data types, but because this is a small dataset and you do not have whole number values, you can go back to the Source step and change the value of the third argument in Excel.Workbook (the delayTypes argument) from true to false. This change allows the Excel.Workbook function to add data types. Figure 6-58 shows the result.

```
fx    = Table.Combine(FilterToGetT_[Data])
```

	Date	1.2 Sales	ABC Product
1	2/26/2024	769.56	Compressor Kit 2
2	10/23/2023	1687.87	Compressor Kit 5
3	9/18/2023	514.09	Compressor Kit 4
4	3/11/2023	810.1	Compressor Kit 2
5	4/15/2024	943.04	Compressor Kit 4

Figure 6-58 *Data types are added using the Excel.Workbook function.*

As shown in Figure 6-59, three lines of M code is all it took to import the four specific Excel tables from the Excel file and append them into a single table. That is M code magic!

```
let
    Source = Excel.Workbook(
        File.Contents("E:\MCodeExcelisfunBook\ExcelSalesData.xlsx"),null,false),
    FilterToGetT_ = Table.SelectRows(Source, each Text.StartsWith([Name], "T_")),
    AppendTables = Table.Combine(FilterToGetT_[Data])
in
    AppendTables
```

Figure 6-59 *Not much code is required to get the tables from the Excel file and append them.*

The Excel.CurrentWorkbook Function

Whereas the Excel.Workbook function can be used in Excel, Power BI, and other apps to import data from an external Excel file, the Excel.CurrentWorkbook function can only be used in an Excel file to import objects from within the current file into the Power Query Editor. You already learned about this function in Chapters 4 and 5. If you work in Excel, this is a great M code function because it is the lead line of M code in many helpful queries, such as queries involved in:

- Building a dynamic folder and file path
- Converting worksheet source data in a cross-tabulated table into a proper dataset
- Appending Excel tables into a combined table on a new worksheet
- Adding the necessary columns to a worksheet Excel table by using the Power Query Editor and loading it to the PivotTable cache (not back to the worksheet)

We have already looked at the first two of these processes in earlier chapters. In this section, we will look at the last two.

Excel.CurrentWorkbook is an argumentless function that extracts objects from the current Excel file (that is, the file where the function is being used) and delivers a table of objects and object names to the Power Query Editor. The returned table has two columns: one for the object and one for the name of the object. The primary key of the returned table is the Name column. These are the objects it can return:

- Excel tables
- User-created defined names (LAMBDA and formula names are not imported.)
- Automatically created defined names when you use these features:
  - Print range
  - Advanced Filter criteria and extract ranges
  - The Filter feature
  - Dynamic arrays

The Excel.CurrentWorkbook function does not import worksheets into the Power Query Editor. (However, the Excel.Workbook function can import worksheets.) In addition, if you have dynamic spilled arrays in your Excel file and you have never manually imported them into the Power Query Editor, the Excel.CurrentWorkbook function will not detect or import the dynamic arrays. However, when you manually import a dynamic array into the Power Query Editor, an automatic defined name is created. It is only after the automatic defined name is created that the Excel.CurrentWorkbook function can "see" the dynamic array and therefore import it as an object from the current Excel file into the Power Query Editor.

> **Note:** The Excel.Workbook function imports worksheets but not dynamic arrays. The Excel. CurrentWorkbook function imports dynamic arrays but not worksheets.

Finally, if you are using the Excel.CurrentWorkbook function to import multiple Excel tables, append them into a single table, and then load the table back to the worksheet, you must prevent recursion from occurring. (With **recursion**, a function calls itself.) Because the Excel.CurrentWorkbook function delivers an Excel table

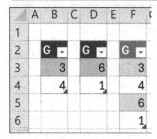

Figure 6-60 *The two G tables are appended into one table.*

Figure 6-61 *When the query output is refreshed, recursion doubles the records in the table.*

Figure 6-62 *Filtering out the name of the query prevents the table from being re-imported.*

to the worksheet, and the function is programmed to import all Excel tables, when you refresh the query, the function imports the original tables plus the query output table (importing itself), thereby calling itself and doubling the size of the table. There are a few simple solutions.

The first way to prevent recursion is to add a single line of M code that filters out the name of the query. This way, when you refresh, the query output table is not allowed to be part of the final output. For example, Figure 6-60 shows two tables with G columns. The two tables have been imported using the Excel. CurrentWorkbook function, appended, and loaded to the worksheet. The query is named TwoTables.

As shown in Figure 6-61, when the query is refreshed, it calls the two G tables and itself, the query output, to double the size of the table.

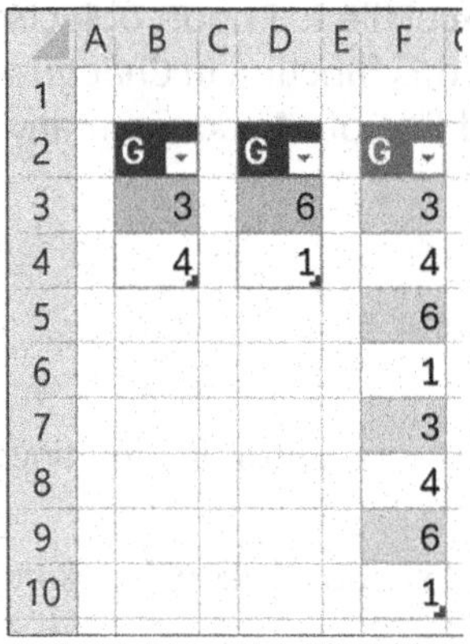

As shown in Figure 6-62, when the query named TwoTables is filtered out as a possible name for the queries being appended, recursion does not occur.

Note: The example shown in Figures 6-60 to 6-62 can be found in the file Recursion.xlsx.

Another way to prevent recursion is to use a special naming convention for the tables being appended and then not use the naming convention to name the append query.

The third way to prevent recursion comes into play when the result of the append operation is to create a PivotTable report. In this case, you do not load the append query to the worksheet; instead, you load it to the PivotTable cache. This way, when you refresh, there is no Excel table query output to cause recursion.

Earlier in this chapter, you used the Excel.Workbook function in the MCodeBook-Start.xlsx file to connect to the source data file, ExcelSalesData.xlsx, in order to import four compressor tables and append them. In this section, you are going to work with the same four compressor sales tables, but this time you will open the ExcelSalesData.xlsx file and from within that file, you will use the Excel. CurrentWorkbook file to import the four tables into the Query Editor, append them, and then load them to a new worksheet. For this example, the source data file and destination file are the same file. To try this example, follow these steps:

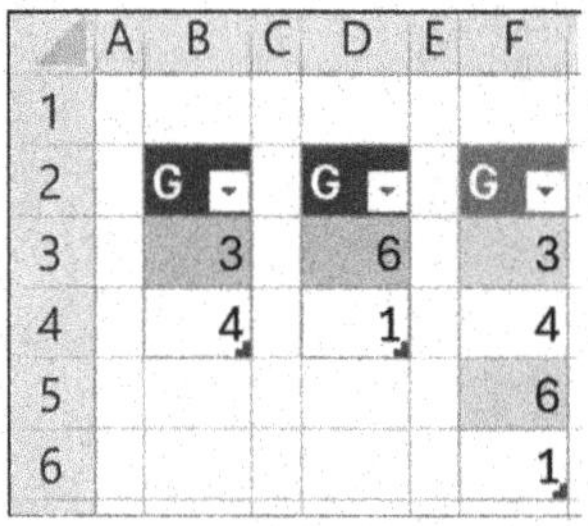

1. Open the file named ExcelSalesData.xlsx and in the Power Query Editor create a blank query and name the query CompressorAppenedSales.

2. As the first query step, create this formula:
    ```
    = Excel.CurrentWorkbook()
    ```

As shown in Figure 6-63, the function returns all the objects in the file. Notice that none of the worksheet objects are imported. Also notice that the Excel. CurrentWorkbook function returns a table with only two columns. You saw earlier in this chapter that the Excel.Workbook function returned a table with five columns. With five columns of attributes, it is almost always going to be easier to find a pattern to help you filter to get the files you want. Luckily, in this example, the names of the Excel tables with the compressor data have a consistent naming convention, with each table name beginning with T_, and the append query name, CompressorAppenedSales, does not follow that convention. So when you filter to include only tables that have a name that begins with T_, you will not encounter the recursion problem.

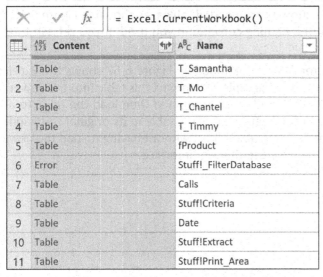

	ABC 123 Content	A^BC Name
1	Table	T_Samantha
2	Table	T_Mo
3	Table	T_Chantel
4	Table	T_Timmy
5	Table	fProduct
6	Error	Stuff!_FilterDatabase
7	Table	Calls
8	Table	Stuff!Criteria
9	Table	Date
10	Table	Stuff!Extract
11	Table	Stuff!Print_Area

fx = Excel.CurrentWorkbook()

Figure 6-63 *Eleven objects are imported, and no worksheets are imported.*

3. To filter to get just the compressor sales tables, create the formula shown in Figure 6-64. Name the step FilterToGetT_. (You can use the user interface to create the formula.)

fx = Table.SelectRows(Source, each Text.StartsWith([Name], "T_"))

	ABC 123 Content	A^BC Name
1	Table	T_Samantha
2	Table	T_Mo
3	Table	T_Chantel
4	Table	T_Timmy

Figure 6-64 *Using Table.SelectRows to filter to get only names that begin with T_.*

4. To append the tables, create the formula shown in Figure 6-65. Name the step AppendTables.

fx = Table.Combine(FilterToGetT_[Content])

	ABC 123 Date	ABC 123 Sales	ABC 123 Product
1	2/26/2024 12:00:00 AM	769.56	Compressor Kit 2
2	10/23/2023 12:00:00 AM	1687.87	Compressor Kit 5

Figure 6-65 *The formula to combine tables.*

5. Add a data type to each column and then close and load the data to a new worksheet. The result is shown in Figure 6-66.

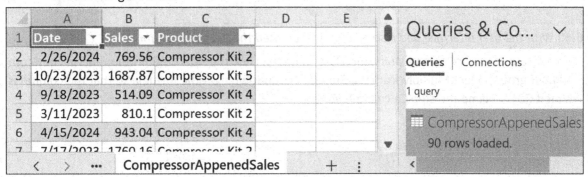

	A	B	C	D	E
1	Date	Sales	Product		
2	2/26/2024	769.56	Compressor Kit 2		
3	10/23/2023	1687.87	Compressor Kit 5		
4	9/18/2023	514.09	Compressor Kit 4		
5	3/11/2023	810.1	Compressor Kit 2		
6	4/15/2024	943.04	Compressor Kit 4		
7	7/17/2023	1760.16	Compressor Kit 2		

Queries & Co... ∨

Queries | Connections

1 query

CompressorAppenedSales
90 rows loaded.

< > ··· CompressorAppenedSales +

Figure 6-66 *The appended table is loaded to the worksheet, and a refresh does not cause recursion.*

Even though you used the Excel.CurrentWorkbook function and appended tables, as shown in Figure 6-66, you do not encounter the recursion error because of the naming convention you used. If you refresh this query, the row count stays at 90.

Now let's try another example of using the Excel.CurrentWorkbook function. Figure 6-67 shows the Excel table named fProduct on the Stuff worksheet. The goal in this example is to import this table into the Power Query Editor; calculate revenue, cost of goods sold (COGS), and gross profit; and then load the table to a PivotTable cache. The benefit of this method is that you can keep the original table in its original state and use Power Query and M code to transform the table for a PivotTable report without having to load the new table back to the worksheet. For this example, you can mostly use the user interface.

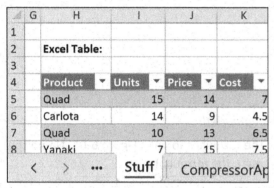

Figure 6-67 *Product units, price, and cost Excel table.*

To try this example, follow these steps:

1. To import the Excel table into the Power Query Editor, in the Data tab, go to the Get & Transform group and select the Get Data dropdown, select From File, and select From Excel Workbook. Name the query ProductSalesAndCOGS.

   Two query steps are automatically created. The second query step adds data types. As shown in Figure 6-68, the first query step uses the Excel.CurrentWorkbook function and a two-way key match lookup to extract and return the fProduct table.

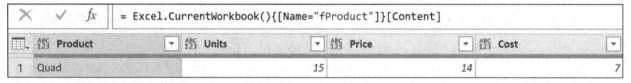

Figure 6-68 *Looking up a specific table never causes a recursion error.*

2. To calculate revenue, select the Units and Price columns, click the Add Column tab, and in the From Number group, select Multiply from the Standard dropdown. Edit the formula so that the column is named Revenue, as shown in Figure 6-69. Name the step CalculateRevenue.

```
= Table.AddColumn(AddDataTypes, "Revenue", each [Units] * [Price], type number)
```

1²3 Units	1.2 Price	1.2 Cost	1.2 Revenue
15	14	7	210

Figure 6-69 *With the user interface and a small edit, you created the Revenue column.*

3. To calculate COGS, select the Units and Cost columns, click the Add Column tab, and in the From Number group, select Multiply from the Standard dropdown. Edit the formula so that the column is named COGS. Name the step CalculateRevenue.

4. To calculate gross profit, select the Revenue column and then the COGS column. Then click the Add Column tab, go to the From Number group, and select Subtract from the Standard dropdown. Name the column Gross Profit and name the step GrossProfit. Figure 6-70 shows the result.

= Table.AddColumn(COGS, "Gross Profit", each [Revenue] - [COGS], type number)				∨
1.2 Cost ▾	1.2 Revenue ▾	1.2 COGS ▾	1.2 Gross Profit ▾	
14	7	210	105	105

Figure 6-70 *Gross Profit formula.*

5. To remove unwanted columns and reorder columns in a single step, hold down the Ctrl key while using the mouse to select the following columns, in this order: Product, Revenue, COGS, Units, Gross Profit. Right-click any one of these selected columns and select Remove Other Columns. Name the step RemoveAndReorder. Figure 6-71 shows the result.

✕ ✓ ƒx	= Table.SelectColumns(GrossProfit,{"Product", "Revenue", "COGS", "Units", "Gross Profit"})				∨
Aᵇc Product	1.2 Revenue ▾	1.2 COGS ▾	1²3 Units ▾	1.2 Gross Profit ▾	▾
1 Quad	210	105	15	105	

Figure 6-71 *Table.SelectColumns removes unwanted columns and reorders the columns in one step.*

6. In the Close group on the Home tab, click the Close & Load dropdown and select Close & Load To. Then, in the Import Data dialog box, select the PivotTable Report option and the New Worksheet option and then click OK. Build a PivotTable that shows revenue, COGS, and gross profit by product. Name the worksheet ProductReport. Figure 6-72 shows the result.

	A	B	C	D
1	**Product** ▾	**Revenue ($)**	**COGS ($)**	**Gross Profit ($)**
2	Aspen	205.25	97.7	107.55
3	Carlota	332	166.4	165.6
4	Quad	673.5	343.5	330
5	Yanaki	292.5	146	146.5
6	**Grand Total**	**1503.25**	**753.6**	**749.65**

‹ › ••• **ProductReport** | Stuff | Compresso

Figure 6-72 *A table from a worksheet, transformed and loaded to a PivotTable.*

Using the Locale Feature to Import Data from Different Locales

Now that you have learned about the usefulness of the Excel.CurrentWorkbook function in an Excel file, you are ready to learn about the using the Locale feature to help import dates, times, and numbers in the correct format.

You use the regional settings in the Control Panel to indicate how numbers, currency, times, and dates are interpreted on your computer. Figure 6-73 shows the regional settings for my computer here in the United States, where I use the format English (United States). Power Query uses the regional settings to interpret the data that you import, and Power Query refers to the regional format on a computer as the **locale**.

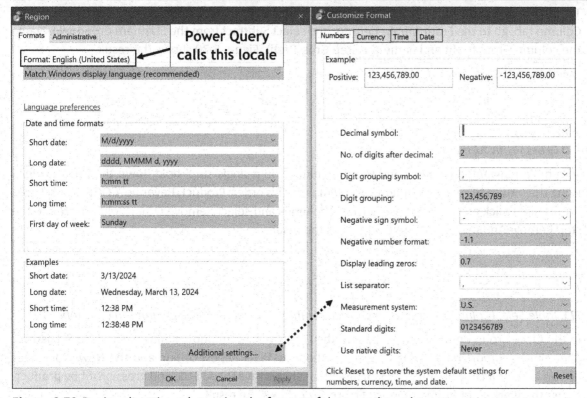

Figure 6-73 *Regional settings determine the format of dates and numbers on your computer.*

The table shown in Figure 6-74 has five columns: The first three columns contain dates, and the last two contain sales numbers. However, because of the regional settings on my computer, the only columns that are interpreted correctly are the Dates MM/DD/YY column and the US Sales column. The Dates DD/MM/YYYY column and the France Sales column are considered text on my computer. However, if the format, or locale, setting were set to French (France), the dates and numbers would be interpreted correctly. The ISO Date column contains dates with a format set by the International Organization for Standardization. The format is YYYYMMDD, and ISO dates can show up in a dataset as text values or number values. In this example, the ISO dates are numbers.

Many times when people are faced with dates and numbers that do not have the correct formatting, they resort to using formulas to convert the dates and numbers to the correct format. However, creating formulas is usually more complicated than using the Using Locale feature or using back-to-back data types for ISO dates.

```
Table.TransformColumnTypes(Source,{{"Dates MM/DD/YY", type date}, {"Dates DD/MM/YYYY", type text},
    {"ISO Date", Int64.Type}, {"US Sales", type number}, {"France Sales", type text}})
```

Dates MM/DD/YY	A^B_C Dates DD/MM/YYYY	1^2_3 ISO Date	1.2 US Sales	A^B_C France Sales
1/22/2018	22/01/2018	20180122	22.95	22,95
1/5/2018	05/01/2018	20180105	1258.32	1 258,32
2/28/2018	28/02/2018	20180228	7555.1	7 555,10

Figure 6-74 *Using different formats for dates and numbers can cause issues.*

To try out the Using Locale feature, follow these steps:

1. Select the LocalDatesQ query in the Chapter06 group and select the last query step, AddDataTypes.

2. As shown in Figure 6-75, click the ABC data type icon at the top left of the Dates DD/MM/YYYY column and select Using Locale.

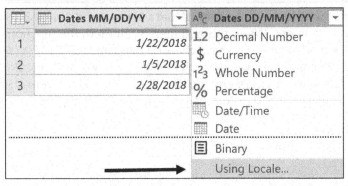

Figure 6-75 *Using Locale helps import dates with different formats, or locales.*

3. As shown in Figure 6-76, complete the Change Type with Locale dialog box so the column has the data type date coming from the locale French (France) and then click OK. Name the step ConvertedFrenchData. Figure 6-77 shows the result.

> ## Change Type with Locale
>
> Change the data type and select the locale of origin.
>
> Data Type
>
> | Date | ▾ |
>
> Locale
>
> | French (France) | ▾ |

Figure 6-76 *The data type is date, coming from the locale French (France).*

```
= Table.TransformColumnTypes(AddDataTypes, {{"Dates DD/MM/YYYY", type date}}, "fr-FR")
```

Dates DD/MM/YYYY	ISO Date	US Sales	France Sales
1/22/2018	20180122	22.95	22,95
1/5/2018	20180105	1258.32	1 258,32
2/28/2018	20180228	7555.1	7 555,10

Figure 6-77 *The third argument to Table.TransformColumnTypes allows you to specify the locale.*

As you can see in Figure 6-77, the Using Locale feature converted the French dates to dates that match the regional settings on my computer. However, it is the third argument in the Table.TransformColumnTypes function that really made the change by referring to the locale code for France: "fr-FR". The arguments for this function are listed here:

```
Table.TransformColumnTypes(
    table as table,
    typeTransformations as list,
    optional culture as nullable text) as table
```

The **table** argument contains the table with the columns where you want to add data types. The **typeTrans-formations** argument contains lists within a list, where each sublist contains the name of the column and the data type that should be applied. The **culture** argument contains the culture code (also known as the locale, or language code), which specifies where the source data came from so that the function can convert the source dates to dates that match the regional setting on the computer in use.

> **Note:** You saw culture codes in Chapter 5, when you learned about the comparer functions. Remember that a full list of locale codes can be found in the Excel file MCodeBook-Start.xlsx, in the worksheet named Locale, or at https://msdn.microsoft.com/en-us/library/cc233982.aspx.

Look back at Figure 6-74, and you'll see that the initial application of data types used the Table. TransformColumnTypes function without the third argument. When this argument is omitted, the function assumes the regional settings from the computer. In this example, you have changed the Dates DD/MM/YYYY column, but you still need to change the France Sales column. However, each time you use the Using Locale feature, it adds a new query step. Rather than do that, you can simply edit the formula to make a French-to-US conversion on two columns in a single step. To do so, you just need to edit the formula as shown in Figure 6-78.

```
= Table.TransformColumnTypes(AddDataTypes,
    {{"Dates DD/MM/YYYY", type date},{"France Sales", type number}}, "fr-FR")
```

Dates DD/MM/YYYY	1²₃ ISO Date	1.2 US Sales	1.2 France Sales
1/22/2018	20180122	22.95	22.95
1/5/2018	20180105	1258.32	1258.32

Figure 6-78 *This formula changes two of the columns from French to US format.*

ISO Dates

Converting ISO dates to proper serial number dates is a simple one- or two-step process. If the ISO dates are text values, the one-step method is simply to apply a date data type, and the ISO dates are converted to proper dates. If the ISO dates are number values, the two-step process is simply to apply a text data type and then, in a separate query step, add the date data type; the ISO dates are then converted to proper dates.

To convert ISO dates to proper dates, follow these steps:

1. In the LocalDatesQ query, select the query step named AddDataTypes. Change the data type on the ISO Date column to text. When you are asked if you want to insert a step in the first dialog box, click Insert. When the second dialog box asks you if you want to replace the existing conversion, click Replace Current. The column now has a text data type applied.

2. Change the data type on the ISO Date column to date.

3. When the first dialog box asks if you want to insert a step, click Insert. When the second dialog box asks you if you want to replace the existing conversion, click Add New Step. Name the new step ConvertISODates. Figure 6-79 shows the result.

Dates MM/DD/YY	Dates DD/MM/YYYY	ISO Date	1.2 US Sales	1.2 France Sales
1/22/2018	1/22/2018	1/22/2018	22.95	22.95
1/5/2018	1/5/2018	1/5/2018	1258.32	1258.32
2/28/2018	2/28/2018	2/28/2018	7555.1	7555.1

Figure 6-79 *All dates are proper dates.*

As you can tell, using the ISO data type trick or the Using Locale feature is much easier than using formulas to convert dates and numbers from one locale to another.

Online Data Sources

Online data sources such as websites, SQL Server databases, and the Power BI semantic models do not use on-premises folder or file paths. Therefore, if you are connected to the internet, you can move the destination file anywhere you like. In addition, any time you want updated data, you can refresh the query. First, let's consider importing data from a website.

A Website as a Data Source

Typically, data that you get from a website is peripheral data, such as a table of data connectors for Power Query from a Microsoft website, a table of financial metrics from the Yahoo! Finance website, or a list of stock ticker symbols from a stock analysis website. Many websites are built so that the M code web connector can import tables of data from the website. But not all websites have the structure or the permissions to allow connections. When you connect to a website, you are connecting to a live data source that you can refresh at any time if you are connected to the internet.

For a web query, if you use the Excel user interface, Excel writes the complicated code for you. To try to connect to the Yahoo! Finance website and extract a table of the most active stocks, open the MCodeBook-Start.xlsx or MCodeBook-Start.pbix file and follow these steps in either Excel, Power BI Desktop, or Dataflow:

1. In Excel, on the Data tab, go to the Get & Transform group and click the From Web button. In Power BI Desktop, on the Home tab, go to the Data group, click the Get Data dropdown, and select Web. In Dataflow, in the Get Data/New Source area, click the Web Page option (and keep in mind that you will need an enterprise-assigned gateway to get through).

2. In the From Web dialog box, paste the web address https://finance.yahoo.com/ and click OK.

3. In the Web Access Content dialog box, select Anonymous and then click the Connect button.

4. On the left side of the Navigator dialog box, click Table 1 and then click the Transform Data button (or the OK button in Power BI) to bring the single table into the Power Query Editor.

5. Name the query WebYahooMostActiveStocks.

6. Click on the Source step. The Source step of this query, shown in Figure 6-80, makes you glad to have the user interface, which frees you from needing to write this code.

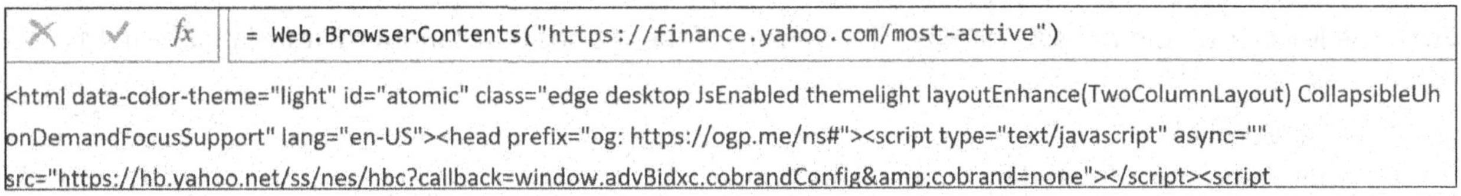

```
X   ✓   fx        = Web.BrowserContents("https://finance.yahoo.com/most-active")

<html data-color-theme="light" id="atomic" class="edge desktop JsEnabled themelight layoutEnhance(TwoColumnLayout) CollapsibleUh
onDemandFocusSupport" lang="en-US"><head prefix="og: https://ogp.me/ns#"><script type="text/javascript" async=""
src="https://hb.yahoo.net/ss/nes/hbc?callback=window.advBidxc.cobrandConfig&amp;cobrand=none"></script><script
```

Figure 6-80 *If the Web.BrowserContents function does not work, try the Web.Contents function.*

The table that results from this code, shown in Figure 6-81, lists the most active stocks, with columns that show important metrics for the stocks. This query could be loaded to the worksheet or the Data Model, and a visual could be created. Any time you wanted an update, all you need to do is refresh the query.

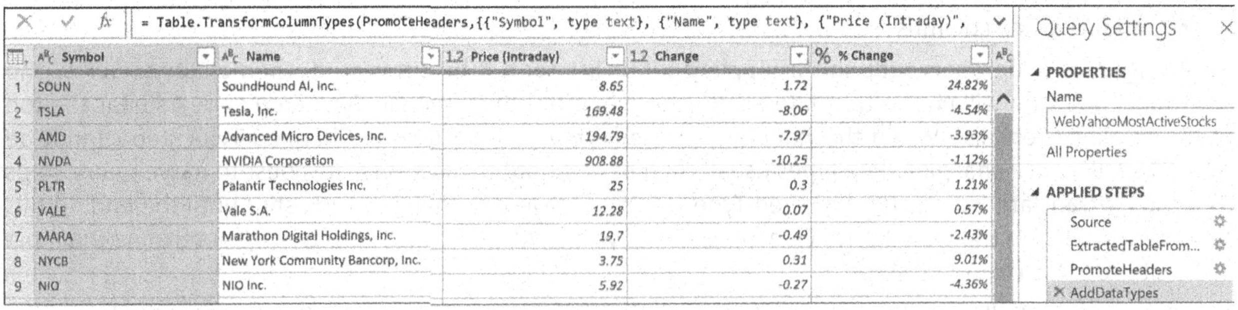

Figure 6-81 *The most active stock query can be refreshed any time the stock market is open.*

An SQL Server Database as a Data Source

SQL Server is one of the most widely used relational database management systems in the world. In the world of data analysis, connecting to an SQL Server database is a common task.

SQL, short for Structured Query Language, is a computer language used to build and query databases. SQL is almost always more efficient at executing queries than M code. Luckily, Microsoft programmed **query folding** into Power Query, which gives you the ability to translate lines of M code into a single SQL query statement and send it back to the more efficient SQL Server environment to execute and make a transformation. This means that for many queries, Power Query will write SQL code for you! SQL is an efficient query language, and this spectacular ability is built into Power Query.

In this section, you will learn how to use the **View Native Query** feature, which allows you to view the SQL code that is written for you. However, when you connect to an SQL Server database, you want to be able to use the user interface to write the M code rather than write your own M code (much as with the web page connector we just discussed). The query folding translator is programmed to understand the M code written by the user interface. For example, when you first connect to an SQL Server database, it creates two M code query steps: The first step delivers a table with database objects, and the second step performs a key match lookup to extract the desired table. With your M code skills, you could easily combine the two steps into one. But as soon as you alter the M code, it is highly likely that the query folding translator will no longer work. In addition, not all M code functions and actions can be translated into SQL.

From the Microsoft help website (https://learn.microsoft.com/en-us/power-query/power-query-folding), here is a list of some of the actions that can be translated from M code to SQL (with the SQL equivalent commands in parentheses):

- Removing columns (SELECT clause)
- Renaming columns (SELECT column aliases)
- Filtering rows, with static values or Power Query parameters (WHERE clause predicates)
- Grouping and summarizing (GROUP BY clause)
- Expanding record columns (source foreign key columns) to achieve a join of two source tables (JOIN clause)
- Non-fuzzy merging of foldable queries based on the same source (JOIN clause)
- Appending foldable queries based on the same source (UNION ALL operator)
- Adding custom columns with simple logic, which implies simple math calculations or the use of basic M code functions like Date.Year (SELECT column expressions)
- Pivoting and unpivoting (PIVOT and UNPIVOT operators)

From the Microsoft help website, here is a list of some of the actions that cannot be translated from M code to SQL:

- Adding data types
- Combining steps created by the user interface
- Merging queries based on different sources
- Appending (UNION) queries based on different sources
- Adding custom columns with complex logic, which implies the use of M functions that have no equivalent functions in the data source
- Adding index columns

Finally, if an M code query step in the Applied Steps list cannot be translated, then all steps below the non-translated step will not be translated. For example, often the Changed Type step appears near the top of the Applied Steps list. When this happens, all steps that come after the Changed Type step cannot be translated. Because changing data types usually can be left until the last step, it is best to move query steps that can be translated above the Changed Type step and leave the Changed Type step until the end. In this section, you will use the View Native Query feature as you build each query step to help determine the most efficient order for the query steps.

Through Highline College, where I work, I have made available to the public an SQL Server database with 7 million rows of boomerang sales data. In this section, you will use that dataset to learn about SQL Server databases. The goal for the exercise is to connect to the SQL Server database and create a simple product COGS report, where you start with a 7 million-row table and generate a 22-row report. Open the MCodeBook-Start. xlsx or MCodeBook-Start.pbix file and then follow these steps:

1. In Excel, Power BI Desktop, or Dataflow, access the user interface SQL Server database connector from the Get Data dropdown menu. The SQL Server Database dialog box appears.

2. As shown in Figure 6-82, in the SQL Server Database dialog box, type pond.highline.edu in the Server textbox. Type BoomData in the Database textbox. Click the OK button.

Figure 6-82 *If you are proficient with SQL, you can write your own code in the Advanced Options area.*

3. As shown in Figure 6-83, in the second SQL Server Database dialog box, on the left, select Database. Type excelisfun in the User Name textbook. Type ExcellsFun! in the Password textbook.

4. In the Select Which Level to Apply These Settings To dropdown, select pond.highline.edu;Boom-Data. Click Connect.

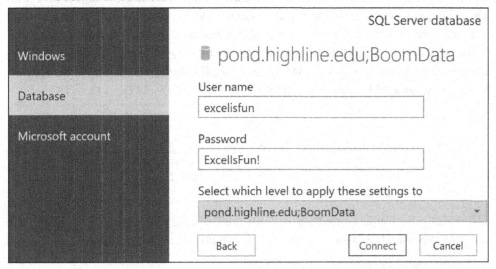

Figure 6-83 *Credentials are required to access pond.highline.edu;BoomData.*

5. As shown in Figure 6-84, in the Encryption Support dialog box, click OK.

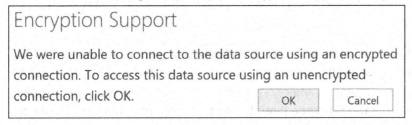

Figure 6-84 *The database is not encrypted.*

6. As shown in Figure 6-85, in the Navigator dialog box, select the fTransactions table on the left and then click the Transform Data button to bring the table into the Power Query Editor. Name the query ProductCOGSReport.

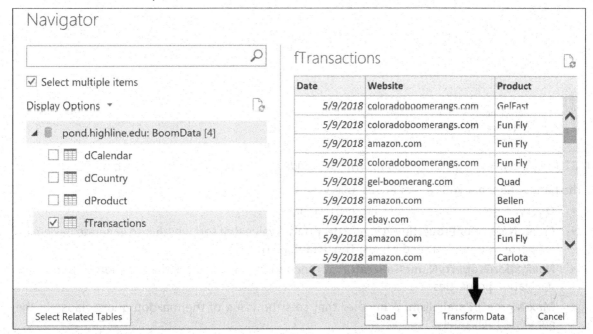

Figure 6-85 *The Navigator dialog box offers tables from the database.*

7.   Three automatic query steps are created. Click on the first step, the Source step.

As shown in Figure 6-82, the first step uses the Sql.Database M code function to deliver a table of database objects and attributes for those objects. The **Name** column shows the name of the database object, such as the name of a table, view, or function. The **Data** column contains the object from the database. The **Schema** column shows the name of the schema, which describes the structure and location of the database. The Schema column tells you where and how the data is stored. The Item column shows the name from the Name column, but the item name may provide additional database connection parameters, such as server name or database name. The Kind column shows the type of object in the database, such as a table, view, or function.

✕ ✓	*fx*	= Sql.Database("pond.highline.edu", "BoomData")			
	A^B_C **Name**	ABC$_{123}$ **Data**	A^B_C **Schema**	A^B_C **Item**	A^B_C **Kind**
1	dCalendar	Table	dbo	dCalendar	Table
2	dCountry	Table	dbo	dCountry	Table
3	dProduct	Table	dbo	dProduct	Table
4	fTransactions	Table	dbo	fTransactions	Table

Figure 6-86 *The Sql.Database M code function allows you to connect to an SQL Server database.*

The arguments for the Sql.Database function are as follows:

```
Sql.Database(
        server as text,
        database as text,
        optional options as nullable record) as table
```

The **server** argument is the name of the server, as text. The **database** argument is the name of the database, as text. The **options** argument allows you to set parameters inside a record. Figure 6-87 shows an example of the use of this argument, where rather than having the Power Query translator write the SQL for you, you can write the SQL code directly into the third argument. Unless you are proficient with SQL, it is better to let the query folding process write it for you.

```
Sql.Database(   "pond.highline.edu",
                "BoomData",
            [   Query="#(lf)
                SELECT dProduct.Product,#(lf)
                    SUM(Quantity*NetStandardCost*[Standard Cost]) AS COGS#(lf)
                FROM fTransactions#(lf)
                    JOIN dProduct#(lf)
                    ON dProduct.Product = fTransactions.Product#(lf)
                WHERE Quantity >= 100#(lf)
                GROUP BY dProduct.Product#(lf)
                HAVING SUM(Quantity*NetStandardCost*[Standard Cost]) >= 50000#(lf)
                ORDER BY dProduct.Product;",
                CommandTimeout=#duration(0, 0, 5, 0),
                HierarchicalNavigation=true,
                MultiSubnetFailover=true    ]   )
```

Figure 6-87 *The third argument allows you to write SQL code and set parameters as a record.*

The parameters that you can set are as follows:

- **Query:** A native SQL query used to retrieve data.
- **CreateNavigationProperties:** A logical (true/false) value that sets whether to generate navigation properties on the returned values. The default is true.
- **NavigationPropertyNameGenerator:** A function that is used for the creation of names for navigation properties.
- **MaxDegreeOfParallelism:** A number that sets the value of the maxdop query clause in the generated SQL query.

- **CommandTimeout:** A duration that controls how long the server-side query is allowed to run before it is canceled. The default is 10 minutes.

- **ConnectionTimeout:** A duration that controls how long to wait before abandoning an attempt to make a connection to the server. The default value is driver dependent.

- **HierarchicalNavigation:** A logical (true/false) value that sets whether to view the tables grouped by their schema names. The default is false.

- **MultiSubnetFailover:** A logical (true/false) value that sets the value of the MultiSubnetFailover property in the connection string. The default is false.

- **ContextInfo:** A binary value that is used to set the CONTEXT_INFO before running each command.

- **OmitSRID:** A logical (true/false) value that, if true, omits the SRID when producing well-known text from geometry and geography types.

- **EnableCrossDatabaseFolding:** A logical (true/false) value that, if true, allows query folding across databases on the same server. The default value is false.

As shown in Figure 6-88, the second step shows that a key match lookup was performed using the primary key columns Schema and Item.

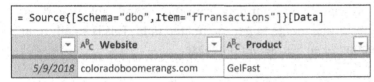

Figure 6-88 *The key match lookup uses the primary key columns Schema and Item.*

8. To view the SQL code generated by Power Query using the View Native Query feature, in the Applied Steps pane, right-click the Navigation step and select View Native Query, as shown in Figure 6-89. Figure 6-90 shows the result.

> **Note:** When you right-click a query step in the Applied Steps pane and search for the View Native Query item in the menu, if it is not grayed out, you know that that step and all steps above it are part of the query folding SQL code. If View Native Query is grayed out, you know that that step and all steps below it will not be part of the SQL code.

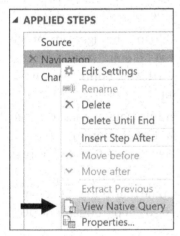

Figure 6-89 *View Native Query is not grayed out, so you know SQL code has been written.*

Native Query

```
select [$Table].[Date] as [Date],
    [$Table].[Website] as [Website],
    [$Table].[Product] as [Product],
    [$Table].[Quantity] as [Quantity],
    [$Table].[RevenueDiscount] as [RevenueDiscount],
    [$Table].[NetStandardCost] as [NetStandardCost],
    [$Table].[CountryCode] as [CountryCode]
from [dbo].[fTransactions] as [$Table]
```

Figure 6-90 *SQL code is automatically created by the query folding process.*

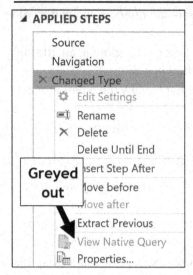

Source

Navigation

✕ Changed Type

  ⚙ Edit Settings

  ▭ Rename

  ✕ Delete

  Delete Until End

Greyed out | Insert Step After

Move before

Move after

Extract Previous

View Native Query

Properties...

Figure 6-91 *When View Native Query is grayed out, no SQL code was written.*

9. As shown in Figure 6-91, right-click the Changed Type step in the Applied Steps pane. Notice that the View Native Query option is grayed out. You do not need a step to add data types because the data types will be imported from the SQL Server database, so you can delete the Changed Type step.

10. To begin to build the COGS report, select the Navigation step and then use the filter dropdown at the top of the Website column to show only coloradoboomerangs.com. Name the step GetColoradoRecords. (Renaming steps will not adversely affect the query folding.) Check to see if the View Native Query feature is grayed out.

In relational databases, when you import a table, if there are related tables created through relationships, the data from the related table will be included in a column with the name of the related table. For example, in Figure 6-92, the value in the first row of the dProduct column is a record with the related dimension table data from the dProduct table. This means that if you want data from the related table, you do not have to perform a merge to get the related data. This is an advantage of connecting to an SQL Server database.

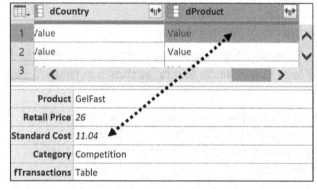

	dCountry	dProduct	
1	Value	Value	∧
2	Value	Value	∨
3	‹	›	

Product	GelFast
Retail Price	26
Standard Cost	11.04
Category	Competition
fTransactions	Table

Figure 6-92 *In a relational database, related dimension table data is pulled into the fact table.*

11. To pull the product standard cost into each row of the fTransactions table, on the right side of the dProduct column header, click the expand arrows, uncheck Use Original Column Name as Prefix, uncheck Select (All Columns), check the Standard Cost column, and click the OK button. Name the step GetCost. Check to see if the View Native Query feature is grayed out.

12. To calculate COGS for each row, select the noncontiguous columns Quantity, NetStandardCost, and Standard Cost and then use the Multiply feature to create the formula. Edit the formula to name the column COGS. Name the step CalculateCOGS. Check to see if the View Native Query feature is grayed out.

13. To remove all columns except Product and COGS, select the Product column and then the COGS column, right-click either column, and select Remove Other Columns. Name the step KeepProductAndCOGS. Check to see if the View Native Query feature is grayed out.

14. Group by the Product column and sum the COGS column. Name the new column Total COGS. Name the step GroupByProduct. Open the View Native Query pane. Figure 6-93 shows the query folding SQL code that was written. Figure 6-94 shows the result of the query.

15. In Excel, load the query as a connection only. In Power BI, uncheck Enable Load.

Native Query

```
select [rows].[Product2] as [Product],
    sum([rows].[COGS]) as [Total COGS]
from
(
    select [_].[Product2] as [Product2],
        case
            when ([_].[Quantity] is null and [_].[NetStandardCost] is null) and [_].[Standard Cost] is null
            then null
            else ((case
                when [_].[Quantity] is null
                then 1
                else [_].[Quantity]
            end) * (case
                when [_].[NetStandardCost] is null
                then 1
                else [_].[NetStandardCost]
            end)) * (case
                when [_].[Standard Cost] is null
                then 1
                else [_].[Standard Cost]
            end)
        end as [COGS]
    from
    (
        select [$Outer].[Product2],
            [$Outer].[Quantity],
            [$Outer].[NetStandardCost],
            [$Inner].[Standard Cost]
        from
        (
            select [_].[Date] as [Date],
                [_].[Website] as [Website],
                [_].[Product] as [Product2],
                [_].[Quantity] as [Quantity],
                [_].[RevenueDiscount] as [RevenueDiscount],
                [_].[NetStandardCost] as [NetStandardCost],
                [_].[CountryCode] as [CountryCode]
            from [dbo].[fTransactions] as [_]
            where [_].[Website] = 'coloradoboomerangs.com' and [_].[Website] is not null
        ) as [$Outer]
        left outer join [dbo].[dProduct] as [$Inner] on ([$Outer].[Product2] = [$Inner].[Product])
    ) as [_]
) as [rows]
group by [Product2]
```

Figure 6-93 *The query folding process created a single SQL statement from the seven M code steps.*

	Product	1.2 Total COGS
1	Alpine	13301929.72
2	Aspen	14880143.78
3	Bellen	31109273.32

Figure 6-94 *This report was executed in the SQL Server database.*

A Power BI Semantic Model as a Data Source

When you use the Data Model environment in Power Pivot or Power BI Desktop, you call the resulting model that you build a *data model*. When you publish a data model to the online Power BI service from either Power Pivot or Power BI Desktop, the uploaded data model becomes a *semantic model*. This is what Microsoft has to say about semantic models:

Semantic models present a mapping of the tables, columns, hierarchies, relationships, measures and other model components that sits between the underlying data sources and the workbooks, reports, dashboards and analysis. Semantic models should match the structure and data security needs of the business. Semantic models serve as the single source of truth that end users can connect to easily and interpret easily so that they can create consistent, data-driven and useful information for decision makers.

A semantic model has two main benefits. First, because it is hosted online, it serves as a single data source (or "single source of truth") for many users. Second, security measures can be added to safeguard the data.

Note: As discussed earlier in this chapter, to have access to the Power BI service, you must be working for an entity that has purchased and deployed a Microsoft enterprise package.

Now here is the funny thing: If you connect to a semantic model in the Power BI service, there is no M code involved at all. In fact, when you connect to a semantic model, no data is imported at all. You actually have a live connection to a single source of truth!

Why did I even mention semantic models if there is no M code in them? Well, because so much of M code query writing goes into creating semantic models (plus the relationships and DAX formulas), I wanted to mention that Power BI is a great place to store semantic models so that the people who use the models to create PivotTables, visuals, and dashboards have a single source of truth. In fact, in Chapter 7, I show an example of M code data modeling and uploading the result as a semantic model to the online Power BI service just to show you.

Summary

In this chapter, you have learned about some of the data connection functions, such as Csv.Document, Xml.Tables, Json.Document, Excel.Workbook, Excel.CurrentWorkbook, and Sql.Database. Importantly, you have learned about on-premises folder and file paths and what to do if a source file is moved. You have also learned about data extraction functions such as File.Contents, Folder.Contents, and Folder.Files. In addition, you have seen how to create a dynamic folder and file path in Excel, and you have learned that online data sources like Dataflow, websites, and SQL Server databases do not use on-premises file paths, which makes them more user friendly. Finally, you have learned how to import dates with the wrong format by using the Using Locale feature and an ISO double-data type trick. In Chapter 7, you will use all of the M code skills that you have learned in the book so far to build effective data models for data analysis.

Chapter 7: Data Modeling

This is the last chapter in the book, and I want it to be the most fun. You'll put to use all the M code skills you have picked up by applying them in some data modeling projects.

Data modeling for Power Pivot and Power BI usually means building a semantic model with a star schema structure. A **star schema model** is a model with a fact table surrounded by dimension tables, where each dimension table is connected to the fact table through a relationship and where the model has premade measures and is constructed to be user friendly. A **fact table** contains the data that you want to summarize or measure (such as sales amounts or units sold). A **dimension table** (also called a lookup table) contains a field with a unique list of entities (such as product IDs) with attributes in subsequent fields or lookup items (such as product prices). A field with a unique list of entities, called a **primary key**, is used to ensure that there are no duplicate records in the dimension table. When a primary key from a dimension table is used in a fact table, it is a **foreign key**. You connect a primary key and a foreign key in a **one-to-many relationship**, where the one side is the primary key, and the many side is the foreign key. A one-to-many relationship helps make lookup formulas easy and allows dimension table attributes to filter reports and visuals.

The **grain**, or **granularity**, of a fact table number indicates the size of the number. For example, the grain of an invoice sales total is larger than the grain of the invoice line detail sales amounts, and the grain of an invoice line detail sales amount is smaller than the grain of the invoice sales total amount. In one of the projects in this chapter, you will use your M code skills to convert two fact tables, each with a different granularity, into one fact table. That will be fun for sure!

In this chapter, you will work through eight projects that put all of your M code skills to work:

- Project 1: Converting seven Excel files, each with a single worksheet object, into a fact table using the From Folder feature and the Combine Files button
- Project 2: Converting seven Excel files, each with a single worksheet object, into a fact table using a custom column
- Project 3: Converting five text files with structural problems into a fact table using the Folders.File function, a parameter, and a custom function
- Project 4: Converting five CSV files with inconsistent column names into a fact table using correct names from a table
- Project 5: Converting seven JSON files with filename attributes into a fact table using the Folders.File function and a custom column formula
- Project 6: Extracting multiple objects and attributes from multiple Excel files and creating a fact table using the Folders.Files function and a custom column formula
- Project 7: Converting two fact tables with different granularities and three dimension tables into four tables that can be used in a star schema semantic model
- Project 8: Converting a single column of badly structured records into a proper table

We end the chapter with a bonus section on source data privacy settings and a bonus example that shows how to create a dynamic folder path to a SharePoint location.

Project 1: Using From Folder and Combine Files to Combine Multiple Excel Files, Each with a Single Object

As you learned when you studied the Excel.Workbook function, an Excel file can have multiple objects within a file. But in some situations—such as with the Oracle database system at Highline College, where I work—a database exports Excel files, each with a single worksheet named Sheet1. This means that there is a single object, not multiple objects, in each Excel file. The Power Query method you use for importing multiple Excel files depends on whether each file has one object or many objects. This first project shows the method you use when each Excel file contains a single object. In Project 6, you will see how to import Excel files that each contain many objects.

As shown in Figure 7-1, in the folder named FromFolderSingleTableExcel, there are seven Excel files. Each file was exported from a database and contains a single worksheet named Sheet1 with a proper table (not an Excel table) with the three columns Data, Product, and Sales. Figure 7-2 shows an example of one of the exported worksheets. I am going to show you two methods to import, extract, and append the seven proper tables:

- In this project, you will use the user interface and the Combine Files feature to create multiple queries, a reusable function, and multiple steps.
- In Project 2, you will write your own more condensed M code.

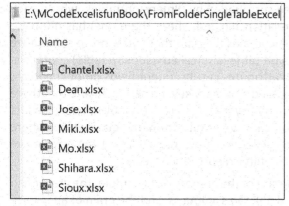

Figure 7-1 *Seven Excel files, each with a single worksheet object.*

	A	B	C
1	Date	Sales	Product
2	2/24/2025	41.05	Carlota
3	5/12/2025	1929.81	Yanaki
4	5/24/2024	2475.21	Carlota
	Sheet1	+	

Figure 7-2 *Each of the seven Excel files has a worksheet named Sheet1 with a proper table.*

Both methods start with using the **From Folder feature**, which imports all the files from a specified folder and delivers the files and file attributes in a table. From this table, you can perform many data modeling tasks, such as:

- Filter to remove unwanted files.
- Use the Combine Files button to easily append tables that have the same structure.
- Clean attribute columns so that you can use the attribute data.
- Use attributes to create new columns in the resulting tables.
- Add custom columns to convert the binary files into proper tables.

To try the first method, follow these steps:

1. Open a new Excel or Power BI file and save the file with the name DataModeling. If you are using Dataflow, create a new query to import tables and name the query SevenExcelFiles.

2. Access the From Folder feature in Excel, Power BI Desktop, or Dataflow:
   - **In Excel:** On the Data tab, go to the Get & Transform group, click the Get Data dropdown arrow, hover over From File, click From Folder, browse to the folder FromFolderSingleTableExcel, and click Open.
   - **In Power BI Desktop:** On the Home tab, go to the Data group, click the Get Data dropdown arrow, and select More. Then, on the right side of the Get Data dialog box, click Folder, click Connect, browse to the folder FromFolderSingleTableExcel, and click OK.
   - **In Dataflow:** In the Get Data area, click the Folder option. You need access to a data gateway in order to access the folder.

3. In the group address dialog box, click Transform Data. Name the query FromFolderSingleTableExcel.

   As shown in Figure 7-3, the **Folder.Files** function returns a table with the files from the specified folder path and all subfolders, as well as additional columns with file attributes. The Content column contains the seven Excel files. The Name column holds the name of each file, and this name can be used to create a new column in the resulting table (as you will see in Project 6). The Extension column, which holds the extension of each file, is useful for filtering out files that you do not want (as you will see in Project 3).

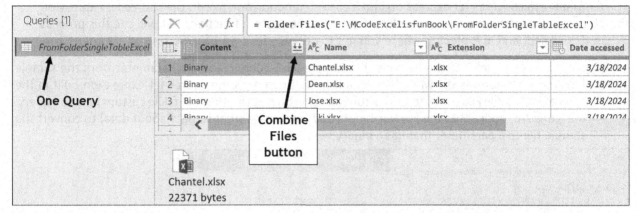

Figure 7-3 *The Folder.Files function returns a table with files from the specified folder.*

At the top of the Content column is the **Combine Files** button. To use this option, you need to ensure that all tables have the same structure, such as the same number of columns, consistent column names and data types, equivalent file types, and even equivalent worksheet names if you are importing Excel files. When you click the Combine Files button, you have to complete the Combine Files dialog box (which varies by file type), and then the option builds four new queries, including a reusable custom function, and adds six new steps to the append query to produce the final appended table.

4. Right-click the Content column and select Remove Other Columns.
5. Click the Combine Files button at the top of the Content column.
6. On the left side of the Combine Files dialog box, select Sheet1 and then click OK. Figure 7-4 shows the result.
7. Load the query as a connection only.

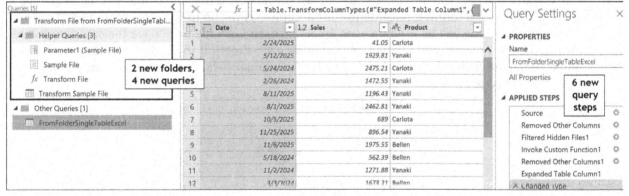

Figure 7-4 *The Combine Files button creates new folders, queries, and query steps.*

Figure 7-4 shows that the Combine File button creates two new folders, four new queries, six new query steps, and a single append table based on the seven worksheets. That is a lot of action from a single click of a button! To understand how these automatically generated components are working together to create the appended table, we need to look at each component, one at a time:

*   As shown in Figure 7-5, the Sample File query extracts an Excel file that it can use as a sample to help build the M code for the custom function that is built in the Fx Transform File query.

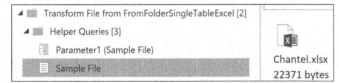

Figure 7-5 *The first step in the automatic process is to select a sample file.*

Note: In M code, a **parameter** is a variable that you can define and store in the Manage Parameters dialog box (like a defined name in the Excel worksheet that is stored in the Name Manager). You can use a defined parameter throughout the Power Query environment. In addition, you can use a parameter to convert a let expression into a custom function and to edit the source let expression so that any changes are automatically reflected in the custom function. You will see this process in this project and in Project 3, where you get to define your own parameter.

- As shown in Figure 7-6, the Parameter1 (Sample File) query creates a parameter from the sample file. This parameter is the M code mechanism that connects the source let expression built in the Transform Sample File query to the custom function built in the Transform File custom function query. In Figure 7-6, notice that the keyword meta adds **metadata** (that is, data about data) to convert the sample file to a parameter that has a binary type.

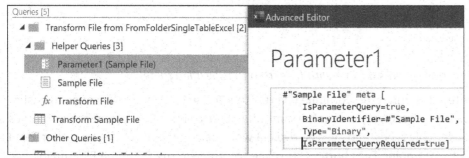

Figure 7-6 *The second step in the automatic process is to build a parameter from the sample file.*

- As shown in Figure 7-7, the Transform Sample File query is the source of the let expression M code that will be used in the final custom function. The let expression has three steps. In the Source step, the parameter is used inside the Excel.Workbook function. The parameter connects the query to the custom function query so that any edits made in this query will be automatically reflected in the custom function query. As shown in Figure 7-8, the Navigation step extracts the single worksheet using a key match lookup based on the primary key columns Item and Kind. The Promoted Headers step promotes the first row of column names to column headers. This is necessary because the object is a worksheet object rather than an Excel table object. Notice that the worksheet name Sheet1 is hard-coded into the formula. Because this is the code that will be used in the custom function, and the custom function will be used on each Excel file, each Excel file must have the same worksheet name, Sheet1 (or some other equivalent name for each sheet). If the worksheets do not have the same name, the code will not work, and you have to manually edit the code in this process or create a different M code solution.

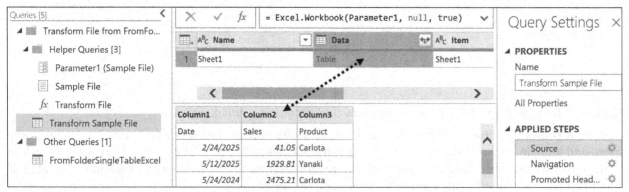

Figure 7-7 *The Excel.Workbook function creates a table with a single worksheet object.*

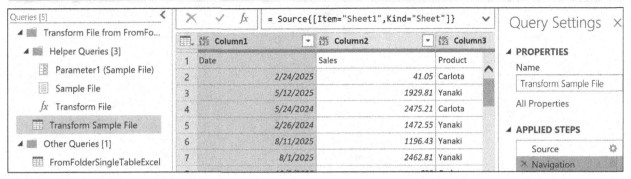

Figure 7-8 *A key match lookup based on the Item and Kind columns.*

- Figure 7-9 shows the let expression that will be transferred to the custom function.

```
Advanced Editor

Transform Sample File                                    Display Options ▾

let
    Source = Excel.Workbook(Parameter1, null, true),
    Sheet1_Sheet = Source{[Item="Sheet1",Kind="Sheet"]}[Data],
    #"Promoted Headers" = Table.PromoteHeaders(Sheet1_Sheet, [PromoteAllScalars=true])
in
    #"Promoted Headers"
```

Figure 7-9 *The let expression created by the Transform Sample File query.*

- Figure 7-10 shows the let expression that was converted to a custom function named Transform File. The function contains a single binary variable named Parameter1. The single input for the function will be the Excel file in each row of the table of Excel files.

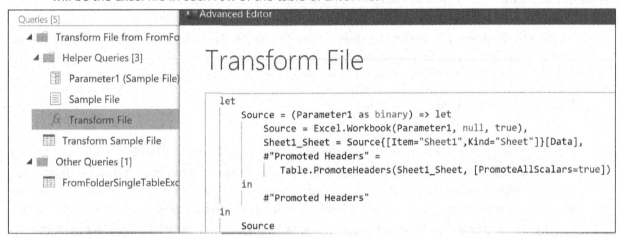

Figure 7-10 *A custom function created from the let expression in the previous step.*

- As shown in Figure 7-11, there are six new query steps added to the query that append the tables into a single fact table. Four of the query steps are standard, but two of the steps are worth noting: Filtered Hidden Files1 filters out hidden files, and, as shown in Figure 7-11, the Invoke Custom Function1 query step invokes the custom function and returns a proper table from each Excel worksheet.

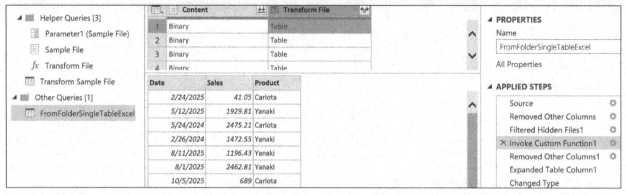

Figure 7-11 *A custom function is invoked to create proper tables from the Excel worksheets.*

Project 2: Using a Custom Column to Combine Multiple Excel Files, Each with a Single Object

The automatic process involved in using the Combine Files button (as described in Project 1) is fast and easy if all the tables have the same structure and if you don't mind a lot of extra queries cluttering up your file. When I am in a hurry and using a file that does not have other queries, I tend to use the Combine File button. However, sometimes it's better to create a custom column solution. As you'll see in this project, a custom column solution is appropriate in three situations:

- When you do not want to clutter the file with many queries
- When the tables being appended do not have a proper table structure (for example, when they are cross-tabulated tables, have inappropriate titles, or are JSON files)
- When the tables being appended look like tables but have small differences, such as inconsistent column names or different file types

This project walks through the process of combining multiple Excel files, each with a single object, by using a custom column. Using the same folder of Excel files as in Project 1, follow these steps:

1. Create a blank query and name it OneQueryAppendExcelFiles. To import the Excel files, create the following formula with your on-premises folder path:

   ```
   = Folder.Files("E:\MCodeExcelisfunBook\FromFolderSingleTableExcel")
   ```

2. Add a custom column with this formula:

   ```
   = Excel.Workbook([Content],true,false)
   ```

3. Name the new column GetExcelTables. Name the query step CCGetExcelTables.

   As shown in Figure 7-12, because each Excel file has a single worksheet object, the table of returned Excel file objects always has a single row. All you need is the worksheet from the Data column. This means you can use a row index lookup to get the worksheet from each row. In addition, in the second argument of the Excel.Workbook function, you smartly used true to promote the first row of column names in each worksheet. Further, because you don't have a lot of data and none of the columns contains integer data, you use false in the third argument of the Excel.Workbook function to infer the data types from the worksheet. By using the second and third arguments in the Excel.Workbook function, you replace two query steps to promote headers and add data types.

```
= Table.AddColumn(Source, "GetExcelTables", each Excel.Workbook([Content],true,false))
```

Date created	Attributes	Folder Path	GetExcelTables
3/7/2024 5:49:04 PM	Record	E:\MCodeExcelisfunBook\FromFolderSingleTableExcel\	Table
3/7/2024 5:49:04 PM	Record	E:\MCodeExcelisfunBook\FromFolderSingleTableExcel\	Table

Name	Data	Item	Kind	Hidden
Sheet1	Table	Sheet1	Sheet	FALSE

Figure 7-12 *Using the Excel.Workbook function in a custom column.*

4. To extract the worksheet from the table of objects in each row, edit the custom column formula as shown in Figure 7-13, so that it becomes:

```
= Excel.Workbook([Content],true,false){0}[Data]
```

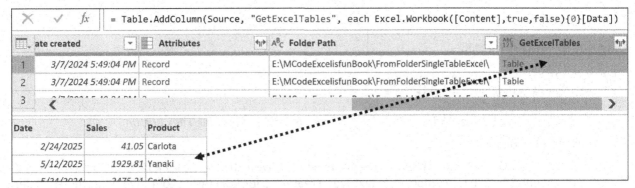

Figure 7-13 *Using a row index lookup to extract the worksheets from each file as a table.*

5. To complete the append, add a new query step and create this formula:

```
= Table.Combine(CCGetExcelTables[GetExcelTables])
```

6. Name the query step CombineWorksheetTables. The resulting fact table is shown in Figure 7-14.

7. Load the query as a connection only.

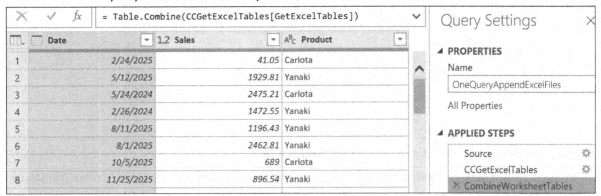

Figure 7-14 *There is less clutter with one query and three steps.*

As the results in Figure 7-14 illustrate, with some M code knowledge, you can build solutions that are more compact and efficient than user interface solutions.

Project 3: Appending Multiple Text Files with Table Structure Problems

Now that you have seen how to import and work with Excel files that each include a single sheet, you're ready to try a more complex data transformation involving multiple text files. The goal of this project is to import and append the tables of data in the text files, as shown in Figure 7-15. In addition, because there is a misplaced Excel file in the folder, you will have to filter out that file, and because M code is case sensitive, you will have to fix the inconsistent file extensions.

As shown in Figure 7-16, the other common problem that you face here is that each text file has three rows of titles that are not part of the proper table. These tables do not have the proper table structure, and therefore you cannot use the Combine Files button to append the tables. In this case, you can build your own sample file, parameter, and let statement for the sample file, as well as a reusable custom function. Although it is easy to just create a custom column, the advantage of using a

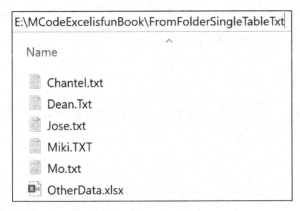

Figure 7-15 *You want to import only the text files.*

parameter and a reusable function is that you can use the function more than one time and, in many cases, it is easier to edit the M code in a separate query than it is to edit in a custom column.

```
Gel·Booms →    →   ¶
Chantel·Sales →    →   ¶
    →    →   ¶
Date → Sales→Product¶
2/24/2025 → 41.05→Carlota¶
5/12/2025 → 1929.81  →  Yanaki¶
5/24/2024 → 2475.21  →  Carlota¶
```

Figure 7-16 *The titles above each table prevent you from using the Combine Files button.*

To try this project, follow these steps:

1. In the Power Query Editor, create a new group named FiveTextFiles. Create a blank query and name it E05AppenedTextTable. To import the text files, create this formula (using your own on-premises folder path):

    ```
    Folder.Files("E:\MCodeExcelisfunBook\FromFolderSingleTableTxt")
    ```

2. Duplicate the query and name this second query A01SampleFile. Figure 7-17 shows the result. (We will come back to this query later.)

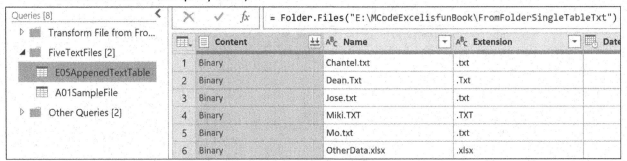

Figure 7-17 *Creating two queries in a group named FiveTextFiles.*

3. In the E05AppenedTextTable query, right-click the Extension column header, hover over Transform, and select Lowercase. Name the query step ExtensionsLowercase.

4. Filter the Extension column to include only records where the extension is equal to .txt. Name the query step FilterKeepTextFiles. Figure 7-18 shows the result.

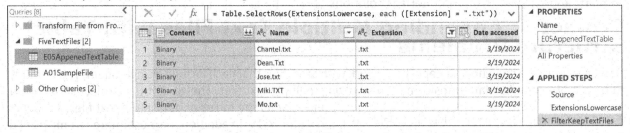

Figure 7-18 *Transforming extensions to lowercase and filtering to include only text files.*

5. In the A01SampleFile query, add a new step and create the following formula:

    ```
    = Source{0}[Content]
    ```

    Press Enter. The step is automatically named Navigation, and two extra query steps are added.

6. Delete the two extra query steps. Figure 7-19 shows the result.

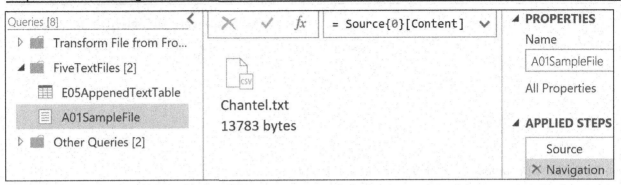

Figure 7-19 *Extracting to get a sample file.*

7. To create a parameter, go to the Home tab, and in the Parameters group, click the Manage Parameters dropdown arrow and select New Parameter. The Manage Parameters dialog box appears.

8. Complete the Manage Parameters dialog box as shown in Figure 7-20 and click OK.

9. Move the parameter to the FiveTextFiles group.

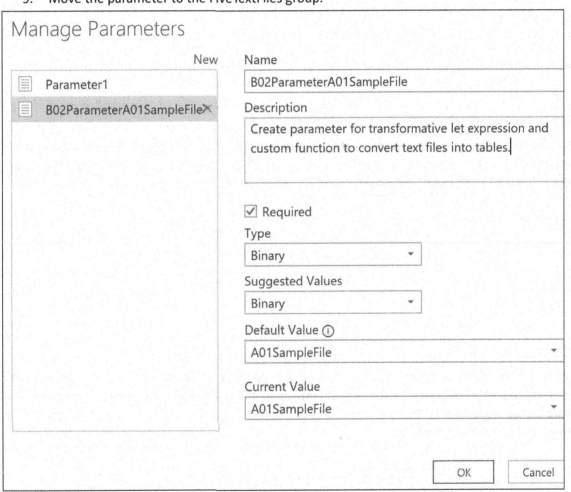

Figure 7-20 *The parameter connects the transformative query to the custom function.*

10. To build the let expression for the custom function, create a blank query in the FiveTextFiles group, name it C03TransformSampleFile, and create this formula as the first step:

    ```
    = Csv.Document(B02ParameterA01SampleFile,null,"#(tab)")
    ```

11. As shown in Figure 7-21, the first three rows are titles and are not part of the proper table. To fix this, add a step and create the following (intentionally incorrect) formula:

    ```
    = Table.Skip(Source,2)
    ```

    Name this query step SkipTitleRows.

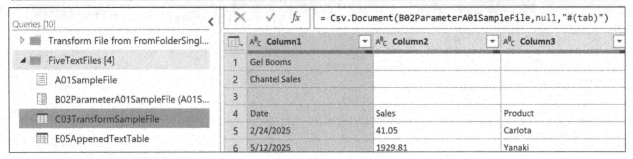

Figure 7-21 *Csv.Document uses the parameter in the first argument.*

12. To promote headers, add a query step and create the following formula:

```
= Table.PromoteHeaders(SkipTitleRows, [PromoteAllScalars=true])
```

Name the query step PromoteHeaders. Figure 7-22 shows the let expression created in C03TransformSampleFile.

```
//C03TransformSampleFile
let
    Source = Csv.Document(B02ParameterA01SampleFile,null,"#(tab)"),
    SkipTitleRows = Table.Skip(Source,2),
    PromoteHeaders = Table.PromoteHeaders(SkipTitleRows, [PromoteAllScalars=true])
in
    PromoteHeaders
```

Figure 7-22 *The let expression that transforms one text file.*

13. To convert the let expression into a reusable custom function, right-click the C03TransformSampleFile query and select Create Function. As shown in Figure 7-23, in the Create Function dialog box, name the custom function query D04FxTextFileToTable. Click OK to close the dialog box.

Create Function

Enter a name for the new function.

Function name

D04FxTextFileToTable|

Parameters: B02ParameterA01SampleFile   [OK]   [Cancel]

Figure 7-23 *Creating the function.*

14. When the new function query appears in the Queries pane, unfortunately, a number of unnecessary folders are created. Figure 7-24 shows that I moved all the queries into the FiveTextFiles group and deleted the extra folders. This figure also shows the resulting custom function let expression from the Advanced Editor on the right.

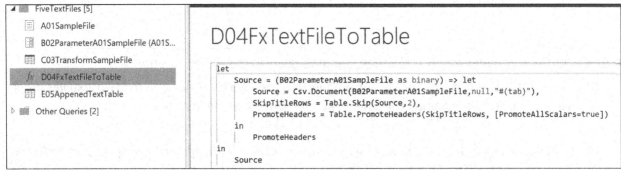

Figure 7-24 *The let expression that defines the custom function.*

15. To use the custom function, select the query E05AppenedTextTable, go to the Add Column tab, and in the General group, click the Invoke Custom Function button. Name the new column E05AppenedTextTable GetTextFiles, select the function query D04FxTextFileToTable, in the argument textbox select the column Content, and click OK. Name the query step InvokeCustomFunction. Figure 7-25 shows that in each row, the text files have not been converted to a proper table.

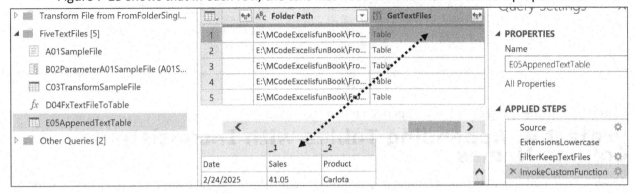

Figure 7-25 *Each row does not have a proper table. There is an error.*

16. Figure 7-25 reveals that there is an error in the transformative query. To fix the error, select the C03TransformSampleFile query and edit the formula in the second step so it becomes the following (see Figure 7-26):

```
= Table.Skip(Source,3)
```

The edit flows through to the custom function and on to the append query, as shown in Figure 7-27.

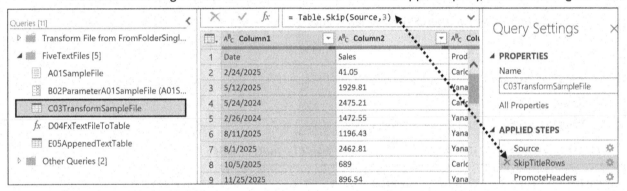

Figure 7-26 *Editing the transformative query.*

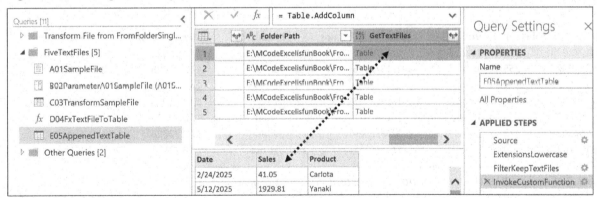

Figure 7-27 *The edit flows through to the append query.*

17. To append the tables, create the following formula:

```
= Table.Combine(InvokeCustomFunction[GetTextFiles])
```

Name the step AppendTables.

18. Add a data type to each of the three columns. Name the query step AddDataTypes.

19. Load the query as a connection only. Figure 7-28 shows the fact table that results.

Figure 7-28 *All the text files are now appended into a fact table.*

Project 4: Appending Tables with Inconsistent Column Names

When you get tables of data from a database, you often get consistent column names. However, in the working world of data analysis, it is common to get tables that do not have a consistent structure; for example, tables may have inconsistent column names.

Figure 7-29 shows a folder named FromFolderCSVInconsistentNames that contains three CSV files. As shown in Figure 7-30, each of these CSV files contains a table, and the tables have inconsistent column names. As you learned in Chapter 2, if you try to append tables with inconsistent column names, you end up with a table with extra columns and null values littered throughout the data. Figure 7-31 shows the awful result of appending the tables from Figure 7-30.

Figure 7-29 *CSV files with tables that contains inconsistent column names.*

SalesTable01.csv

Extra Space	($)	OK
Date	Sales ($)	Product
1/10/2025	119.99	Quad
1/11/2025	255.12	Sunset
1/12/2025	234.01	Quad
1/13/2025	373.39	Carlota
1/14/2025	233.34	Aspen
1/15/2025	379.21	Quad
1/16/2025	409.9	Aspen

SalesTable02.csv

OK	OK	OK
Date	Sales	Product
1/15/2025	512.12	Yanaki
1/18/2025	459.2	Yanaki
1/22/2025	167.87	Bellen
1/25/2025	201.34	Quad
1/15/2025	597.65	Aspen
1/18/2025	233.07	Bellen
1/22/2025	100	Carlota

SalesTable03.csv

Extra s	Extra Space	Extra s
Dates	Sales	Products
1/10/2025	523.36	Quad
1/11/2025	110	Carlota
1/12/2025	274.25	Yanaki
1/13/2025	33.1	Yanaki
1/14/2025	779.95	Sunset
1/15/2025	391.2	Sunset
1/16/2025	200.23	Bellen

Figure 7-30 *Three tables that do not have consistent column names.*

Date	Sales ($)	Product	Date	Sales	Dates	Sales	Products
1/10/2025	119.99	Quad	null	null	null	null	null
1/11/2025	255.12	Sunset	null	null	null	null	null
1/12/2025	234.01	Quad	null	null	null	null	null
1/13/2025	373.39	Carlota	null	null	null	null	null
1/14/2025	233.34	Aspen	null	null	null	null	null
1/15/2025	379.21	Quad	null	null	null	null	null
1/16/2025	409.9	Aspen	null	null	null	null	null
null	null	Yanaki	1/15/2025	512.12	null	null	null
null	null	Yanaki	1/18/2025	459.2	null	null	null
null	null	Bellen	1/22/2025	167.87	null	null	null
null	null	Quad	1/25/2025	201.34	null	null	null
null	null	Aspen	1/15/2025	597.65	null	null	null
null	null	Bellen	1/18/2025	233.07	null	null	null
null	null	Carlota	1/22/2025	100	null	null	null
null	null	null	null	null	1/10/2025	523.36	Quad
null	null	null	null	null	1/11/2025	110	Carlota
null	null	null	null	null	1/12/2025	274.25	Yanaki
null	null	null	null	null	1/13/2025	33.1	Yanaki
null	null	null	null	null	1/14/2025	779.95	Sunset
null	null	null	null	null	1/15/2025	391.2	Sunset
null	null	null	null	null	1/16/2025	200.23	Bellen

Figure 7-31 *Appending tables with inconsistent column names leads to this type of mess.*

There are multiple ways to deal with this issue. The method you will use in this project involves appending correct column names. To try it, follow these steps:

1. Create a group named InconsistentColumnNames. (You will save the two queries for this example in this group.)

2. Create the query CCN (for Correct Column Names) in Excel, Power BI Desktop, or Dataflow:

   - **In Excel:** As shown in Figure 7-32, import the Excel table from the ColumnNames worksheet.

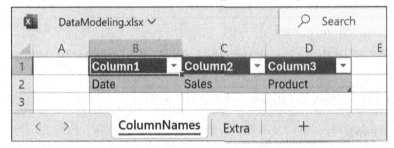

Figure 7-32 *In Excel, import the table with the correct column names.*

   - **In Power BI Desktop or Dataflow:** Create a blank query and write the intrinsic table function formula shown here:

```
= #table(
     type table [Column1 = text, Column2 = text, Column3 = text],
   {{"Date", "Sales", "Product"}})
```

   Name the query CCN.

3. Create a blank query and name it InconsistentColumnNames. To import the CSV files, create this formula (using your own on-premises folder path):

```
Folder.Files("E:\MCodeExcelisfunBook\FromFolderCSVInconsistentNames")
```

4. Add a custom column with the column name GetCsvTables, the query step name GetCsvTables, and the following formula:

    ```
    Table.Skip(Csv.Document([Content]))
    ```

    As shown in Figure 7-33, the formula accomplishes these three goals:

    - Using only the first argument in the Csv.Document function allows the function to assume the following defaults: columns = infer number of columns, delimiter = comma, encoding = 65001 UFT-8.
    - Using only the first argument in the Table.Skip function allows the function to assume the default of skipping the first row. By removing the first row, you remove the inconsistent column names.
    - Not using the Table.PromoteHeaders function causes the process to assume the consistent column names Column1, Column2, and Column3. These default column names equate with the column names from the table with the correct column names.

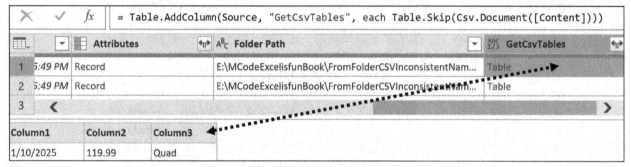

Figure 7-33 *Extracting tables from the CSV files and removing inconsistent column names.*

5. Create the formula to append the CSV files, as shown in Figure 7-34, and name the query step AppendWithCNamesInFirstRow. Notice that because all the CSV tables have the same default column names, the append works perfectly.

| | | fx | = Table.Combine(GetCsvTables[GetCsvTables]) |

	ABC Column1	ABC Column2	ABC Column3
1	1/10/2025	119.99	Quad
2	1/11/2025	255.12	Sunset

Figure 7-34 *Appending CSV tables with default column names.*

6. Edit the formula as shown in Figure 7-35 so that it can append the correct column names to the top of the table.

| | | fx | = CCN & Table.Combine(GetCsvTables[GetCsvTables]) |

	ABC Column1	ABC Column2	ABC Column3
1	Date	Sales	Product
2	1/10/2025	119.99	Quad
3	1/11/2025	255.12	Sunset

Figure 7-35 *Appending the correct column names to the first row in the appended table.*

7. Promote the column names to headers as shown in Figure 7-36.

| | | fx | = Table.PromoteHeaders(AppendWithCNamesInFirstRow, [PromoteAllScalars=true]) |

	ABC Date	ABC Sales	ABC Product
1	1/10/2025	119.99	Quad
2	1/11/2025	255.12	Sunset

Figure 7-36 *Promoting the correct column names to column headers.*

8. Add data types as shown in Figure 7-37.
9. Load the query as a connection only.

	Date	1.2 Sales	Aᴮ𝒸 Product
1	1/10/2025	119.99	Quad
2	1/11/2025	255.12	Sunset
3	1/12/2025	234.01	Quad
4	1/13/2025	373.39	Carlota
5	1/14/2025	233.34	Aspen
6	1/15/2025	379.21	Quad

Figure 7-37 *After you add data types, the result is a single fact table.*

Project 5: Appending JSON Tables with Filename Attributes

As you have seen, to deal with the common problem of inconsistent column names, you need to build a solution. In cases like the one in Project 4, the formulas are relatively easy to write, and building a custom column is quick and easy; in such cases, I do not bother to create reusable custom functions. Sometimes, though, you need to append JSON tables, which are actually records and not tables, so you can't use the Combine Files button with them. This project walks you through how to deal with these records.

As shown in Figure 7-38, the folder FromFolderSingleTableJson contains three JSON files. None of these records has structural problems, as you can see in the records from the Chantel.json file shown in Figure 7-39. However, say that you need to add to each table a new column that lists the sales rep name—which is the same as the filename for the table. For example, in the file Chantel.json, you need to create a new attribute column that lists the name Chantel in each row of the table. Once the new column is added to each table, you can append the tables to get a final fact table.

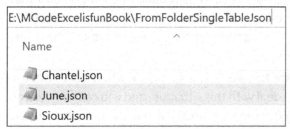

Figure 7-38 *Three JSON files, each of which contains sales records.*

```
[¶
··{¶
····"Dates":·"10/6/2025",¶
····"Products":·"Rang",¶
····"Sales":·220.62¶
··},¶
··{¶
····"Dates":·"8/8/2024",¶
····"Products":·"Icarus",¶
····"Sales":·266.31¶
··},¶
```

Figure 7-39 *An example of the first two records in the Chantel.json file.*

To walk through this project, follow these steps:

1. Create a new query that connects to the folder FromFolderSingleTableJson and imports a table containing the JSON files. Name the query FromFolderSingleTableJson. Figure 7-40 shows the result. As you can see, the Name column shows the whole filename, but in this case, you do not want to include the file extension.

	Content	↕ A^B_C Name	▼	A^B_C Extension	▼	🕘 Date acc
	fx	= Folder.Files("E:\MCodeExcelisfunBook\FromFolderSingleTableJson")				
1	Binary	Chantel.json		.json		3/20/
2	Binary	June.json		.json		3/20/
3	Binary	Sioux.json		.json		3/20/

Figure 7-40 *Importing the JSON files using the Folder.Files function.*

2. To extract the sales rep name from the Name column, select the Name column, click the Transform tab, go to the Text Column group, and click the Extract dropdown arrow and select Text Before Delimiter. Enter a period delimiter in the Text Before Delimiter dialog box and click OK. Name the query step GetSalesRepName. Figure 7-41 shows the result.

	Content	↕ A^B_C Name	▼	A^B_C Extension	▼	🕘 Date accessed	▼	🕘 Date
	fx	= Table.TransformColumns(Source, {{"Name", each Text.BeforeDelimiter(_, "."), type text}})						
1	Binary	Chantel		.json		3/20/2024 11:54:50 AM		3/
2	Binary	June		.json		3/20/2024 11:54:50 AM		3/

Figure 7-41 *Extracting the sales rep name in the Name column.*

3. To convert the JSON files to tables by extracting the list of records from the file and converting the list to a table, add a custom column, name the column GetJsonTables, name the query step CCGetJsonTables, and create this formula:

```
Table.FromRecords(Json.Document([Content]))
```

Figure 7-42 shows that the formula successfully created a table in each row, but each table is missing a column for the sales rep names. In addition, because there is a table in each row and that table needs to access the sales rep name in the same row in the Name column, you must use the Table.AddColumn function a second time in this formula, and it must be wrapped around the Table. FromRecords function.

As you learned in Chapter 3, you cannot have two back-to-back iterating table functions that both use the keyword each. But you learned a few methods to deal with this situation, and you can use the one that you like. My favorite is to use a let expression. With the let expression, you can define a variable in the scope of the first Table.AddColumn function because it has access to the Name column. Once you define the variable with the let expression, you can use it anywhere in your formula.

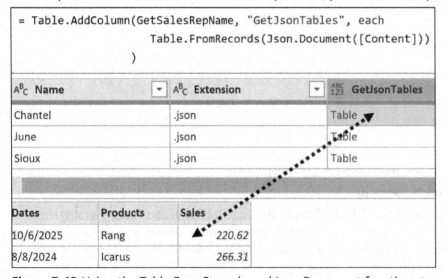

Figure 7-42 *Using the Table.FromRecords and Json.Document functions to create tables.*

4. To use a let express, open the Custom Column dialog box by clicking the gear icon next to the GetJsonTables query step in the Applied Steps pane and create the formula shown in Figure 7-43. Figure 7-44 shows that each table in each row now has a new SalesRep column.

Custom column formula (i)

```
= let Name = [Name] in
  Table.AddColumn(
      Table.FromRecords(Json.Document([Content])),
      "SalesRep",
      each Name)
```

Figure 7-43 *Defining a variable in the scope of the first Table.AddColumn function.*

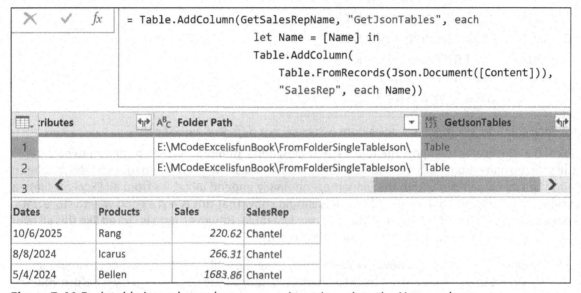

```
= Table.AddColumn(GetSalesRepName, "GetJsonTables", each
              let Name = [Name] in
              Table.AddColumn(
                  Table.FromRecords(Json.Document([Content])),
                  "SalesRep", each Name))
```

:ributes		AᵇC Folder Path		₁₂₃ GetJsonTables	
1		E:\MCodeExcelisfunBook\FromFolderSingleTableJson\		Table	
2		E:\MCodeExcelisfunBook\FromFolderSingleTableJson\		Table	
3					

Dates	Products	Sales	SalesRep
10/6/2025	Rang	220.62	Chantel
8/8/2024	Icarus	266.31	Chantel
5/4/2024	Bellen	1683.86	Chantel

Figure 7-44 *Each table in each row has a new column based on the Name column.*

5. Use the Table.Combine function to append the tables. Name the query step AppendTables.
6. Add a data type to each column. Name the query step AddDataTypes.
7. Load the query as a connection only. Figure 7-45 shows the resulting fact table.

	Dates	AᵇC Products	1.2 Sales	AᵇC SalesRep
1	1/13/2024	Aspen	1078.07	Chantel
2	1/14/2024	Sunset	1859.77	June
3	2/10/2024	Rang	1075.91	Chantel

Figure 7-45 *The final fact table is complete and includes a SalesRep column.*

Project 6: Importing Multiple Excel Files, Each with Multiple Objects

You have worked through five projects where you created fact tables from multiple files, each with a single object. Next, you will see how to import multiple Excel files and extract multiple objects from each file.

For this project, you have three Excel files in the folder named FromFolderMultipleObjectsExcel, as shown in Figure 7-46. Figure 7-47 shows the Bellingham file, which contains four worksheets. On each worksheet is an Excel table with the sales for the sales rep whose name appears on the worksheet tab. Each Excel table has between 25,000 and 100,000 rows of sales data. (Together, all the tables have more than 900,000 rows of data.) In addition, the city name is included in the filename.

E:\MCodeExcelisfunBook\FromFolderMultipleObjectsExcel

🟩	Bellingham.xlsx	7,098 KB
🟩	Olympia.xlsx	6,237 KB
🟩	Sumner.xlsx	7,952 KB

Figure 7-46 *Three city Excel files that contain sales rep compressor sales data.*

Bellingham.xlsx • Saved to this PC ∨

	A	B	C
1	Date ▾	Sales ▾	Product ▾
2	4/3/2023	1460.59	Compressor Kit 6
3	5/2/2023	101.48	Compressor Kit 2
4	12/2/2023	592.72	Compressor Kit 1
5	5/16/2024	454.63	Compressor Kit 3
6	4/18/2023	782.95	Compressor Kit 3

< > **Cisco** | Chantel | Ty | Miki

Figure 7-47 *Each sales rep's compressor sales data is stored on a different worksheet.*

For each Excel file, the goal is to import the four Excel tables, add a different SalesRep column to each table that lists the sale rep name from each Excel table name (which is not shown here), add to each table a column that contains the city name from within the filename, and finally append all tables from all Excel files into a single fact table. The company that created these files should know that this is not a good way to store data. Data that belongs in one fact table should be stored in one fact table. However, data is stored like this all over the world. Luckily, Power Query and M code come to the rescue!

> **Note:** In Chapter 6, I showed you how to use an Excel dynamic folder path to connect to a folder of files. If you want to try that here, go back to Chapter 6, look up the details, and try it before you begin the steps. If you do not want to try it, or if you are working in Power BI Desktop or Dataflow, then you can just use an on-premises folder path.

To import the three Excel files, create a new query and connect to the folder FromFolderMultipleObjectsExcel. For an on-premises path, Figure 7-48 shows an example of the formula. For the dynamic path, Figure 7-49 shows an example of the formula. Name the query FactTableFromExcelFiles.

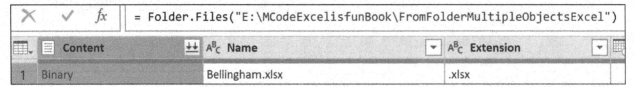

```
fx    = Folder.Files("E:\MCodeExcelisfunBook\FromFolderMultipleObjectsExcel")
```

▦ ▾	🗎 Content	↧↧ AᵇC Name	▾ AᵇC Extension	▾ ▦
1	Binary	Bellingham.xlsx	.xlsx	

Figure 7-48 *On-premises path inside Folder.Files.*

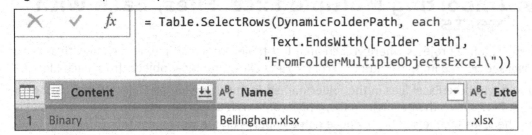

```
fx    = Table.SelectRows(DynamicFolderPath, each
                Text.EndsWith([Folder Path],
                "FromFolderMultipleObjectsExcel\"))
```

▦ ▾	🗎 Content	↧↧ AᵇC Name	▾ AᵇC Exte
1	Binary	Bellingham.xlsx	.xlsx

Figure 7-49 *Dynamic folder path in an Excel workbook file.*

The dynamic formula in Figure 7-49 has the folder name hard-coded into the formula, but if the destination file and source data folder move to the same new location, there is no need to update the path because everything is dynamic.

I show two different methods to approach this project:

- For the first method, you will use a mix of the user interface and writing M code, and when you combine tables, you will use the Table.ExpandTableColumn function.

- For the second method, you will write most of the M code, and when you combine tables, you will use the Table.Combine function.

Back in Chapter 5, you learned about the two functions Table.Combine and Table.ExpandTableColumn. In that chapter, you saw that the performance of the Table.Combine function was slightly better, and it did not hard-code column names coming from external sources into formulas, as the Table.ExpandTableColumn function did.

To try the first method—using a mix of the user interface and M code and using the Table.ExpandTableColumn function when you combine tables—follow these steps:

1. To extract the objects from each Excel file, add a custom column with the Excel.Workbook function. Name the new column GetExcelObjects, as shown in Figure 7-50. Name the query step CCGetExcelObjects. Notice that the Item column lists the names of objects. Any object that starts with T_ is an Excel table.

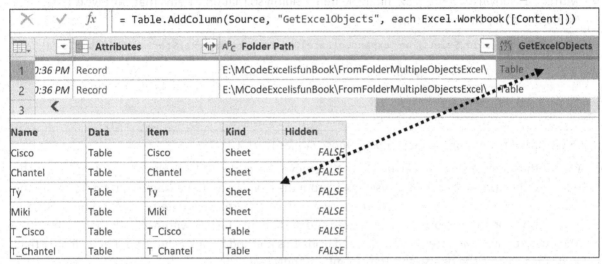

Figure 7-50 *Each row contains a table of Excel objects.*

2. Click the expand button at the top of the GetExcelObjects column and check only the columns Data and Item. Name the query step ExpandGetExcelObjects. The finished formula should look like this:

```
= Table.ExpandTableColumn(CCGetExcelObjects,"GetExcelObjects",
    {"Data", "Item"}, {"Data", "Item"}
    )
```

3. The Table.ExpandTableColumn function delivers a table with many columns. To extract the Date, Name, and Item columns, rather than add a new step, you can create a column/table lookup formula by using the field access operator. Edit your formula by adding the column/table lookup formula element directly after the closing parenthesis for the Table.ExpandTableColumn function, as shown here:

```
= Table.ExpandTableColumn(CCGetExcelObjects,"GetExcelObjects",
    {"Data", "Item"}, {"Data", "Item"}
    )[[Data],[Name],[Item]]
```

As shown in Figure 7-51, the Data column now contains the Excel tables with sales data. The Name column lists the filename, with the city name attribute that you want in the final table. The Item column contains the names and references for all Excel objects. However, you want this column to show only the Excel table objects whose names start with T_.

```
✕  ✓  fx    = Table.ExpandTableColumn( CCGetExcelObjects,"GetExcelObjects",
                                      {"Data", "Item"}, {"Data", "Item"}
                                    )[[Data],[Name],[Item]]
```

⊞. 123 Data	↔ ABc Name	▼	123 Item	▼
1 Table	Bellingham.xlsx		Cisco	
2 Table	Bellingham.xlsx		Chantel	
3 Table	Bellingham.xlsx		Ty	
4 Table	Bellingham.xlsx		Miki	
5 Table	Bellingham.xlsx		T_Cisco	

Figure 7-51 *Expanding the GetExcelObjects column and extracting three columns.*

4. To filter the table so that the Item column contains only the Excel table objects whose names start with T_, as shown in Figure 7-52, filter the Item column so that only items that start with T_ remain. Name the query step FilterKeepT_.

```
✕  ✓  fx    ⊨ Table.SelectRows(ExpandGetExcelObjects, each Text.StartsWith([Item], "T_"))
```

⊞. 123 Data	↔ ABc Name	▼	123 Item	▼
1 Table	Bellingham.xlsx		T_Cisco	
2 Table	Bellingham.xlsx		T_Chantel	

Figure 7-52 *Filtering to get just the Excel tables whose names start with T_.*

5. Create the formula shown in Figure 7-53 to remove the prefix T_ from the sales rep names in the Item column and remove the extension .xlsx from the city names in the Name column. To create the formula shown in the figure, start in the user interface, where you create two steps, and then copy the list transformation from the second step and paste it into the list within a list in the first formula. Then delete the second step. (I recommend using this method because one step seems cleaner than two steps.) Name the query step TransformItemAndName.

```
✕  ✓  fx    = Table.TransformColumns(FilterKeepT_,
                  {{"Item", each Text.AfterDelimiter(_, "T_"), type text},
                   {"Name", each Text.BeforeDelimiter(_, "."), type text}})
```

⊞. 123 Data	↔ ABc Name	▼	ABc Item	▼
1 Table	Bellingham		Cisco	
2 Table	Bellingham		Chantel	

Figure 7-53 *Making column transformations on the Item and Name columns.*

6. Click the expand button at the top of the Data column and include all the columns from the Excel tables. Name the query step ExpandGetSalesRecords. As shown in Figure 7-54, the column names are hard-coded into the formula. If this hard-coding would be a problem, you can instead use the inconsistent column name technique you learned about in Project 4.

```
= Table.ExpandTableColumn(TransformItemAndName, "Data", {"Date", "Sales", "Product"}, {"Date", "Sales", "Product"})
```

Date	▼	123 Sales	▼	123 Product	▼	ABc Name	▼	ABc Item	▼
4/3/2023		1460.59		Compressor Kit 6		Bellingham		Cisco	
5/2/2023		101.48		Compressor Kit 2		Bellingham		Cisco	

Figure 7-54 *Expanding to get the sales records.*

7. Create a formula similar to the one shown in Figure 7-55 to rename the Name column City and the Item column SalesRep. Name the query step NameCitySRColumns.

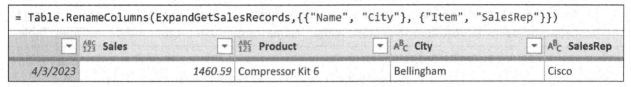

```
= Table.RenameColumns(ExpandGetSalesRecords,{{"Name", "City"}, {"Item", "SalesRep"}})
```

▾ 123 Sales	▾ 123 Product	▾ ABC City	▾ ABC SalesRep
4/3/2023	1460.59 Compressor Kit 6	Bellingham	Cisco

Figure 7-55 *Renaming columns.*

8. Add data types to the columns. Name the query step AddDataTypes.
9. Load the query as a connection only.

   Figure 7-56 shows the resulting fact table.

Date	1.2 Sales	ABC Product	ABC City	ABC SalesRep
4/3/2023	1460.59	Compressor Kit 6	Bellingham	Cisco
5/2/2023	101.48	Compressor Kit 2	Bellingham	Cisco
12/2/2023	592.72	Compressor Kit 1	Bellingham	Cisco
5/16/2024	454.63	Compressor Kit 3	Bellingham	Cisco
4/18/2023	782.95	Compressor Kit 3	Bellingham	Cisco
6/22/2023	1789.8	Compressor Kit 3	Bellingham	Cisco
5/16/2024	1104.16	Compressor Kit 1	Bellingham	Cisco
5/8/2024	2196.59	Compressor Kit 6	Bellingham	Cisco
8/13/2023	2010.2	Compressor Kit 2	Bellingham	Cisco
10/1/2024	1528.43	Compressor Kit 1	Bellingham	Cisco
5/18/2023	1179.99	Compressor Kit 3	Bellingham	Cisco
4/15/2023	648.7	Compressor Kit 3	Bellingham	Cisco
1/22/2024	1440.97	Compressor Kit 5	Bellingham	Cisco

PROPERTIES
Name
ExcelFilesToFactExpandButton
All Properties

APPLIED STEPS
- Source ⚙
- CCGetExcelObjects ⚙
- ExpandGetExcelObjects
- FilterKeepT_ ⚙
- TransformItemAndName
- ExpandGetSalesRecords ⚙
- NameCitySRColumns
- × AddDataTypes

Figure 7-56 *The fact table created from 12 Excel tables in three Excel workbooks is done!*

For the second method—which involves writing most of the M code and using the Table.Combine function to combine tables—you must have a list of tables, and those tables must have all the attributes as columns before you combine. In contrast, recall that the Table.ExpandTableColumn function allows you to expand a column of tables and take attribute columns from the expanded table with it. For example, earlier in this section, when you used the first method, you expanded the GetExcelObjects column, and the Name column with the filename was automatically expanded into a new column. In order to use the Table.Combine function at that point, the tables in each row of the column would already have to have a Name column with the filenames. Well, you can make that happen, but performance will go down. You would not have to hard-code the column names, but on a large dataset, the query refresh time would be quite slow. When I timed the two methods, the Table.Combine method was faster on small datasets but much slower on datasets containing more than 1 million rows. Nevertheless, I will show you how to do this second method.

To try the second method, follow these abbreviated steps:

1. To connect to the folder of files, create a new query using the steps shown in Figure 7-48 (for an on-premises path) or Figure 7-49 (for a dynamic folder path).

2. Create a custom column with the column name and formula shown in Figure 7-57. Name the query step CCGetExcelObjects. Notice that the formula has to use a Table.AddColumn function to add the Name column to each table in the column.

New column name

GetExcelObjects

Custom column formula ⓘ

```
= let N = [Name] in
  Table.AddColumn(
      Excel.Workbook([Content]),
      "City",
      each Text.BeforeDelimiter(N,".")
  )
```

Figure 7-57 *Creating a formula to add the Name column to the table with Excel objects.*

3. As shown in Figure 7-58, wrap the Table.SelectRows function around the Table.Combine function to keep only rows where the item name starts with T_. Name the query step AppendAndFilterObjectTables.

```
= Table.SelectRows(
      Table.Combine(CCGetExcelObjects[GetExcelObjects]),
      each Text.StartsWith([Item],"T_"))
```

	A^B_C Name	Data	A^B_C Item	A^B_C Kind
1	T_Cisco	Table	T_Cisco	Table
2	T_Chantel	Table	T_Chantel	Table

Figure 7-58 *Filtering the combined table to get Excel tables that start with T_.*

4. Create a custom column with the column name and formula shown in Figure 7-59. Name the query step CCCreateExcelTables. Notice that the formula uses back-to-back Table.AddColumn functions inside the Table.AddColumn function generated by the custom column to add attribute columns to each table in the column.

New column name

CreateExcelTables

Custom column formula ⓘ

```
= let C = [City], N = [Name] in
   Table.AddColumn(
       Table.AddColumn([Data],"City",each C),
       "SalesRep",
       each Text.AfterDelimiter(N,"T_"))
```

Figure 7-59 *Adding City and SalesRep columns to each table in the column.*

5. As shown in Figure 7-60, use the Table.Combine function to combine the tables into the final fact table. Name the query step AppendToGetFactTable.

```
= Table.Combine(CCCreateExcelTables[CreateExcelTables])
```

Date	1.2 Sales	A^B_C Product	City	SalesRep
4/3/2023	1460.59	Compressor Kit 6	Bellingham	Cisco
5/2/2023	101.48	Compressor Kit 2	Bellingham	Cisco
12/2/2023	592.72	Compressor Kit 1	Bellingham	Cisco
5/16/2024	454.63	Compressor Kit 3	Bellingham	Cisco
4/18/2023	782.95	Compressor Kit 3	Bellingham	Cisco
6/22/2023	1789.8	Compressor Kit 3	Bellingham	Cisco
5/16/2024	1104.16	Compressor Kit 1	Bellingham	Cisco
5/8/2024	2196.59	Compressor Kit 6	Bellingham	Cisco
8/13/2023	2010.2	Compressor Kit 2	Bellingham	Cisco
10/1/2024	1528.43	Compressor Kit 1	Bellingham	Cisco

Query Settings

PROPERTIES
Name
ExcelFilesToFactTableCombine

All Properties

APPLIED STEPS
Source ⚙
CCGetExcelObjects ⚙
AppendObjectTables
CCCreateExcelTables ⚙
✕ AppendToGetFactTable

Figure 7-60 *Five steps to create the final fact table.*

Project 7: Combining Two Fact Tables into One Fact Table

Now that you have seen two methods to combine Excel objects into a fact table, you are ready to see how to create one fact table from two fact tables, each with a different granularity.

The goal of data analysis is to convert data into useful information to help make data-driven decisions. The useful information that results from data analysis tells you where to start the data analysis process and how to model the data so that you can get the types of reports and visuals you need.

For this project, the report you need is like the one shown in Figure 7-61, which contains sales values, invoice shipping cost values, and invoice discount values. In addition, you need to be able to slice and filter the report with attributes like product category, product, and year. The problem is that the sales and cost data—the fact data—is stored in two fact tables, each with a different grain.

Category	Product	Total Sales($)	TotalShipping Cost($)	TotalInvoice Discount($)	InvoiceShipCosts As%OfSales	InvoiceDiscount As%OfSales
⊟Australian Round	Majestic Beaut	58,399.30	2,880.77	5,044.32	4.93%	8.64%
	Sunbell	60,031.76	2,709.62	4,847.44	4.51%	8.07%
	Sunset	62,367.07	2,611.89	4,892.85	4.19%	7.85%
	Yanaki	50,801.54	1,718.87	4,165.82	3.38%	8.20%
Australian Round Total		231,599.67	9,921.15	18,950.43	4.28%	8.18%
⊟Beginner	Aspen	54,343.84	1,548.71	4,424.16	2.85%	8.14%
	Crested Beaut	48,935.67	2,111.72	3,892.44	4.32%	7.95%
	Eagle	39,480.79	2,133.68	3,021.50	5.40%	7.65%
	Kangaroo	40,101.41	1,387.81	3,164.04	3.46%	7.89%
Beginner Total		182,861.71	7,181.92	14,502.14	3.93%	7.93%
⊟Freestyle	Carlota	64,381.91	1,871.00	5,264.67	2.91%	8.18%
	Carlota Doublers	126,097.50	2,294.69	11,600.20	1.82%	9.20%
	Quad	81,032.18	1,025.36	7,380.74	1.27%	9.11%
Freestyle Total		271,511.59	5,191.05	24,245.61	1.91%	8.93%
Grand Total		685,972.97	22,294.12	57,698.18	3.25%	8.41%

Year:
- 2017
- 2018
- 2019

Figure 7-61 *You need a report with sales, invoice shipping cost, and invoice discount.*

As shown in Figure 7-62, the fInvoiceTotalsPQ table stores the facts (shipping costs and invoice discount) and foreign key attributes (date and sales rep ID) at the invoice total grain, and the fLineItemInvoiceSalesPQ table stores the facts (quantity and unit price) and foreign key attributes (invoice number and product ID) at the invoice line-item sales grain. In addition, the dimension tables (dDatePQ and dSalesRepPQ) can only filter fInvoiceTotalsPQ at the invoice total grain, and the dimension tables (fInvoiceTotalsPQ and dProductPQ) can only filter fLineItemInvoiceSalesPQ at the invoice line-item sales grain. It is impossible to create the report you need from the data structure as it currently exists.

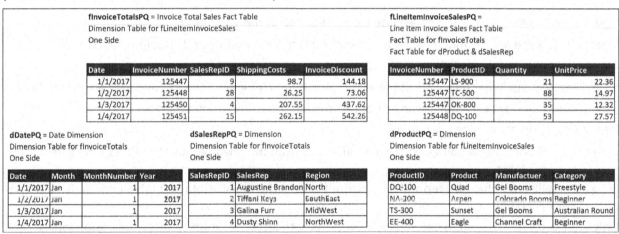

Figure 7-62 *Two fact tables with different grains and three dimension tables.*

The data model shown in Figure 7-63 will not work for what you need to do. The dDatePQ and dSalesRepPQ tables can filter the fInvoiceTotalsPQ table but not the fLineItemInvoiceSalesPQ table. Similarly, the dProductPQ table can filter the fLineItemInvoiceSalesPQ table but not the fInvoiceTotalsPQ table. The data model that you need to create is shown in Figure 7-64. The key is that you need to determine the sales, invoice discount, and invoice shipping costs—all at the invoice line-item sales grain.

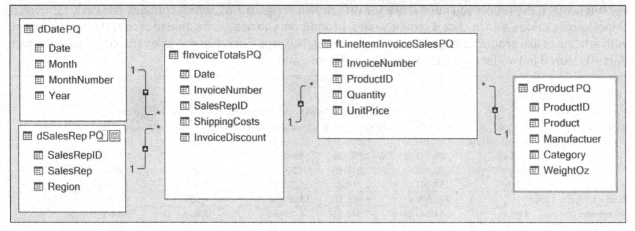

Figure 7-63 *This data model will not allow you to create the report you want.*

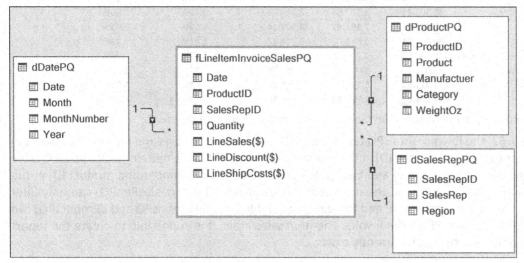

Figure 7-64 *This data model works because the facts are all at the same grain.*

In summary, these are the fundamental problems you face for reporting and visualizing in this scenario:

- Sales rep and date attributes only work at the invoice total grain. Product attributes do not.
- Product attributes only work at the invoice line-item sales grain. Sales rep and date attributes do not.
- You cannot create reports with attributes from all three dimension tables.

Here are the keys to creating a solution:

- You will allocate shipping and discount amounts from the fInvoiceTotalsPQ table to the fLineItemInvoicePQ table.
- You will bring the sales rep and date attributes from the fInvoiceTotalsPQ table into the fLineItemInvoicePQ table.

Only after you take these steps can you create reports with attributes from all three dimension tables.

You will import all five tables into Power Query, and then all the transformations will be made in the fLineItemInvoiceSalesPQ table. You will primarily use the user interface to create your query steps. To try this data modeling project, follow these steps:

1. In the Power Query Editor, go to the Queries pane and create a new group named TwoFactTablesIntoOne.

2. As shown in Figure 7-65, import the five Excel tables from the Excel file named TwoFactTablesDimensionsSource.xlsx into the TwoFactTablesIntoOne group.

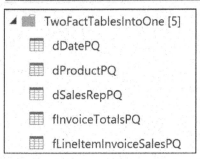

Figure 7-65 *Importing five Excel Tables from the file TwoFactTablesDimensionsSource.xlsx.*

3. In the fLineItemInvoiceSalesPQ table, as shown in Figure 7-66, calculate invoice line-item sales. Name the query step CalcLineSales.

```
= Table.AddColumn(AddDataTypes, "LineSales($)", each [Quantity] * [UnitPrice], type number)
```

ABC ProductID	123 Quantity	1.2 UnitPrice	1.2 LineSales($)	
125447 LS-900	21	22.36	469.56	

Figure 7-66 *Calculating sales at the invoice line-item grain.*

4. As shown in Figure 7-67, create a left outer join between the fLineItemInvoiceSalesPQ and dProductPQ tables. Name the query step JoinWithProduct.

```
= Table.NestedJoin(CalcLineSales,
    {"ProductID"}, dProductPQ, {"ProductID"}, "dProductPQ", JoinKind.LeftOuter)
```

123 Quantity	1.2 UnitPrice	1.2 LineSales($)	dProductPQ	
21	22.36	469.56	Table	

Figure 7-67 *Creating a left outer join to look up product details.*

5. As shown in Figure 7-68, expand the dProductPQ column to look up the product weight. Name the query step GetProductWeight.

```
= Table.ExpandTableColumn(JoinWithProduct, "dProductPQ", {"WeightOz"}, {"WeightOz"})
```

123 Quantity	1.2 UnitPrice	1.2 LineSales($)	1.2 WeightOz	
21	22.36	469.56	6.5	
224	12.58	2817.92	6.5	

Figure 7-68 *Looking up the product weight.*

6. As shown in Figure 7-69, calculate the invoice line-item shipping weight. Later you will use the invoice line weight as the numerator and total invoice weight as the denominator to create a shipping cost allocation rate. Name the query step CalcLineShipWeight.

```
= Table.AddColumn(GetProductWeight, "LineShipWeight", each [Quantity] * [WeightOz], type number)
```

1.2 UnitPrice	1.2 LineSales($)	1.2 WeightOz	1.2 LineShipWeight	
21	22.36	469.56	6.5	136.5
224	12.58	2817.92	6.5	1456

Figure 7-69 *Calculating the shipping weight at the invoice line-item grain.*

7. As shown in Figure 7-70, group by invoice number and calculate total line-item sales, calculate total shipping line-item weight, and group all the invoice line-item records from the table. The beauty of this calculation is that it allows you to move from the invoice line-item grain up to the invoice total grain, all while keeping a table of invoice line-item records that you can use later to expand back down to the invoice line-item grain. Name the query step GroupToInvoiceGrain.

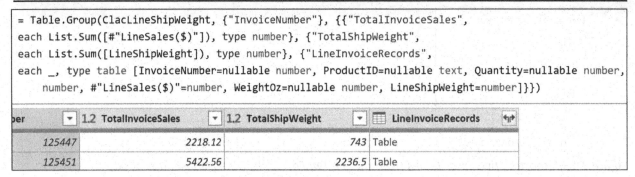

```
= Table.Group(ClacLineShipWeight, {"InvoiceNumber"}, {{"TotalInvoiceSales",
each List.Sum([#"LineSales($)"]), type number}, {"TotalShipWeight",
each List.Sum([LineShipWeight]), type number}, {"LineInvoiceRecords",
each _, type table [InvoiceNumber=nullable number, ProductID=nullable text, Quantity=nullable number,
    number, #"LineSales($)"=number, WeightOz=nullable number, LineShipWeight=number]}})
```

ber	1.2 TotalInvoiceSales	1.2 TotalShipWeight	LineInvoiceRecords
125447	2218.12	743	Table
125451	5422.56	2236.5	Table

Figure 7-70 *Grouping to move up to the invoice total grain.*

8. As shown in Figure 7-71, create a left outer join between the fLineItemInvoiceSalesPQ and fInvoice-TotalsPQ tables. Name the query step JoinWithfInvoiceTotal.

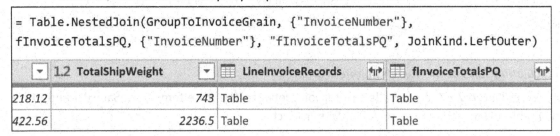

```
= Table.NestedJoin(GroupToInvoiceGrain, {"InvoiceNumber"},
fInvoiceTotalsPQ, {"InvoiceNumber"}, "fInvoiceTotalsPQ", JoinKind.LeftOuter)
```

1.2 TotalShipWeight	LineInvoiceRecords	fInvoiceTotalsPQ
218.12	743 Table	Table
422.56	2236.5 Table	Table

Figure 7-71 *Creating a left outer join to look up invoice total details.*

9. As shown in Figure 7-72, expand the fInvoiceTotalsPQ table to look up the foreign keys (Date and SalesRepID) and the invoice totals (ShippingCosts and InvoiceDiscount). Name the query step GetInvoiceItems.

```
= Table.ExpandTableColumn(JoinWithfInvoiceTotal, "fInvoiceTotalsPQ",
{"Date", "SalesRepID", "ShippingCosts", "InvoiceDiscount"},
{"Date", "SalesRepID", "ShippingCosts", "InvoiceDiscount"})
```

1²₃ SalesRepID	1.2 ShippingCosts	1.2 InvoiceDiscount
9	98.7	144.18
15	262.15	542.26

Figure 7-72 *Expanding to get the invoice total detail.*

10. As shown in Figure 7-73, calculate the allocation rate for the invoice discount amount by dividing the invoice total amount discount by sales. Name the query step CalcInvoicePercentDis.

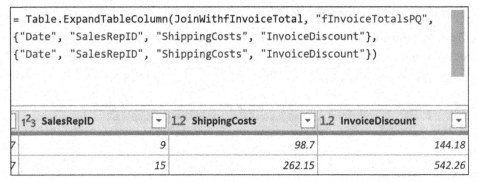

```
= Table.AddColumn(GetInvoiceItems, "InvoicePercentDiscount",
    each [InvoiceDiscount] / [TotalInvoiceSales], type number)
```

gCosts	1.2 InvoiceDiscount	1.2 InvoicePercentDiscount
98.7	144.18	0.065000992
262.15	542.26	0.100000738

Figure 7-73 *Dividing the invoice total value discount by sales.*

11. As shown in Figure 7-74, expand the LineGrainRecords column to move from the invoice total grain back down to the invoice line-item grain. Name the query step ExpandToLineInvoiceGrain.

```
= Table.ExpandTableColumn(CalcInvoicePercentDis, "LineGrainRecords", {"ProductID", "Quantity",
    "LineSales($)", "LineShipWeight"}, {"ProductID", "Quantity", "LineSales($)", "LineShipWeight"})
```

ABc ProductID	▼	1.2 Quantity	▼	1.2 LineSales($)	▼	1.2 LineShipWeight	▼	▦
LS-900		21		469.56		136.5		
TC-500		88		1317.36		484		

Figure 7-74 *Expanding to get back down to the invoice line-item grain.*

12. As shown in Figure 7-75, to allocate the invoice discount to the invoice line-item grain, multiply the invoice discount percentage by the line sales. Name the query step CalcLineDiscountAmount.

```
= Table.AddColumn(ExpandToLineInvoiceGrain, "LineDiscount($)",
    each Number.Round([InvoicePercentDiscount] * [#"LineSales($)"],2,2), type number)
```

Costs	▼	1.2 InvoiceDiscount	▼	1.2 InvoicePercentDiscount	▼	1.2 LineDiscount($)	▼
98.7		144.18		0.065000992		30.52	
98.7		144.18		0.065000992		85.63	

Figure 7-75 *Allocating the total invoice discount down to the invoice line-item grain.*

13. As shown in Figure 7-76, calculate the allocation rate for the invoice shipping costs. Name the query step CalcLineShipCosts.

```
= Table.AddColumn(
        CalcLineDiscountAmount, "LineShipCosts($)",
        each Number.Round([LineShipWeight] / [TotalShipWeight] * [ShippingCosts],2,2),
        type number)
```

unt	▼	1.2 InvoicePercentDiscount	▼	1.2 LineDiscount($)	▼	1.2 LineShipCosts($)	▼
144.18		0.065000992		30.52		18.13	
144.18		0.065000992		85.63		64.29	

Figure 7-76 *Multiplying the shipping costs allocation rate by the shipping costs.*

14. Select the Date, ProductID, SalesRepID, Quantity, LineSales($), LineDiscount($), and LineShipCosts($) columns, in this order, and then remove the other columns. Name the query step SelectColumnsForFactTable. Figure 7-77 shows the result.

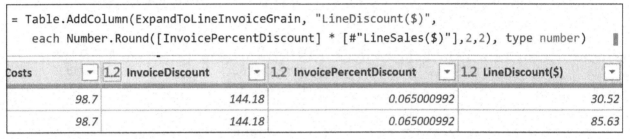

Figure 7-77 *The finished fact table at the invoice line-item grain.*

15. Load fInvoiceTotalsPQ as a connection only. Load the other four tables to the Data Model.

    The Power Query M code section of the project is complete. Even though this is not a book about relationships and DAX, Figure 7-78 shows what the finished data model could look like.

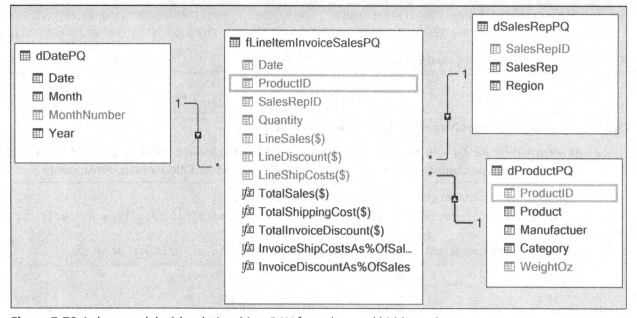

Figure 7-78 *A data model with relationships, DAX formulas, and hidden columns.*

Figures 7-78 to 7-82 show the process of publishing and consuming a semantic model once the Power Query M code process has converted the data to a semantic model that can easily create the required report.

Manufactuer	TotalSales($)	TotalInvoiceShipCosts($)	TotalInvoiceDiscount($)	InvoiceShipCostsAs%OfSales	InvoiceDiscountAs%OfSales
⊟ **Channel Craft**	**78,013.59**	**3,498.79**	**5,551.13**	**4.48%**	**7.12%**
Eagle	43,272.20	2,200.90	2,993.43	5.09%	6.92%
Kangaroo	34,741.39	1,297.89	2,557.70	3.74%	7.36%
⊟ **Colorado Booms**	**181,872.87**	**6,863.32**	**14,825.61**	**3.77%**	**8.15%**
Aspen	54,392.76	1,804.12	4,475.89	3.32%	8.23%
Crested Beaut	45,979.54	2,047.76	3,541.41	4.45%	7.70%
Yanaki	81,500.57	3,011.44	6,808.31	3.69%	8.35%
⊟ **Gel Booms**	**450,586.64**	**13,759.10**	**39,402.87**	**3.05%**	**8.74%**
Carlota	55,654.10	1,614.75	4,519.55	2.90%	8.12%
Carlota Doublers	131,763.75	2,371.24	12,336.48	1.80%	9.36%
Majestic Beaut	65,364.10	3,400.76	5,512.50	5.20%	8.43%
Quad	80,805.62	1,155.10	7,334.36	1.43%	9.08%
Sunbell	55,673.09	2,690.54	4,554.36	4.83%	8.18%
Sunset	61,325.98	2,526.71	5,145.62	4.12%	8.39%
Total	**710,473.10**	**24,121.21**	**59,779.61**	**3.40%**	**8.41%**

Year
☐ 2017
☐ 2018
■ 2019

Figure 7-79 *A visual in Power BI created from the new data model.*

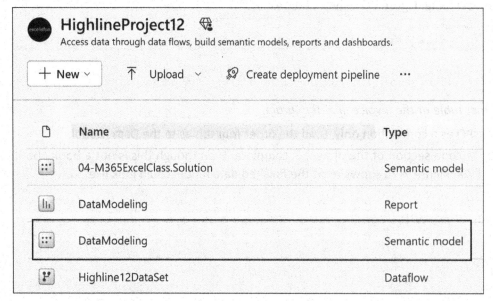

Figure 7-80 *If you have access to the Power BI service, you can publish the sematic model.*

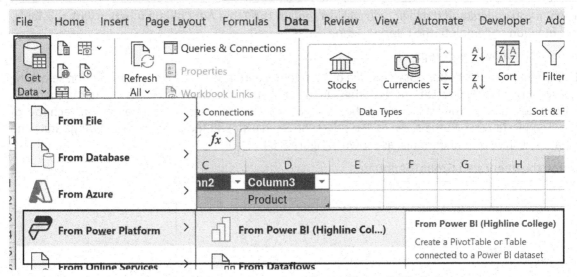

Figure 7-81 *The semantic model (the single source of truth) is available in Excel.*

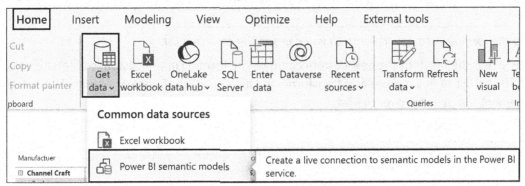

Figure 7-82 *The semantic model (the single source of truth) is available in Power BI.*

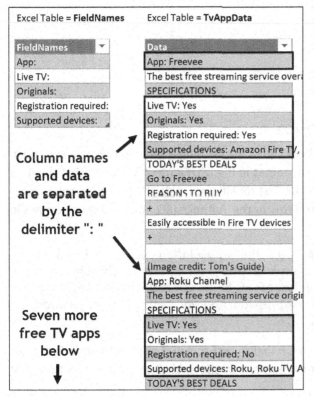

Figure 7-83 *This is bad data because it lacks the proper structure to allow analysis.*

Project 8: Converting a Single Column of Badly Structured Records into a Proper Table

In this project, say that you have two tables, named FieldNames and TvAppData, as shown in Figure 7-83. The FieldNames table contains a list of the column names that you will use to identify which rows in the TvAppsData table have records that belong in the final table. The TvAppsData table contains data about free TV apps available on various devices. The problem with this table is that the column names and data associated with the columns are stored in the same cell. In addition, most of the data in the column is extraneous data and does not belong in the final table. There are nine apps with associated data that you need to extract from the TvAppsData table and convert into a proper fact table.

The first task is to filter the TvAppData table to include only rows where a column name is listed. To filter, you use the Table.SelectRows function. However, because the formula element inside the second argument of the Table.SelectRows function is difficult to understand, initially you will use the Table.AddColumn function to visualize the formula element in each row of the table, and then, when you understand the logic, you will just replace the Table.AddColumn function with the Table. SelectRows function to complete the filtering action.

To try this project, follow these steps:

1. Open either the MCodeBook-Start.xlsx file or MCodeBook-Start.pbix file. In the Query Editor, select the query named FieldNamesQ from the Other Queries folder. Notice that it contains a buffered list of the correct field names. The list is buffered because you will have to use that query output in each row of the TvAppData table. In the same folder, select the Source step in the query named TvAppDataQ and create a custom column formula, as shown in Figure 7-84.

2. Name the query step GroupToAppData.

New column name
SeeList

Custom column formula ⓘ

```
= let d = [Data] in
  List.Transform(FieldNamesQ, each Text.StartsWith(d, _))
```

Figure 7-84 *Adding the formula to a new column so you can see the resulting list.*

Figure 7-85 shows the result of the new custom column. The formula in the custom column iterates over the buffered list of field names and transforms the list into a list of Boolean values. This is the formula element that iterates over the list:

```
Text.StartsWith(d, _)
```

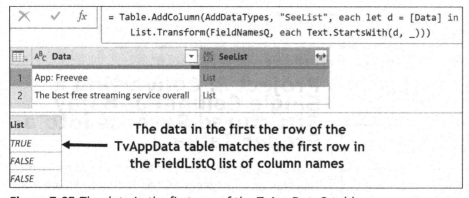

Figure 7-85 *The data in the first row of the TvAppDataQ table.*

For each row in the buffered list, this formula checks whether the single value in the Data column in the TxAppData table starts with any of the column names in the list. Figure 7-85 shows that the data in the first row of the TvAppData table matches the first row in the FieldListQ list of column names. Figure 7-86 shows that the data in the second the row of the TvAppDataQ table matches no rows in the FieldListQ list of column names.

> **Note:** The formula element in Figure 7-84 is running a sub-array, FieldNamesQ, over the larger array in the Data column. In the Excel worksheet, this is much more complicated to do; it involves BYROW and LAMBDA functions. As the technical editor of this book, Geert Delmulle, says about M code functions: "Every argument can be an entire expression. And since let...in is an expression as well, things can get very elaborate very quickly."

3. From the list of Boolean values, you must run an OR logical test to see if one of the rows in the list contains TRUE, so edit the formula in the third argument of the Table.AddColumn function so it becomes:

```
List.AnyTrue(List.Transform(FieldNamesQ, each Text.StartsWith(d, _)))
```

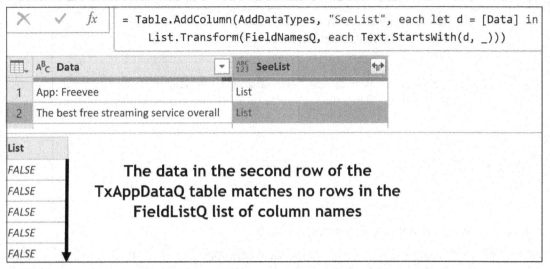

Figure 7-86 *In the second row, the FieldNamesQ list contains all false values.*

Figure 7-87 shows a Boolean value in each row of the TvAppData table that indicates that the row should be included in the filtered table. However, notice that the name of the column with the Boolean values is SeeList. The purpose of creating the column with the Table.AddColumn function was to visualize what is happening inside the formula. Now that you can see that the formula element delivers a Boolean value in each row of the table that you want to filter, you can edit the formula so that, rather than adding a column to the table, it will filter the table.

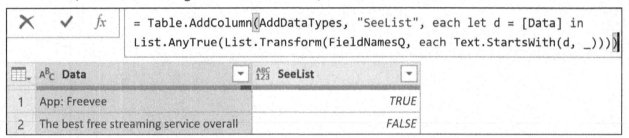

Figure 7-87 *The List.AnyTrue function runs an OR logical test.*

4. As shown in Figure 7-88, remove the column name SeeList from the second argument of the Table. AddColumn function and then replace the Table.AddColumn function with the Table.SelectRows function. The result is a table with only records where the cell contains a field name.

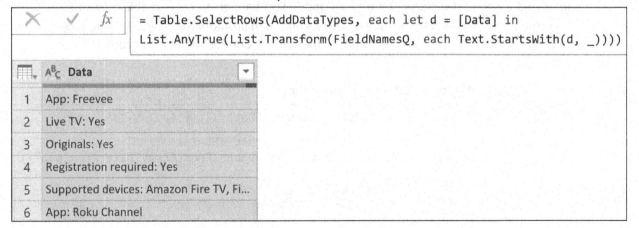

Figure 7-88 *The table is filtered to include only rows that start with a column name.*

5. The next step is to split the Data column by the delimiter : (a colon followed by a space) to keep the column name in the first column and push the data associated with the column name to the second column. The formula to accomplish this is shown in Figure 7-89.

```
       ✗  ✓  fx   = Table.SplitColumn(GroupToAppData, "Data",
                        Splitter.SplitTextByEachDelimiter({": "}), {"Data.1", "Data.2"})
```

	A^B_C Data.1	A^B_C Data.2
1	App	Freevee
2	Live TV	Yes
3	Originals	Yes
4	Registration required	Yes
5	Supported devices	Amazon Fire TV, Fire TV Stick, Apple TV, Chromecast, Playstation 3, Pla...
6	App	Roku Channel

Figure 7-89 *Splitting the columns to get column names and data.*

6. As you learned back in Chapter 5, you can group vertical cells together based on a reoccurring value in a column if you use the fourth and fifth arguments of the Table.Group function. To group together records that sit under the text item App but before the next occurrence of the term App, create the formula shown in Figure 7-90.

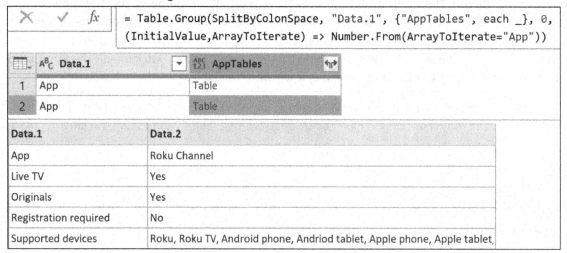

```
       ✗  ✓  fx   = Table.Group(SplitByColonSpace, "Data.1", {"AppTables", each _}, 0,
                        (InitialValue,ArrayToIterate) => Number.From(ArrayToIterate="App"))
```

	A^B_C Data.1	ABC 123 AppTables
1	App	Table
2	App	Table

Data.1	Data.2
App	Roku Channel
Live TV	Yes
Originals	Yes
Registration required	No
Supported devices	Roku, Roku TV, Android phone, Andriod tablet, Apple phone, Apple tablet,

Figure 7-90 *Grouping to get a table of records for each free TV app.*

7. Figure 7-90 shows that the second row contains an improperly structured table with the column names and associated data for the free TV app Roku Channel. To convert this data to a properly structured table, you need to transpose the data and then promote the headers. To do this, edit the grouping calculation in the third argument of the Table.Group function so it becomes:

    ```
    Table.PromoteHeaders(Table.Transpose(_))
    ```

    Figure 7-91 shows the completed Table.Group formula.

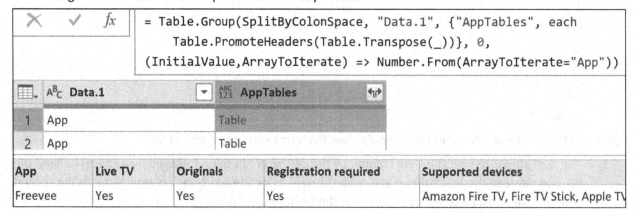

```
       ✗  ✓  fx   = Table.Group(SplitByColonSpace, "Data.1", {"AppTables", each
                        Table.PromoteHeaders(Table.Transpose(_))}, 0,
                        (InitialValue,ArrayToIterate) => Number.From(ArrayToIterate="App"))
```

	A^B_C Data.1	ABC 123 AppTables
1	App	Table
2	App	Table

App	Live TV	Originals	Registration required	Supported devices
Freevee	Yes	Yes	Yes	Amazon Fire TV, Fire TV Stick, Apple TV

Figure 7-91 *Transposing the table and then promoting headers.*

8. To complete the process, append the tables in the AppTables column by using the Table.Combine function. Then add data types to all the columns. Figure 7-92 shows the finished fact table. Figure 7-93 shows the full let expression for this transformation.

	A^B_C App	A^B_C Live TV	A^B_C Originals	A^B_C Registration required	A^B_C Supported devices
1	Freevee	Yes	Yes	Yes	Amazon Fire TV, Fire TV
2	Roku Channel	Yes	Yes	No	Roku, Roku TV, Android
3	Pluto TV	Yes	No	No	Amazon Fire TV, Fire TV
4	Tubi	No	Yes	No	Amazon Fire TV, Fire TV

Figure 7-92 *It's hard to believe we got a proper fact table from the original bad data.*

```
TVAppDataQ

let
    Source = Excel.CurrentWorkbook(){[Name="TvAppData"]}[Content],
    FilterByFieldName = Table.SelectRows(Source,
        each let d = [Data] in  List.AnyTrue(List.Transform(FieldNamesQ,each Text.StartsWith(d,_)))),
    SplitByDelimiter = Table.SplitColumn(FilterByFieldName,
        "Data", Splitter.SplitTextByEachDelimiter({": "}), {"Data.1", "Data.2"}),
    GroupGetAppRecords = Table.Group(SplitByDelimiter,"Data.1",
        {"AppTVTable", each Table.PromoteHeaders(Table.Transpose(_))},
        0, (InitialValue,ArrayToIterate) => Number.From(ArrayToIterate="App")),
    CombineTables = Table.Combine(GroupGetAppRecords[AppTVTable]),
    AddDataTypes = Table.TransformColumnTypes(CombineTables,
        {{"App", type text}, {"Live TV", type text}, {"Originals", type text},
        {"Registration required", type text}, {"Supported devices", type text}})
in
    AddDataTypes
```

Figure 7-93 *Using a let expression to create a proper fact table from lots of bad data.*

This project shows that there is almost nothing that M code can't do!

Bonus Topic: Privacy Levels and Data Security

Now that you've walked through a number of projects, I want to take you on a little detour and discuss privacy levels, data security, and the Formula.Firewall error. This background knowledge will help you understand the bonus example at the end of this chapter, which involves dynamically connecting to SharePoint server files from within an Excel file.

For each data source, you can assign one of four privacy levels to help protect sensitive data (so that it is viewed only by authorized users) and to determine if data sources can be combined or folded with other data (to avoid unwanted or illegal leakage of data). Although a restrictive privacy level can increase data security, it may reduce functionality and impact performance. You face a tradeoff between security and performance.

Note: This section does not provide a step-by-step example, but the files you downloaded include the files used to create the figures in this section. Look for them in the folder named Firewall.

As shown in Figure 7-94, you can set the privacy level for each data source by using the Edit Permissions button in the Data Source Settings dialog box.

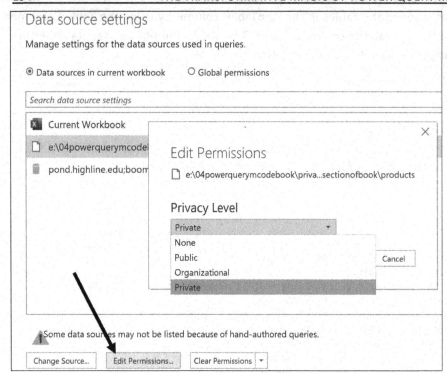

Figure 7-94 *You can set the privacy level for each data source.*

These are the four data source privacy settings:

- **None:** This setting applies no privacy settings. If you select this level, be careful to ensure that privacy regulations are otherwise maintained. You might use this privacy setting in a controlled development environment for testing and performance reasons.

- **Public:** This setting gives everyone visibility into the data. Public data can be combined with and folded into public, organizational, and private sources, but then the data is no longer public; it assumes the final location's privacy status. Examples include data from Google, Wikipedia, and other public web pages.

- **Organizational:** This setting limits the visibility of a data source to a trusted group of people. The data source is isolated from all public data sources but is visible to other organizational data sources. Organizational data can be combined with and folded into other organizational data or into a private data source. It is okay to bring public data into data designated as organizational, but then it all becomes organizational. Examples include a Power BI report stored in a workspace, data from an organizational SQL Server database, and files shared on an intranet SharePoint site with permissions enabled for a trusted group.

- **Private:** This setting is useful for a data source that contains sensitive or confidential information, where the visibility of the data source may be restricted to authorized users. A data source with this setting is completely isolated from other data sources and can't be bidirectionally combined with other sources. It is okay to bring public or organizational data into data designated as private, but then it all becomes private. Examples of private data include a workbook with student financial aid data, a text file with an employee review, and protected customer data.

Once you set the privacy level for each data source, the next step in securing data is to set the global rule for how data can be combined based on privacy levels. To set this global rule, in the Power Query Editor go to File, Options and Settings, Query Options, Global, Privacy. Figure 7-95 shows the Privacy Levels options in the Query Options dialog box. As you can see, there are three global settings for determining how data is combined:

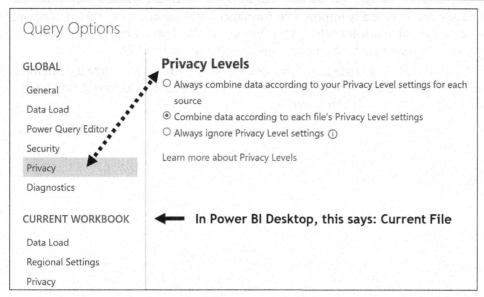

Figure 7-95 *Global rules for combining data.*

- **Always Combine Data According to Your Privacy Level Settings for Each Source:** When you choose this option, data combinations are controlled by the options you set for each individual data source. Each time you use a data source in your Excel or Power BI Desktop app, the data source privacy level settings are used. When you choose this option, the settings you select for a given data destination file, as shown in Figure 7-96, are ignored.

- **Combine Data According to Each File's Privacy Level Settings:** When you choose this option, you can determine the data combining rule for the current data destination file, as shown in Figure 7-96. Merging data across privacy isolation zones will result in some data buffering. This setting may decrease performance and functionality.

- **Always Ignore Privacy Level Settings:** Privacy levels are ignored. This setting can improve performance and functionality, but with this setting, Power Query cannot ensure the privacy of data.

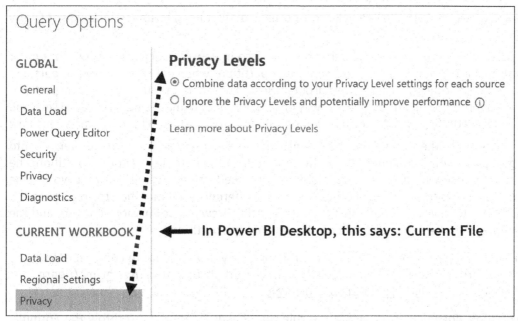

Figure 7-96 *Current file rules for combining data.*

These are the two settings for determining how data is combined (refer to Figure 7-96):

- **Combine Data According to Your Privacy Level Settings for Each Source:** When you choose this option, data combinations are controlled by the options you set for each individual data source.

- **Ignore the Privacy Levels and Potentially Improve Performance:** When you choose this option, you can override individual data source privacy settings for the current file. For example, if you have this setting for the current file, you can combine a private file into an organizational file.

As shown in Figure 7-97, in Dataflow there is a single checkbox option that determines how data is combined. By checking this option, you can combine data sources. You can open the Dataflow Options dialog box by going to the Home tab, Options group, Options button, Privacy.

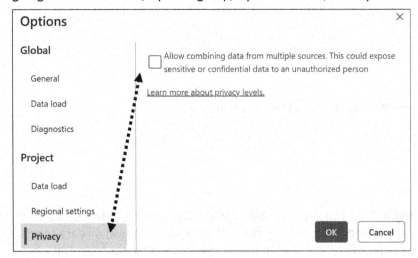

Figure 7-97 *Dataflow has a single checkbox setting.*

Formula.Firewall Error

What happens if you try to combine data sources that have incompatible privacy levels? You will get the dreaded Formula.Firewall error. The Formula.Firewall error exists to prevent unintentional data leakage between data sources from the query folding process. As discussed in Chapter 6, with query folding, Power Query converts the M code into SQL code so that it can be sent back to the source to be executed more efficiently than is possible with M code. For example, you would not want sensitive data like federally protected student financial aid data to be leaked through the query folding process.

In order to understand when the Formula.Firewall error occurs, you first need to understand Power Query partitions.

Power Query uses partitions to wall off data. A **partition** is an area in Power Query that consists of one or more query steps and that is considered walled off from other partitions when data is combined. A partition could be a single query step, another query, an external database, or another data source. When one partition references another partition, it must go through a gateway or security check to make sure it is okay to combine the data. This gateway is called a firewall. Microsoft documentation describes a firewall and partitions this way:

When a query is evaluated with the Firewall on, the Firewall divides the query and all its dependencies into partitions (that is, groups of steps). Anytime one partition references something in another partition, the Firewall replaces the reference with a call to a special function called Value.Firewall. In other words, the Firewall doesn't allow partitions to access each other directly. All references are modified to go through the Firewall. A partition that references another partition must get the Firewall's permission to do so, and the Firewall controls whether the referenced data will be allowed into the partition.

> **Note:** You can think of a partition as a query step or a query. If you want a more comprehensive description of how partitions are determined, visit the Microsoft documentation at https://learn.microsoft.com/en-us/power-query/data-privacy-firewall.

According to the Microsoft documentation, this is the rule that Power Query uses to throw the Formula.Firewall error: "A partition may either access compatible data sources, or reference other partitions, but not both." In this rule, you can see that there are two situations where you will get an error:

- When combining incompatible data sources within a partition
- When a partition tries to reference other partitions and directly access data sources

For the first situation, there are two Formula.Firewall messages that you might get:

- "Formula.Firewall: Query 'Query1' (step 'Source') is accessing data sources that have Privacy Levels which cannot be used together. Please rebuild this data combination."
- "Formula.Firewall: Information is required about data privacy."

As an example of this error, Figure 7-98 shows a query step that appends the SQL Server database dProduct table, which has the privacy level None, with the CSV file dProductsNew table, which has the privacy level Private. Because the two data sources are in the same query step and have different privacy levels, a message states that data privacy information is required.

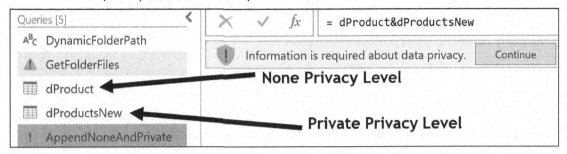

Figure 7-98 *Appending two tables with different privacy levels is not allowed.*

If you click the Continue button, the Privacy Levels dialog box shown in Figure 7-99 pops up. As you can see in the figure, the Privacy Levels dialog box offers two options:

- By checking the checkbox, you can ignore privacy levels for the current file. When this checkbox is checked, the option Ignore the Privacy Levels and Potentially Improve Performance, shown back in Figure 7-96, is selected. This will allow you to continue with the append.
- The textbox with the dropdown arrow to the right of the SQL pond.highline.edu data source allows you to change the privacy level for the data source. If you use the textbox to change the privacy level, the change will be reflected in the data source's privacy level settings, as shown back in Figure 7-95. If you choose a compatible privacy level, you can continue the append.

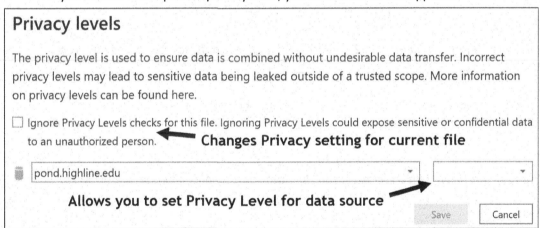

Figure 7-99 *You can change privacy level settings to resolve the issue.*

Although combining incompatible data sources within a partition yields an error, if a partition references another partition with an incompatible data source, there is no error. This is because the firewall buffers the referenced data and stores it in memory, as if it came from nowhere. This, in turn, prevents any further folding against the first partition's data source.

For the second situation (when a partition tries to reference other partitions and directly access data sources), this is the Formula.Firewall message you see: "Formula.Firewall: Query 'Query1' (step 'Source') references other queries or steps, so it may not directly access a data source. Please rebuild this data combination."

As an example of this error, Figure 7-100 shows the DynamicFolderPath query, which retrieves a dynamic folder path in an Excel workbook. (You saw an example of this in Chapter 6.) However, as shown in Figure 7-101, when you use the DynamicFolderPath query in the GetFolderFiles query to try to get the files from the dynamic folder path, you get the Formula.Firewall error. As shown in Figure 7-102, this error occurs because the GetFolderFiles query, partition 1, references the DynamicFolderPath query, partition 2, which in turn tries to access a data source directly. As Figure 7-103 illustrates, this violates the rule that a partition cannot reference another partition and directly access its data sources. Figure 7-104 shows a possible solution to this problem: If you bring the direct path to the data source into partition 1 (the GetFolderFilesTwoStep query), then you no longer have a reference to another partition, and you do not get the error. Figure 7-105 shows the result when the Folder.Files function successfully delivers the files from the folder path.

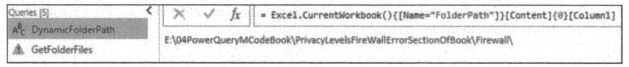

Figure 7-100 *The query delivers a direct path to a data source.*

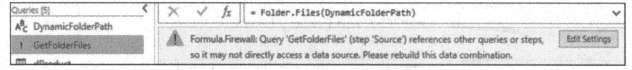

Figure 7-101 *This query uses a query that delivers a direct path to a data source.*

Partition01 GetFolderFiles	→Reference→	Partition02 DynamicFolderPath	→Direct Data Source→	E:\04PowerQueryMCo deBook\PrivacyLevels FireWallErrorSectionO fBook\Firewall\

Figure 7-102 *The sequence that leads to the Formula.Firewall error.*

Partition01 references Partition02 AND Direct Data Source	→Formula.Firewall error

Figure 7-103 *Partition 1 referencing partition 2 and accessing a direct data source causes an error.*

```
//GetFolderFilesTwoSteps
let
    Source = Excel.CurrentWorkbook(){[Name="FolderPath"]}[Content]{0}[Column1],
    FolderFiles = Folder.Files(Source)
in
    FolderFiles
```

Figure 7-104 *The same partition with direct access to the data source yields no error.*

Figure 7-105 *Without a reference to another partition, there is no error.*

As shown in Figure 7-106, another way to solve this problem is to create a custom function that executes the Excel.CurrentWorkbook formula that retrieves the dynamic folder path. Because the function is not executed until it is invoked, when you invoke the function inside the Folder.Files function, as shown in Figure 7-107, the direct data source is accessed in the same partition as the Folder.Files function, and you do not get an error.

```
//fxDynamicPath
let
    DynamicPath = () => Excel.CurrentWorkbook(){[Name="FolderPath"]}[Content]{0}[Column1]
in
    DynamicPath
```

Figure 7-106 *Creating a function to get the dynamic path.*

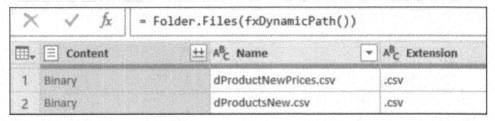

Figure 7-107 *Without a reference to another partition, there is no error.*

Another situation that involves the Formula.Firewall error and a dynamic folder path from an Excel worksheet is shown in Figures 6-20 to 6-25 in Chapter 6. In that example, you saw how to create a query to retrieve the dynamic folder path from the Excel worksheet. But rather than leaving it as a direct link to a data source, you landed the full table of objects from the folder. Then, in subsequent queries, when you wanted to access files through the dynamic folder path, rather than reference a query with a direct data source link, you referenced a table of objects, extracted the object that you wanted from the table, and thereby avoided the Formula. Firewall error.

Performance Without Folding

To illustrate the tradeoff between security and performance, take a look at Figures 7-108 to 7-111. Figure 7-108 shows the ddPriceIncreasePublic query, which is used to pull a price increase factor from the Excel worksheet; this query has the privacy level Public. Figure 7-109 shows the fTransactionsPrivate query, which is pulling data from an SQL Server database; this query has the privacy level Private. The fTransactionsPrivate query pulls the factor from the ddPriceIncreasePublic query into the query and uses it as a factor with the Quantity and Retail Price columns from the SQL Server database. Figure 7-110 shows that through the folding process, the public data is used in a private data source. (The inverse would not be possible.) This query runs very fast. Because the calculations are made on the SQL Server database side, there is no delay in calculating the values for the column. However, if you change the privacy level for the Excel data source to Private, as shown in Figure 7-111, when you right-click the step to view the native query SQL code, the View Native Query option is grayed out. This indicates that the price increase data was not sent back to the SQL Server database. The query takes a full minute to calculate the values for the column because the evaluation is done by Power Query rather than the database.

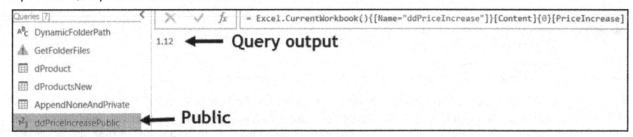

Figure 7-108 *The query has the Public privacy level.*

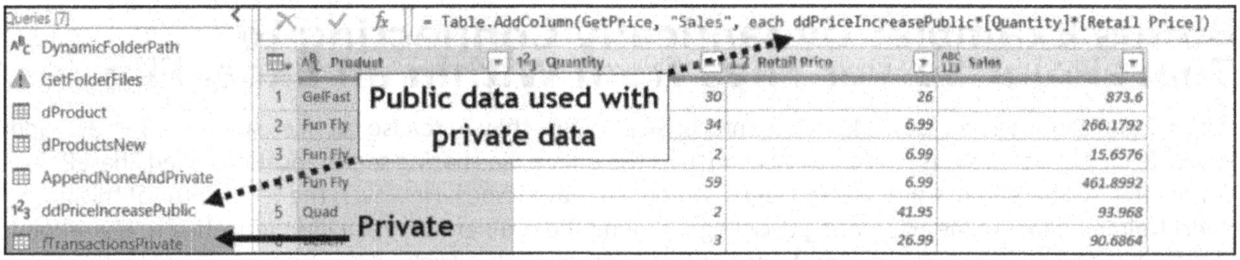

Figure 7-109 *The formula multiplies price increase by quantity by retail price.*

Native Query

```
select [_].[Product2] as [Product],
    [_].[Quantity] as [Quantity],
    [_].[Retail Price] as [Retail Price],
    (1.12E+000 * [_].[Quantity]) * [_].[Retail Price] as [Sales]
from
(
    select [$Outer].[Product2],
        [$Outer].[Quantity],
        [$Inner].[Retail Price]
    from
    (
        select [Product] as [Product2],
            [Quantity] as [Quantity]
        from [dbo].[fTransactions] as [$Table]
    ) as [$Outer]
    left outer join [dbo].[dProduct] as [$Inner] on ([$Outer].[Product2] = [$Inner].[Product])
) as [_]
```

ddPriceIncreasePublic data sent back to SQL Server database through folding

Figure 7-110 *By viewing the native query, you see that the public data was used in the SQL Server database.*

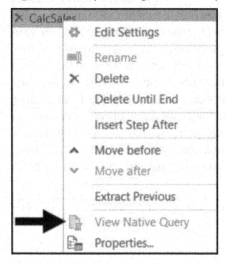

Figure 7-111 *View Native Query is grayed out because of the privacy level.*

In this section, you have learned that understanding privacy levels, the Formula.Firewall, and the implications of privacy levels on performance are key to building solutions that are safe and that perform well. Next, you will see how you can use your knowledge of the Formula.Firewall error to build a solution that allows you to dynamically connect to a folder of files from a SharePoint Server location.

Bonus Example: Dynamically Connecting to SharePoint Server Files from Within an Excel File

When organizations purchase a Microsoft enterprise package, they purchase services such as Office 365 and Power BI Online Services, as well as services such as the online file sharing server location called SharePoint. Connecting to SharePoint using Power Query is known to have issues. However, the tech editor of this book, Geert Delmulle, taught me an amazing trick to get around the problem of manually connecting to SharePoint files from within an Excel file, and this bonus example presents that trick.

The goal for this example is to build a dynamic SharePoint folder path in an Excel file and connect in a fully automated fashion to a folder of files that is in the same SharePoint location as the Excel file itself. There is no manual action required by the user at all (like finding and copying a URL from somewhere). The path will automatically update whenever the source data folder and destination file are moved to the same SharePoint location. This example elaborates on the Excel dynamic folder path trick you learned about in Chapter 6.

Because this project involves an enterprise-level license, I will show you an example using the Highline College SharePoint server that I have access to, but this is not an example you can directly follow along with. However, you can go and look at the solutions that I created from this section of the book in the MCodeBookSharePointSolutions folder provided with the download material.

> **Note:** I'm going to show you a query that illustrates the result from each step. To avoid getting a Formula.Firewall error, you need to set your privacy level for the current file to Always Ignore Privacy Level Settings (refer to Figure 7-95).

Here's how I carry out this trick:

1. Figure 7-112 shows my SharePoint file and folder in File Explorer. Figure 7-113 shows the .txt files inside the data folder that I would like to dynamically access from within the Excel file.

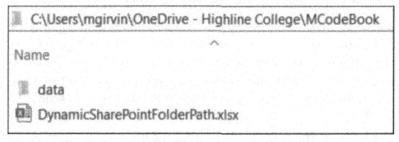

Figure 7-112 *File Explorer does not show the true SharePoint URL address.*

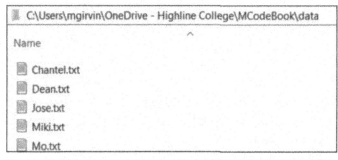

Figure 7-113 *From within the Excel file, I want to dynamically connect to these .txt files.*

2. Although File Explorer does not show the correct folder path, the worksheet formula shown in Figure 7-114 has no problem detecting the correct SharePoint folder path. (You saw this type of formula in Chapter 6.) In addition, this figure shows the defined name that points to the cell B2, which contains the dynamic SharePoint folder path.

> **Note:** Figures 7-112 and 7-113 show the correct local path to the local synchronization folder of SharePoint, as created and managed by the OneDrive synchronization agent.

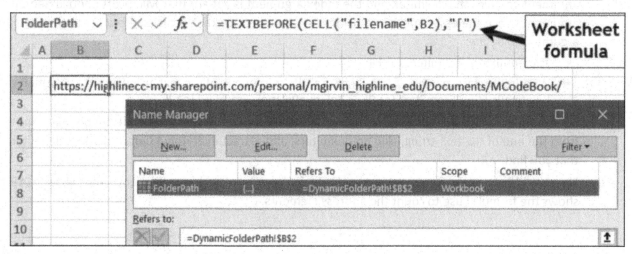

Figure 7-114 *This Excel worksheet formula detects the full SharePoint path.*

3. As shown in Figure 7-115, I can create a formula to import the defined name and look up the SharePoint folder path. At this point, if I saved the query and then referenced this query in other

queries, I would get a Formula.Firewall error. Because I do not want that, I will leave this as the first step in the query and build the rest of the query in this partition.

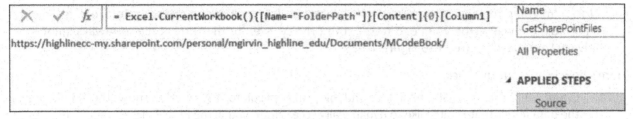

Figure 7-115 *M code formula to look up the SharePoint address from the defined name.*

4. As shown in Figure 7-114, the M code formula to retrieve the SharePoint folder path is the same formula that you used in Chapter 6 to retrieve the on-premises folder path (refer to Figure 6-20). However, there are some important differences in the retrieved SharePoint path:

    -   The result has a different syntax now: It's a URL that contains two essential parts—the URL to the SharePoint site and the hierarchy of subfolders from the SharePoint site to the destination folder (where my Excel file lives).

    -   The component parts of the address use the delimiter /, whereas the delimiter \ is used in the case of an on-premises folder path.

5. Figure 7-116 shows the edit I can make to the formula so that I can remove the last character from the folder path.

```
X   ✓   fx   = Text.BeforeDelimiter(Source,"/",{0,RelativePosition.FromEnd})
```
https://highlinecc-my.sharepoint.com/personal/mgirvin_highline_edu/Documents/MCodeBook

Figure 7-116 *Removing the last character from the dynamic folder path.*

Figure 7-116 shows that I used the TextBeforeDelimiter function. The three arguments for this function are listed here:

```
Text.BeforeDelimiter(
     text as nullable text,
     delimiter as text,
     optional index as any) as any
```

The **text** argument contains the text from which I want to extract a sub-text string, the **delimiter** argument contains the delimiter, and the **index** argument is yet another Microsoft undocumented argument. Nevertheless, I infer from using the user interface that I can create a list in the index argument to define:

-   The number of delimiters to skip

-   Whether to start searching for delimiters at the start or end of the text, using one of two options: RelativePosition.FromStart (or 0) or RelativePosition.FromEnd (or 1)

For example, in Figure 7-116, the formula element {0,RelativePosition.FromEnd} can be read "Start from the end of the text string, skip no delimiters, and extract everything before the first delimiter that you find."

6. Figure 7-117 shows the formula I use to split the folder path into address elements, and Figure 7-118 shows the formula I use to count the address elements.

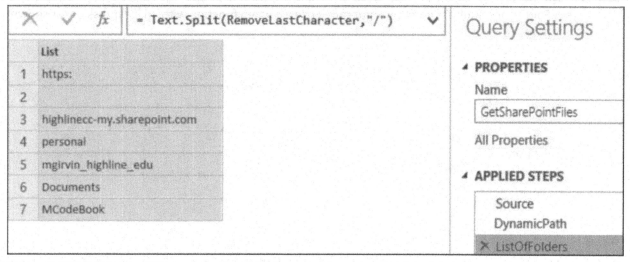

Figure 7-117 *Splitting a URL to get a list of folder names.*

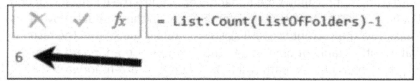

Figure 7-118 *Creating a formula to count forward slashes.*

7. As shown in Figure 7-119, I use the List.Accumulate formula to find the SharePoint site. The formula delivers a record value with a table of objects, and the position of the forward slash indicates where the location was found.

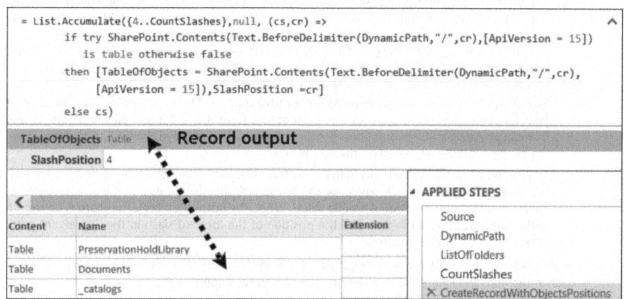

Figure 7-119 *Using a List.Accumulate formula to find the active SharePoint folder.*

Here is the process I go through with the List.Accumulate function to create the record:

- The list argument in List. Accumulate contains this formula element:

  ```
  {4..CountFolders}
  ```

- In the list, I start at the fourth forward slash (to avoid the first part of the URL and look at just the folders with potential files) and iterate until that last possible forward slash.

- I skip the second argument by using a null value because I do not need a seed.

- For the accumulator function argument, I use a custom function with an if expression, as shown here:

```
(cs,cr) =>
if try SharePoint.Contents(
       Text.BeforeDelimiter(Source,"/",cr),
       [ApiVersion = 15])
  is table
    otherwise false
then
[TableOfObjects =
  SharePoint.Contents(
      Text.BeforeDelimiter(Source,"/",cr),
      [ApiVersion = 15]),
  SlashPosition =cr]
else cs
```

- The **try/otherwise** keyword combination allows me to handle errors, like the IFERROR function in Excel worksheet or DAX formulas. The try/otherwise combination in the formula above tests to see if the path result based on the current forward slash is a table value. When the result is a table value, a record value with a table of objects and the position of the forward slash are delivered. If the result is not a table, the next path result based on the current forward slash is tested to see if it is a table.

- The **is** keyword is a comparative operator that equates the two sides of the equal sign to deliver a true or false value. In the formula above, the logical test is "Output of SharePoint.Contents function = table value?"

- The **SharePoint.Contents** and **SharePoint.Files** functions are parallel to the Folder.Contents and File.Contents functions that you used when dealing with on-premises folders in Chapter 6. For the SharePoint.Contents and SharePoint.Files functions, an optional record can be used to specify the ApiVersion for the site: 14 or 15 or "Auto". When this is not specified, API version 14 is used. When Auto is specified, the server version will be automatically discovered, if possible; otherwise, the version defaults to 14. Non-English SharePoint sites require at least version 15. The SharePoint.Contents function delivers a table with a column of files and folders. The SharePoint. Files function delivers a table with a column of files from the folder and all subfolders. In the formula above, the SharePoint.Contents function is used to retrieve the files and folders from the current path result, based on the current forward slash.

- Finally, the if expression that is used in the custom function in the List.Accumulate accumulator argument iterates through each position of a forward slash until it finds that the output from the SharePoint.Contents function is a table value. When the output is a table, a record is delivered with a table of files and folders and the position of the forward slash in the SharePoint path where the table was discovered.

8. As shown in Figure 7-120, my next step is to get the root SharePoint folder path. I need a forward slash at the end, and Figure 7-121 shows the formula to accomplish that.

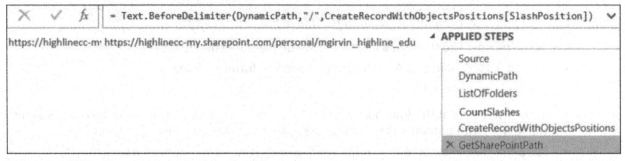

Figure 7-120 *Getting the SharePoint root folder path.*

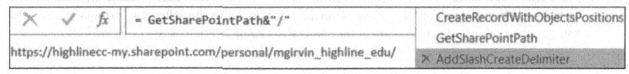

Figure 7-121 *Adding a forward slash to the end of the path.*

9. Once I have the root folder with a forward slash at the end, I make that the delimiter to dynamically extract the current folder path from the Source step full folder path, as shown with the formula in Figure 7-122.

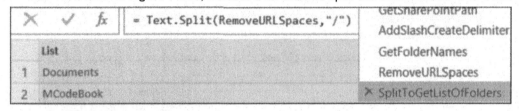

Figure 7-122 *Extracting the folder path for the location of the Excel file.*

10. Because a folder path address may have the URL characters set for spaces, which is the set of characters "%20", I can create a new step named RemoveURLSpaces and create this formula as insurance against a broken query:

```
= Replacer.ReplaceText(GetInvisableFolder,"%20"," ")
```

11. As shown in Figure 7-123, I create a formula to split the folder names into a list.

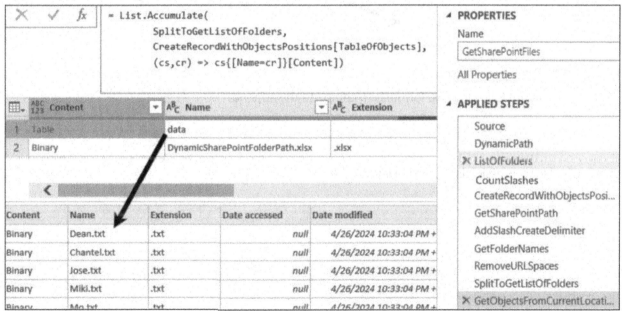

Figure 7-123 *Splitting the folder names to get a list of the names.*

12. Figure 7-124 shows the formula that iterates over the list of folder names. Because this formula refers to the direct SharePoint location, I would get a Formula.Firewall error if I had not set the current file to ignore privacy levels.

Figure 7-124 *Iterating to get the table of objects from the current SharePoint folder.*

13. As shown in Figure 7-124, in the first argument of the List.Accumulate function, I iterate over the list of folder names: SplitToGetListOfFolders.

In the second argument of the List.Accumulate function, I use the following formula element to retrieve the table of objects that are in the same SharePoint location as the Excel file:

```
CreateRecordWithObjectsPositions[TableOfObjects]
```

This is the seed at the start of the iterative process.

The custom function in the third argument performs a two-way lookup to retrieve the table of files and folders from the Content column when the name in the Name column matches the folder name from the list of names in the first argument of the List.Accumulate function.

14. To filter down to a table with .txt files from the folder data, I create the formula shown below, which first filters the previous step and then performs a two-way lookup:

```
= Table.SelectRows(
       GetObjectsFromCurrentLocation,
       each ([Name] = "data")){0}[Content]
```

(No figure is shown for this formula.) I named the step FilterGetDataFolderContent.

15. To extract and fix the .txt tables, I create the formula shown in Figure 7-125. I named this step CCToGetTxtTables.

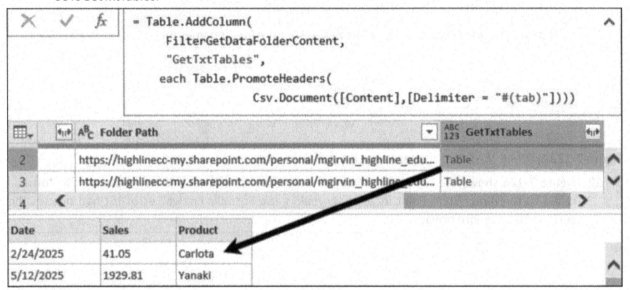

Figure 7-125 *Getting the .txt tables.*

16. I create the following two formulas to complete the append:

```
= Table.Combine(CCToGetTxtTables[GetTxtTables])
= Table.TransformColumnTypes(AppendTables,{{"Date", type date}, {"Sales",
type number}, {"Product", type text}})
```

The finished let expression is shown in Figure 7-126.

```
//GetSharePointFiles
let
    Source = Excel.CurrentWorkbook(){[Name="FolderPath"]}[Content]{0}[Column1],
    DynamicPath = Text.BeforeDelimiter(Source,"/",{0,RelativePosition.FromEnd}),
    ListOfFolders = Text.Split(DynamicPath,"/"),
    CountSlashes = List.Count(ListOfFolders)-1,
    CreateRecordWithObjectsPositions = List.Accumulate({4..CountSlashes},null, (cs,cr) =>
        if try SharePoint.Contents(Text.BeforeDelimiter(DynamicPath,"/",cr),[ApiVersion = 15])
            is table otherwise false
        then [TableOfObjects = SharePoint.Contents(Text.BeforeDelimiter(DynamicPath,"/",cr),
            [ApiVersion = 15]),SlashPosition =cr]
        else cs),
    GetSharePointPath =
        Text.BeforeDelimiter(DynamicPath,"/",CreateRecordWithObjectsPositions[SlashPosition]),
    AddSlashCreateDelimiter = GetSharePointPath&"/",
    GetFolderNames = Text.AfterDelimiter(DynamicPath,AddSlashCreateDelimiter),
    RemoveURLSpaces = Replacer.ReplaceText(GetFolderNames,"%20"," "),
    SplitToGetListOfFolders = Text.Split(RemoveURLSpaces,"/"),
    GetObjectsFromCurrentLocation =
    List.Accumulate(
        SplitToGetListOfFolders,
        CreateRecordWithObjectsPositions[TableOfObjects],
        (cs,cr) => cs{[Name=cr]}[Content]),
    FilterGetDataFolderContent =
        Table.SelectRows(GetObjectsFromCurrentLocation, each [Name] = "data"){0}[Content],
    CCToGetTxtTables = Table.AddColumn(
     FilterGetDataFolderContent,
     "GetTxtTables",
     each Table.PromoteHeaders(
             Csv.Document([Content],[Delimiter = "#(tab)"]))),
    AppendTables = Table.Combine(CCToGetTxtTables[GetTxtTables]),
    AddDataTypes =
        Table.TransformColumnTypes(AppendTables,
        {{"Date",type date},{"Sales",type number},{"Product",type text}})
in
    AddDataTypes
```

Figure 7-126 *Finished M code to dynamically connect to a SharePoint folder.*

To avoid the Formula.Firewall error, as shown in Figure 7-127, I can build a custom function to get the table of SharePoint objects; then, as shown in Figure 7-128, I can invoke the function as the second step in a query after a step that accesses the dynamic folder path to get the direct data source. As shown in Figure 7-129, the query returns a table of objects from the SharePoint location. As an alternative, as shown in Figure 7-130, I can build a custom function to grab the dynamic SharePoint path from the Excel worksheet, and then, as shown in Figure 7-131, I can run back-to-back functions to get the full table of objects from the SharePoint folder without getting the Formula.Firewall error.

The good news is that just as with the dynamic Excel folder path you created in Chapter 6, you can use solutions like the ones shown in Figures 7-127 to 7-131 to move the Excel file to any new location on the SharePoint site, and everything will update like a charm!

```
//FxSharePointFolderContents

(SharePointFullPath as text) as table=>
let
    RecordWithObjectsPositions = List.Accumulate({4..List.Count(Text.Split(SharePointFullPath, "/"))-1},null,
        (cs,cr) =>
        if try SharePoint.Contents(Text.BeforeDelimiter(SharePointFullPath,"/",cr),[ApiVersion = 15])
            is table otherwise false
        then [TableOfObjects = SharePoint.Contents(Text.BeforeDelimiter(SharePointFullPath,"/",cr),
            [ApiVersion = 15]),SlashPosition =cr]
        else cs),
    ListOfFolders = Text.Split(Replacer.ReplaceText(
        Text.AfterDelimiter(SharePointFullPath,"/",RecordWithObjectsPositions[SlashPosition]),"%20"," "),"/"),
    GetObjectsFromCurrentLocation = List.Accumulate(ListOfFolders,RecordWithObjectsPositions[TableOfObjects],
        (cs,cr) => cs{[Name=cr]}[Content])
in
    Table.SelectColumns(GetObjectsFromCurrentLocation,{"Content","Name"})
```

Figure 7-127 *This reusable function retrieves the objects from SharePoint.*

```
//InvokeFunctionToGetTableOfObjects
let
    Source = Text.BeforeDelimiter(
                Excel.CurrentWorkbook()
                    {[Name="FolderPath"]}[Content]{0}[Column1],"/",
                {0,RelativePosition.FromEnd}),
    InvokeCustomFunction = FxSharePointFolderContents(Source)
in
    InvokeCustomFunction
```

Figure 7-128 *Using a direct data source and a custom function to avoid getting a Formula.Firewall error.*

	✕ ✓ *fx*	= FxSharePointFolderContents(Source)	
▦▾	ABC 123 Content	▾	AB C Name	▾
1	Table	data
2	Binary	DynamicSharePointFolderPath.xlsx

Figure 7-129 *The query returns a table of objects from the SharePoint location.*

```
//FxExcelsDynamicPath
let
    Source = () => Text.BeforeDelimiter(
                Excel.CurrentWorkbook()
                    {[Name="FolderPath"]}[Content]{0}[Column1],"/",
                {0,RelativePosition.FromEnd})
in
    Source
```

Figure 7-130 *Creating a custom function to get the path from the Excel worksheet.*

	✕ ✓ *fx*	= FxSharePointFolderContents(FxExcelsDynamicPath())	
▦▾	ABC 123 Content	▾	AB C Name	▾
1	Table	data
2	Binary	DynamicSharePointFolderPath.xlsx

Figure 7-131 *Invoking back-to-back functions to avoid the Formula.Firewall error.*

Conclusion

You have reached the end of the book. I hope you've had fun learning about M code. Understanding the magic of M code will give you power over your data and make you the go-to person in your job. Thanks for reading, and I'll see you next book or at https://www.youtube.com/@excelisfun.

Index

A

adding
  date values, 28–30
  time values to date values, 30–31
aggregate functions
  changing in Group By feature, 5
  in Group By feature, 94
  for list values, 37
and operator, 19
appending
  with custom column, 166–167
  with From Folder and Combine
    Files features, 161–166
  with inconsistent column names,
    172–175
  JSON tables with filename at-
    tributes, 175–177
  tables, 41–42, 81–84
  text files with structure problems,
    167–172
approximate match lookups, 69–77
  custom columns, creating with
    custom function, 70–74
  custom columns, creating with let
    expression, 75–76
  defined, 56
  List.Accumulate function, 76–77
  reusable custom functions, 74–75
  Table.Buffer function, 69–70
as keyword, 20
automatic data type detection,
    toggling, 125

B

banker's rounding, 98
base one, 56
base zero, 56
binary values, 42–43
blank queries, creating, 14
blank row after group, adding,
    118–119
buffering, 70

C

CELL function (Excel), 127–129
column lookups, 37, 61–63
combination frequencies, finding,
    119–120
Combine Files feature, 161–166
combining. See appending; joining
comments, 44
comparer argument (Table.Group
    function), 103–104

Comparer.FromCulture function,
    104–105, 107–108
comparer functions, 104–113
  creating custom, 106–107
  cultures, characters from, 104–105,
    107–108
  date column with empty cells,
    grouping on, 109–110
  ignoring case, 105–106, 108–109
  single-column tables, grouping data
    from, 111–113
Comparer.OrdinalIgnoreCase
    function, 105–106, 108–109
comparing lists, 91–93
conditional columns, creating, 18
cross-tabulated tables, 78
CSV (comma-separated values) files
  defined, 121
  importing, 121–125
Csv.Document function, 121–125,
    137–138
custom columns
  combining Excel files, 166–167
  creating, 19
  creating with custom function,
    70–74
  creating with let expression, 75–76
  Table.UnpivotOtherColumns
    function, 80–81
custom functions
  comparer functions, creating,
    106–107
  custom columns, creating, 70–74
  defined, 7, 44
  each keyword/underscore, creating
    with, 49–50
  in function arguments, creating,
    48–49
  function-expression syntax rules,
    44
  as query steps in let expressions,
    creating, 50–51
  recursion, 51–54
  reusable, creating, 74–75
  reusable function queries, creating,
    45–48

D

data connectors
  Csv.Document function, 121–125,
    137–138
  Dataflow as dynamic data source,
    133–136
  Data Source Settings dialog box,
    126–127
  dynamic paths in Excel, 127–129
  Excel.CurrentWorkbook function,
    128–129, 145–149

Excel.Workbook function, 141–145
  Folder.Contents function, 129–133
  Folder.Files function, 129–133
  ISO dates, 152
  Json.Document function, 139–141
  Locale feature, 149–152
  online data sources, 152–160
  on-premises paths, 125–149
  text files, importing, 137–138
  Xml.Tables function, 138–139
Dataflow, 1
  blank queries, creating, 14
  duration values, 21
  as dynamic data source, 133–136
  From Folder feature, 162
  load data locations, 9
  on-premises paths, changing, 126
  Power Query user interface, 3
  Sql.Database function in, 67
data models
  appending JSON tables with
    filename attributes, 175–177
  appending tables with inconsistent
    column names, 172–175
  appending text files with structure
    problems, 167–172
  combining Excel files with custom
    column, 166–167
  combining Excel files with From
    Folder and Combine Files
    features, 161–166
  combining fact tables into one,
    182–189
  defined, 159
  dynamic SharePoint connections
    from Excel files, 200–208
  elements of, 161
  importing multiple Excel files with
    multiple objects, 177–182
data sources
  CSV versus text files, 121–125
  online, 152–160
  on-premises paths. See on-premises
    paths
  privacy levels, 193–200
  SharePoint connections from Excel
    files, 200–208
Data Source Settings dialog box,
    126–127
data type detection, toggling, 125
data types
  defined, 11
  list of, 11
  operators/operands, 12–13
  source values, relationship with,
    11–12
Date.AddDays function, 28
date column with empty cells,
    grouping on, 109–110

Date.DayOfWeekName function, 28
Date.From function, 32
Date.Month function, 28
dates/times
    adding/subtracting date values,
        28–30
    calculating hours elapsed, 31, 34–35
    datetime values, 25–26
    datetimezone values, 26–27
    date values, 22–24
    duration values, 17, 20–22
    extracting year, 28
    ISO dates, 152
    Locale feature, 149–152
    time values, 24–25
datetime values, 25–26
    adding time values to date values,
        30–31
    calculating hours elapsed, 34–35
datetimezone values, 26–27
date values, 22–24
    adding/subtracting, 28–30
    adding time values to, 30–31
Date.Year function, 28
DAX formulas
    as base one, 56
    defining variables in formulas, 32
    worksheet formulas/PivotTables/M
        code, comparison, 1–2
Day.EndOfMonth function, 28
decimal-precision floating-point
        system, 100
delimiters, 122
dimension tables, 161
dot-dot operator, 37
double-precision floating-point
        system, 100
drill-down lookups, 63–65
duplicating queries, 131
Duration.Hours function, 29
Duration.TotalHours function, 29
duration values
    adding/subtracting dates, 28–30
    defined, 17
    examples, 20–22
dynamic arrays, importing, 145
dynamic paths in Excel, 127–129
dynamic SharePoint connections
        from Excel files, 200–208

E

each keyword
    custom functions, creating, 49–50
    defined, 5, 6
editing
    function queries, 47
    M code, locations for, 3–5

empty cells, grouping on column
        with, 109–110
encoding types, 122
errors
    Formula.Firewall, 196–199
    in key match lookups, 61
exact match lookups, 56–69
    column lookups, 61–63
    defined, 56
    drill-down lookups, 63–65
    key match lookups, 58, 60–61
    row index lookups, 57–58, 59–60
exact match or next smaller lookups.
        See approximate match
        lookups
Excel
    as base one, 56
    blank queries, creating, 14
    date values, 22
    defining variables in formulas, 32
    dynamic paths, 127–129
    From Folder feature, 162
    INDEX function, 56–57
    load data locations, 8
    on-premises paths, changing, 126
    Power Query user interface, 2
Excel.CurrentWorkbook function,
        66–69, 128–129, 145–149
Excel files
    combining with custom column,
        166–167
    combining with From Folder
        and Combine Files features,
        161–166
    dynamic SharePoint connections,
        200–208
    importing, 141–149
    importing with multiple objects,
        177–182
Excel.Workbook function, 141–145
expressions
    defined, 7
    evaluation precedence, 12–13
    operators/operands, 12–13
Extensible Markup Language (XML)
        files, 138–139
extracting
    columns as lists, 37
    records from tables, 38–39, 49–50
    year from date, 28

F

fact tables
    combining into one, 182–189
    defined, 161
field access operator, 19, 57
File.Contents function, 125, 137

filename attributes, appending JSON
        tables, 175–177
firewalls, 196
Folder.Contents function, 129–133
Folder.Files function, 129–133, 162
folding. See query folding
foreign keys, 161
Formula.Firewall error, 130, 196–199
formulas. See DAX formulas;
        worksheet formulas
From Folder feature, 161–166
full outer joins, 86–87
function arguments, creating in
        custom functions, 48–49
function queries
    editing, 47
    reusable, creating, 45–48
function query steps, creating custom
        functions, 50–51
functions. See custom functions; M
        code functions; Power Query
        functions
function values, 44–55

G

Gaussian rounding, 98
generalized identifiers, 7
grain, 161, 182–189
granularity, 161, 182–189
Group By feature, 3–5, 93–120
    blank row after group, adding,
        118–119
    combination frequencies, 119–120
    comparer argument (Table.Group
        function), 103–104
    comparer functions, 104–113
    groupKind argument (Table.Group
        function), 100–103
    Number.Round function, 98–100
    running counts, 118
groupKind argument (Table.Group
        function), 100–103

H

half-even rounding, 98
hard-coding M code values, 11
history of Power Query, 1
hours elapsed, calculating, 31, 34–35

I

identifiers
    defined, 6
    expressions and, 7
    spaces in, 7
if expressions, 18–19

importing
  CSV (comma-separated values)
    files, 121–125
  with custom column, 166–167
  dynamic arrays, 145
  Excel files, 141–149
  Excel files with multiple objects,
    177–182
  with From Folder and Combine
    Files features, 161–166
  JSON files, 139–141
  with Locale feature, 149–152
  from online data sources, 152–160
  text files, 137–138
  text files with structure problems,
    appending, 167–172
  XML files, 138–139
inconsistent column names, ap-
    pending tables with, 172–175
INDEX function (Excel), 56–57
initialization syntax, 36, 38
in keyword, 6
inner joins, 86
is keyword, 204
ISO dates, 152

J

joining
  lists, 37
  records, 39
  tables, 41–42, 85–93
join operator, 30
Json.Document function, 139–141
JSON (JavaScript Object Notation)
    files, 139–141
  appending with filename attributes,
    175–177

K

key match lookups
  defined, 58
  retrieving records/values, 60–61
keywords, 6

L

left anti joins, 85, 87–93
left outer joins, 85–93
let expressions, 5, 6–8
  custom columns, creating, 75–76
  defining variables in formulas,
    32–34
  custom function query steps,
    creating, 50–51
let keyword, 6
List.Accumulate function, 54–55,
    76–77, 203–206
List.Distinct function, 97, 116–117

List.Last function, 37, 73–74
list literals, 36
List.Max function, 37, 102, 117
List.Min function, 37, 102, 117
List.Sort function, 97, 113–115
List.Sum function, 37
list values, 36–38
  comparing, 91–93
  extracting minimum/maximum,
    117
  extracting unique, 116–117
  sorting, 113–115
  tables/records, relationship with, 35
List.Zip function, 37
load data locations, 8–9
Locale feature, 104–105, 107–108,
    149–152
logical operators, 19
logical values, 14–15
lookup operator, 58, 60
lookups. See M code lookups
lookup tables, 161

M

match columns, 56
M code
  as base zero, 56
  locations for editing, 3–5
  Power Query, relationship with, 1
  user interface, 2–3
  worksheet formulas/PivotTables/
    DAX formulas, comparison,
    1–2
M code functions
  data connectors. See data con-
    nectors
  defined, 7
M code lookups
  approximate match lookups, 69–77
  column lookups, 61–63
  custom columns, creating with
    custom function, 70–74
  custom columns, creating with let
    expression, 75–76
  defined, 56
  drill-down lookups, 63–65
  exact match lookups, 56–69
  key match lookups, 58, 60–61
  List.Accumulate function, 76–77
  reusable custom functions, 74–75
  row index lookups, 57–58, 59–60
  Table.Buffer function, 69–70
M code values
  binary values, 42–43
  data types, 11
  datetime values, 25–26
  datetimezone values, 26–27
  date values, 22–24

defined, 10
duration values, 17, 20–22
function values, 44–55
hard-coding, 11
list of, 10
list values, 36–38
logical values, 14–15
null values, 13–14
number values, 16–18
operators/operands, 12–13
primitive values, 35
record values, 38–39
table values, 39–41
text values, 15–16
time values, 24–25
type values, 11
merging
  tables, 85–93
  time values with date values, 30–31
metadata, 164
multiple objects, importing Excel files
    with, 177–182

N

night shift calculations, 31
None privacy setting, 194
not operator, 19
nullable logical data type, 20
null values, 13–14
Number.From function, 32
Number.RoundDown function, 33
Number.Round function, 98–100
number values, 16–18

O

one-to-many relationships, 161
online data sources, 152–160
  Power BI semantic models, 159–160
  SQL Server databases, 153–159
  websites, 152–153
online Power BI service, 1
online Power Query. See Dataflow
on-premises paths
  changing, 125–126
  Dataflow as dynamic data source,
    133–136
  Data Source Settings dialog box,
    126–127
  defined, 125
  dynamic paths in Excel, 127–129
  Excel.CurrentWorkbook function,
    145–149
  Excel.Workbook function, 141–145
  Folder.Contents function, 129–133
  Folder.Files function, 129–133
  Json.Document function, 139–141
  text files, importing, 137–138

tips for, 136
Xml.Tables function, 138–139
operands, 12
operators
    datetime values, 25
    datetimezone values, 26
    date values, 23
    defined, 12
    duration values, 21
    list of, 6
    logical values, 14
    number values, 16
    precedence, 12–13
    text values, 15
    time values, 24
order of operations, 12–13
Organizational privacy setting, 194
or operator, 19

P

parameters, 164
partitions, 196
performance, query folding and,
        199–200
PivotTables
    history of Power Query, 1
    worksheet formulas/DAX for-
        mulas/M code, comparison,
        1–2
Power BI Desktop
    blank queries, creating, 14
    From Folder feature, 162
    history of Power Query, 1
    load data locations, 8
    on-premises paths, changing, 126
    Power Query user interface, 2
    semantic models, 159–160
Power Query. See also query folding
    history of, 1
    M code, relationship with, 1
    partitions, 196
    user interface, 2–3
Power Query functions, 7
primary keys, 161
    determining presence of, 65–66
    drill-down lookups and, 63–65
    functions to create, 66–69
primitive values, 35
privacy levels, 193–200
Private privacy setting, 194
Public privacy setting, 194

Q

query folding
    defined, 196
    performance and, 199–200
    SQL Server databases and, 153–159

query steps (variables)
    defined, 7
    defining in formulas, 32–34
quotation marks in identifiers, 7

R

record literals, 38
record values
    examples, 38–39
    tables/lists, relationship with, 35
recursion
    with custom functions, 51–54
    preventing, 145–146
    simulating, 54–55
referencing queries, 131
regional settings, 104–105, 107–108,
        149–152
reusable custom functions, creating,
        74–75
right anti joins, 86
right outer joins, 86
rounding numbers, 98–100
row index lookups
    defined, 57–58
    retrieving records/values, 59–60
row lookup, 38–39, 49–50
row positional index operator, 57
running counts, 118

S

security, privacy levels and, 193–200
semantic models, as online data
        sources, 159–160
SharePoint, 136, 200–208
SharePoint.Contents function, 204
SharePoint.Files function, 204
single-column tables, grouping data
        from, 111–113
sorting
    lists, 113–115
    tables, 115–116
source values, relationship with data
        types, 11–12
spaces in identifiers, 7
Sql.Database function, 66–69, 156
SQL Server databases, as online data
        sources, 153–159
star schema models, 161
subtracting date values, 28–30

T

tab-delimited text files, importing,
        137–138
Table.AddColumn function, 19–20,
        41, 48
Table.AddIndexColumn function,
        118

Table.AddKey function, 68–69
Table.Buffer function, 69–70
Table.Combine function, 81–84, 97,
        181–182
Table.ExpandTableColumn function,
        81–84, 179–181
Table.FromRecords function, 140
Table.Group function, 36, 41, 93–120
    arguments, list of, 96
    blank row after group, adding,
        118–119
    combination frequencies, 119–120
    comparer argument, 103–104
    comparer functions, 104–113
    groupKind argument, 100–103
    running counts, 118
Table.Keys function, 65–66
Table.NestedJoin function, 89
Table.PromoteHeaders function, 138
Table.SelectColumns function, 62
Table.SelectRows function, 71
Table.Sort function, 115–116
Table.UnpivotOtherColumns
        function, 78–81
table values, 39–41
    combining/appending tables, 41–42
    records/lists, relationship with, 35
    sorting, 115–116
Text.BeforeDelimiter function, 202
TEXTBEFORE function (Excel), 128
text encoding, 122
text files
    defined, 121
    importing, 137–138
    with structure problems, ap-
        pending, 167–172
Text.From function, 32, 102
Text.Proper function, 109
Text.Remove function, 54
text values, 15–16
times. See dates/times
time values, 24–25
    adding to date values, 30–31
    calculating hours elapsed, 31
try/otherwise keyword combination,
        204
type keyword, 6
type values, 11

U

underscore, 38, 49–50
unpivoting tables, 78–81
user interfaces, 2–3

V

values. See M code values
variables (query steps)
    defined, 7
    defining in formulas, 32–34
View Native Query feature, 153–159

W

websites, as online data sources,
    152–153
worksheet formulas
    defining variables, 32–34
    PivotTables/DAX formulas/M code,
       comparison, 1–2

X

XML (Extensible Markup Language)
    files, 138–139
Xml.Tables function, 138–139

Y

years, extracting from dates, 28